MW01002246

DAILY
DEVOTIONS
for
Peace of Mind

DAILY
DEVOTIONS
for
Peace of
Mind

365 MEDITATIONS
FOR WOMEN

BARBOUR
PUBLISHING

© 2023 by Barbour Publishing, Inc.

ISBN 978-1-63609-483-0

Adobe Digital Edition (.epub) 978-1-63609-625-4

Please see pages 373–374 for a list of scripture translations used in this book.

Published by Barbour Publishing, Inc., 1810 Barbour Drive, Uhrichsville, Ohio 44683, www.barbourbooks.com

Our mission is to inspire the world with the life-changing message of the Bible.

Printed in China.

Introduction

*Find inspiration and encouragement
in this devotional based on Isaiah 26:3.*

The prophet Isaiah wrote that God would "keep in perfect peace all who trust in you" (NLT). These 365 readings will give you solid biblical truth for an unsettled and unsettling world—reminding you that:

- God knows exactly what's going on
- He always cares deeply for His own
- He remains in ultimate control of everything

Peace of mind is available (and attainable) by any woman who will take God and His Word to heart. How about you? These powerful daily devotions will point the way.

Day 1

DECIDING TO TRUST

*Let the morning bring me word of your
unfailing love, for I have put my trust in you.*
PSALM 143:8 NIV

How did your day begin today? Did you arise early and enjoy the peaceful quiet of the morning after a good night's sleep? Or maybe you spent a sleepless night tending to the needs of a sick child, and you faced the day running on empty.

We don't know if David was a morning person or a night owl, but he chose to start his day looking for visible reminders of God's unfailing love. It might have been easy to remember God's love for him if he had witnessed a glorious morning sunrise, but if the night had been stormy and he was dealing with spooked sheep in the midst of a downpour, God's unfailing love may have felt a little distant.

Regardless of the circumstances, David decided to trust in God first thing in the morning. Whether or not conditions were favorable for faith, David believed in God's unfailing love—even if he couldn't see it in the world around him.

That's a decision any one of us can—and should—make.

Day 2

WORKS OF ART

*Yet you, Lord, are our Father. We are the clay, you
are the potter; we are all the work of your hand.*
ISAIAH 64:8 NIV

The great sculptor Michelangelo once said, "The true work of art is but a shadow of the divine perfection." Even a master like Michelangelo acknowledged that no matter how talented an artist might be, God is the only one capable of perfection. Everything else in this world is flawed.

Each person is as the earthly clay, put together by the one true God, the potter of perfection. God has created each individual by the work of His hand, designed in His own image. Although He has blessed each person with different gifts and attributes, each human being has this in common: God our creator is the quintessential master artist.

Next time you look in the mirror and aren't happy with what you see, remember that God does not make junk. He makes nothing cheap. For God, the master potter, created each person just the way He saw fit. You are a work of art. You are here for a reason. You were made for this time. And you have a purpose.

Day 3

LINKING HEARTS WITH GOD

*"You will receive power when the Holy
Spirit comes on you; and you will be my
witnesses. . .to the ends of the earth."*
ACTS 1:8 NIV

God knows our hearts. He knows what we need to make it through a day. So in His kindness, He gave us a gift in the form of the Holy Spirit. As a counselor, a comforter, and a friend, the Holy Spirit acts as our inner compass. He upholds us when times are hard and helps us hear God's directions. When the path of obedience grows dark, the Spirit floods it with light. What revelation! He lives within us. Therefore, our prayers are lifted to the Father, to the very throne of God. Whatever petitions we have, we may rest assured they are heard.

We can rejoice in the fact that God cared enough to bless our lives with the Spirit to direct our paths. God loves the praises of His people, and these praises revive the Spirit within you. If you are weary or burdened, allow the Holy Spirit to minister to you. Seek the Holy Spirit and His wisdom, and ask Him to revive and refresh your inner person. Place your hope in God and trust the Spirit's guidance, and He will never let you down.

Day 4

PRAY FOR JESUS' RETURN

*The end of all things is near. Therefore be alert
and of sober mind so that you may pray.*
1 PETER 4:7 NIV

World peace is an ever-present concern and likely one that God's people take to Him in prayer. It seems overwhelming to pray for something that appears impossible, but when Christians pray for peace, they pray knowing that Jesus will fulfill His promise of coming back. How long will it take for Him to return? No human knows. In the meantime, Christians persistently pray for His return and try to live peacefully in a chaotic world.

Around AD 600, Jerusalem fell to the Babylonians. The Jews were exiled to Babylonia and held captive for seventy years. God told the prophet Jeremiah to tell His people to settle there and live normally. He said they should seek peace in the place in which they lived until He came back to get them (Jeremiah 29:4–7).

Today's Christians are similar to those Jews. They live normally in an evil world seeking peace on earth while holding on to the promise of Jesus' return.

Paul wrote, "Brothers and sisters, whatever is true, whatever is noble, whatever is right, whatever is pure, whatever is lovely, whatever is admirable. . .think about such things. . . . And the God of peace will be with you" (Philippians 4:8–9 NIV).

May God's peace be with you today and every day until Jesus comes.

Day 5

FOCUS ON TODAY

*Don't brag about tomorrow, since you
don't know what the day will bring.*
PROVERBS 27:1 NLT

What do you have on your plate today? What about tomorrow? Do you remember the plans you have next week? And that trip you have later this month? What about the work thing you have next year?

If we take an honest look at this verse, we see there is no point in worrying about tomorrow, just as there is no point in worrying about next year! Nothing is set in stone. Even today is a fluid river of moments, susceptible to change.

We will find that we can be happier in life by simply taking each day as it comes. If we are not focused on our calendar of events, and instead decidedly focused on each moment of *this* day, we will have the ability to enjoy moments that otherwise would have passed us by. The hilarious thing your child just said that bubbles into laughter. The sweet message from your husband that warms your heart. A lunch date with a friend that encourages your soul. These are all moments we can revel in and enjoy, rather than thinking about the next thing on the list or schedule.

Today, let's keep our focus on only the events of *today*. We will find fulfillment, laughter, and a reduction in stress if we refuse to borrow the worries of tomorrow.

Day 6

FAULTLESS

*To him who is able to keep you from stumbling and to
present you before his glorious presence without fault and
with great joy—to the only God our Savior be glory,
majesty, power and authority, through Jesus Christ our
Lord, before all ages, now and forevermore! Amen.*
JUDE 24–25 NIV

The Lord is able to keep you from stumbling. What an encouragement this is. You no longer have to fear the pitfalls and road bumps in life. Christ took the fall for you when He was separated from His Father on the cross to take away your every sin. Because He was forsaken, you never will be.

Thinking about standing in the presence of God, the ultimate judge, can be terrifying. But this verse promises that those who are in Christ can stand completely faultless in the overwhelming glory and holiness of God. Your sins are no match for Christ's sacrifice; therefore, they have been washed completely away and totally obliterated. You can come into the presence of God with great joy. What a beautiful thing to know that no matter what happens in this life, you have an eternity of time to spend with God in unspeakable joy as a blameless and loved child.

The Lord holds all glory, majesty, dominion, and authority from eternity past, present, and future. He is the God who protects and cares for you—of course He can keep you from stumbling.

Day 7

FOCUS ON JESUS

*Keep your eyes on Jesus, who both began
and finished this race we're in.*
HEBREWS 12:2 MSG

It can happen in a split second. Your life is suddenly turned upside down. Your mother is rushed to the emergency room. Your doctor utters the word *cancer*. Layoffs leave you jobless. Dark clouds quickly obscure your vision. Emotions reel out of control. Questions without answers rush through your mind. Life has been dramatically altered in the blink of an eye.

If you have not encountered such an experience, it's likely that someday you will. Prepare yourself now. Remember that when life throws us curveballs, we may be caught off guard, but God never is. He knows all things; past, present, and future. Since He knows what lies ahead, He can safely navigate us through the chaos.

When our heads are spinning and tears are flowing, there is only one thing to remember: focus on Jesus. He will never leave you nor forsake you. When you focus on Him, His presence envelops you. Where there is despair, He imparts hope. Where there is fear, He imparts faith. Where there is worry, He imparts peace. He will lead you on the right path and grant you wisdom for the journey. When the unexpected trials of life come upon you, remember this: focus on Jesus.

SONG OF FREEDOM

*God sets the lonely in families, he leads
out the prisoners with singing; but the
rebellious live in a sun-scorched land.*
PSALM 68:6 NIV

God understands what it's like to be lonely. If your biological or adoptive family has let you down, your circle of friends and your church family are also a part of God's plan for your life.

God knows what it is to be imprisoned under false pretenses. Sometimes our own rebellious choices lead us into a prison of our own making, and sometimes we find ourselves falsely accused by others. Regardless of how we arrive there, God promises to deliver us from our captive state, and He leads the way in song.

Most of the Bible's musical citations refer to humanity worshipping God through song. But in this verse (and also in Zephaniah 3:17), God's voice sings over us.

Close your eyes. Listen carefully. Do you hear God's song of freedom and salvation? He's singing to you. Consider that for a moment: God is singing to you. His musical voice calls you from captivity into freedom and from loneliness into loving community. Will you join Him in His song?

Day 1

WATCHING OVER YOU

*I often think of the heavens your hands have made,
and of the moon and stars you put in place.*
PSALM 8:3 CEV

Almost three thousand years ago, the psalmist David looked with awe at the clear night sky. He gazed at the moon and the twinkling stars and marveled at the greatness of God. How could someone so immensely creative care about us lowly humans?

In the summer of 1969, another man wondered the same thing. American astronaut Edwin "Buzz" Aldrin saw the night sky with a new perspective—from the surface of the moon. Aldrin and Neil Armstrong were the first humans to walk on the moon. One can only imagine the thoughts that filled their minds. For Aldrin, it was a deeply religious experience. As he stood on the moon's surface and gazed up at the sky, he remembered the words of the psalmist David as written in the King James Version of the Bible. He quoted those words in a television interview from space. Aldrin said, "When I consider thy heavens, the work of thy fingers, the moon and the stars, which thou has ordained; what is man, that thou art mindful of him? and the son of man, that thou visitest him?" (Psalm 8:3–4 KJV).

Three thousand years apart, two different men looked up at the sky, contemplating the same God. That same God is watching over you today.

Day 10

STRENGTH TO PERSEVERE

*He went there to register with Mary, who was pledged
to be married to him and was expecting a child.*
LUKE 2:5 NIV

You probably recognize Luke 2:5 from the story of Jesus' birth. It's an unassuming verse, one we might read without much thought.

Caesar Augustus decreed that a census be taken of the entire Roman world, and everyone went to his own town to register. Joseph and Mary traveled from Nazareth to Bethlehem, where she gave birth to Jesus (Luke 2:1–7). Those are the simple facts.

The Bible doesn't tell us that the journey from Nazareth to Bethlehem was almost a hundred miles. The route would take the couple through rugged terrain, up and down steep hills. That must have been a concern for the two, since Mary was nearing the end of her pregnancy. The trip would take a minimum of five days on foot, and at night, Joseph and Mary would need safe places to camp. That Mary completed the trip is in itself a miracle.

Mary and Joseph aren't the only ones who face life's ups and downs. Most people—spouses, friends, coworkers—experience "rugged terrain" in their relationships. God understands! This entire life is a journey of faith. When we're tired and face steep hills to climb, He'll give us strength to persevere.

Day 11

DEATH'S STING IS GONE

O death, where is thy sting?
O grave, where is thy victory?
1 CORINTHIANS 15:55 KJV

This verse personifies both death and the grave. In ancient paintings, death is sometimes depicted as a crowned skeleton with a dart in his hand. Like an ox goad, the dart's sharp point continually irritates and taunts.

The apostle Paul explains that the sting of death is sin, and sin is the parent of death. Yet through the death and resurrection of Christ, we have atonement for our sins. So Christians no longer need to fear death and the grave. Or as Paul said, "But thanks be to God, which giveth us the victory through our Lord Jesus Christ" (verse 57 KJV).

Earlier in this passage, Paul declared that when Jesus returns all believers—alive and dead—will receive new, glorified bodies that are imperishable and immortal (verses 50–54).

So the question in 1 Corinthians 15:55 is rhetorical. Because of Christ, the deadly darts of sin no longer hold sway over us. Sin has lost its power, death has no sting, and our shackles are loosed! We have nothing to fear, and everything to gain.

Day 12

THE PROCESS OF GOD'S PRESENCE

*And Moses and Aaron went into the tent of meeting,
and when they came out they blessed the people, and the
glory of the LORD appeared to all the people. And fire
came out from before the LORD and consumed the burnt
offering and the pieces of fat on the altar, and when all
the people saw it, they shouted and fell on their faces.*

LEVITICUS 9:23–24 ESV

God wanted His presence to be made known among His people,
the Israelites. But for His presence to be fully realized among His
chosen, there was a long process they had to go through.

First, Moses would hear a word (or two) from God. Then, in
conjunction with Aaron's leadership, Moses and his brother carried
out the Lord's detailed plan. They communicated God's messages
for building the tabernacle and His instructions for the offering
and atonement of sins. They helped their fellow people obey and
follow God so that they might experience His forgiving presence.

Sister in Christ, continue to follow God's path. Keep looking
up and leaning into His Word, reading the Bible every day. As
you remain faithful and obedient on this straight and narrow path
He has called you to, you *will* experience His awesome presence.

WHEN WE ASK "WHY?"

*"Sir," Gideon replied, "if the LORD is with us, why has
all this happened to us? And where are all the miracles
our ancestors told us about? Didn't they say, 'The LORD
brought us up out of Egypt'? But now the LORD has
abandoned us and handed us over to the Midianites."*

JUDGES 6:13 NLT

You've heard it hundreds of times: "If God really cared, then why
did this happen?" "If He really loved me, why did that happen?"

The "why" question has plagued humankind all along. We've
somehow convinced ourselves that God is cruel for not rescuing
us from our hard times.

Yes, life is hard. That's a fact. An indisputable one. Parents lose
children. Loved ones pass away unexpectedly. Injustices occur. We
can cry out to the heavens, "Why, Lord?" or we can continue to
trust God even during the hardest seasons.

The truth is we won't have all the answers in this life. But
there's a day coming when we will, and He can heal our broken
hearts in the interim.

BECAUSE JESUS IS, YOU WILL. . .

I assure you, most solemnly I tell you,
that I Myself am the Door for the sheep.
JOHN 10:7 AMPC

Just as God revealed Himself to Moses, identifying Himself as the "I AM" (Exodus 3:14 AMPC), Jesus revealed Himself to His followers as the I AM (John 4:26; 6:20; 13:19). Yet Jesus goes even further to describe Himself, saying He is the bread of life (John 6:35, 41, 48, 51); the light of the world (John 8:12); the door of the sheep (John 10:7, 9); the resurrection and the life (John 11:25); the good shepherd (John 10:11, 14); the way, the truth, and the life (John 14:6); and the true vine (John 15:1, 5)! Thus:

Because Jesus is the bread of life, you will never be hungry or thirsty.

Because Jesus is the light of the world, you'll never get lost in the darkness.

Because Jesus is the door of the sheep, you will be safe from predators.

Because Jesus is the resurrection and the life, you will never die.

Because Jesus is the good shepherd, you will never get lost.

Because Jesus is the way, the truth, and the life, you will find your path through the truth and knowledge of God.

Because Jesus is the true vine, you can attach yourself to Him, allowing His life to flow in and through you.

THE SWEETNESS OF TEARS

*When I heard these things, I sat down and wept. For
some days I mourned and fasted and prayed before
the God of heaven. Then I said: "LORD, the God of
heaven, the great and awesome God, who keeps his
covenant of love with those who love him and keep
his commandments, let your ear be attentive and your
eyes open to hear the prayer your servant is praying
before you day and night for your servants, the people of
Israel. I confess the sins we Israelites, including myself
and my father's family, have committed against you."*

NEHEMIAH 1:4–6 NIV

Humans tend to quickly swipe away tears of any kind. And yet there
can be a cleansing effect to tears and a benefit to some kinds of
sorrow. That is, if our hearts are trying to get right with God, then
those tears are sweet, and that kind of remorsefulness is beautiful.

Nehemiah wept over the sins committed by the Israelites. He
mourned and fasted and prayed. And when he prayed, he added
himself to the confessions, which was right and good.

Yes, tears and repentance and heartfelt prayers can be good and
lovely things because they can bring you closer to God—which
will ultimately bring you joy!

Day 16

HOLY CONTROLLER

A person's steps are directed by the LORD.
How then can anyone understand their own way?
PROVERBS 20:24 NIV

Lots of successful people pride themselves on knowing where they're headed. Just going where the wind blows? No way! They've set the trajectory, and that's where they'll land. But sometimes even best-laid plans. . .miss the target. They veer off course; they peter out midair. We miscalculate. Maybe we couldn't really see the target in the first place.

Proverbs 20:24 expresses this "unknowableness" in life—the fact that we can't fathom everything that unfolds in our lives because we aren't the one at the controls. Some translations, like the New International Version, highlight the mystery. Some, like the New Living Translation, seem resigned: "The LORD directs our steps, so why try to understand everything along the way?" Others, like The Message, point to God's providence: "The very steps we take come from God; otherwise how would we know where we're going?" Yet no matter what the translation, the conclusion is the same. Map and maneuver all you want, but God is Lord over every step. (See also Proverbs 16:9 and Proverbs 19:21.) Now, that reality could bother you, or it could be a cause for praise and for peace.

Trust God with your eternal destiny. And trust Him with each step you take along the way.

PERFECT PEACE

*You will keep in perfect peace all who trust in you,
all whose thoughts are fixed on you! Trust in the
LORD always, for the LORD GOD is the eternal Rock.*
ISAIAH 26:3–4 NLT

Our lives are a series of moments. And that's what our minds get caught up in, the day-to-day minutiae, the little niggling worries, the what-ifs, the how-comes, and the why-fors. But God wants us to have a different perspective, not an in-the-moment viewpoint but an eternal one. Because when we look at the big picture, our day-to-day worries—the ones that get our hearts beating out of control and our thoughts ricocheting around in our heads—are really nothing to be upset about.

That takes trust in a power so much higher than ourselves. But when we have that trust, that confidence in the eternal Rock who can never be moved, we are blessed with a peace that blesses us within, keeping us healthy in mind, body, spirit, soul, and heart. Such a calm also blesses those around us, for it's contagious.

So fix your mind on the one who sees and knows so much more than you ever will. Put your confidence in the one who has your name written on the palm of His hand. Practice being in His presence during quiet hours. And then, the moment stress and chaos begin creeping in, call God to mind, and He will surround you with that big-picture, perfect peace.

HOW GOD LOVES HIS DAUGHTERS

*"Why should our father's name disappear
from his clan because he had no son? Give us
property among our father's relatives."*
NUMBERS 27:4 NIV

The promised land of Israel was to be divided among the twelve tribes of Jacob. One of his descendants, Zelophehad, only had daughters, no sons. At that time, women were not allowed to inherit. But his five daughters went to Moses and asked for the land that would have belonged to their father.

Moses is so shocked by their request that, instead of making a ruling himself or consulting with his leaders, he takes their request to God to ask what to do. The culture perpetuated the lie that God didn't care about women. God acted in a counter-cultural manner and granted the women their request.

This story also shows that our spiritual inheritance is not determined by our earthly parents. The women admitted their father had died in his sin of unbelief, but God did not hold that sin against them. He provided the inheritance and blessings their earthly father could not.

These women demonstrated their faith in God's Word by asking for their share of the land *before* any of it had even been conquered. After God led Israel to conquer the land, they reminded Joshua of their inheritance.

God, the perfect Father, is passionately concerned about the unique challenges of being a woman in this world. He wants us to come to Him and ask for His blessings.

NEVER STOP PRAYING

*The effective, fervent prayer of
a righteous man avails much.*
JAMES 5:16 NKJV

Augustine's mother, Monica, was a devout Christian, but her son was an undisciplined child. Even despite Monica's constant warnings to stay away from fornication, Augustine found himself father to a son and a member of a cult.

Years later, she begged him not to travel to Rome, but despite her advice, he went. She was able to persuade him to listen to the bishop. The words of the sermon lingered as he sat in a nearby garden. A child's song, "Take Up and Read," drew him to the Bible, and Saint Augustine was converted that moment.

Monica could have given up on her wayward son. But she was never willing to accept Augustine as he was in his state of godlessness. She kept praying until she got results.

Jesus tells us to pray relentlessly, like a man who knocks on his neighbor's door in the middle of the night for bread. He said, "Ask and it will be given to you; seek and you will find; knock and the door will be opened to you. For everyone who asks receives; the one who seeks finds; and to the one who knocks, the door will be opened" (Luke 11:9–10 NIV).

Don't give up on your prayers. The answer is closer than you know.

Day 20

An Unseen Pathway

Your road led through the sea, your pathway through the mighty waters—a pathway no one knew was there!
PSALM 77:19 NLT

You have read the story. The Israelites, fleeing bondage in Egypt, arrive at the edge of the Red Sea with the Egyptians on their heels. At just the right moment, God parts the sea and every last Israelite passes through to the other side! And in the next instant, their pursuers are caught up in the raging waters, horses and chariots along with them.

Great story. Nice tale of long ago. Awesome movie clip. But wait. This is more than a fantasy. It really happened! And the miraculous part is that God still makes paths for you today.

When you find yourself between a rock and a hard place, cry out to God. When circumstances lead you to a dead end, lift your eyes toward heaven. God is the "great I Am," meaning that He is what you need in each moment. At times of anxiety or fear, you need the Prince of Peace. Other times, when filled with gratitude, you sing praises to the King of Glory.

Then there are Red Sea moments. At such crossroads, rely on Yahweh, the Lord who provides unseen pathways, who makes a way where there seems to be no way (Isaiah 43:16–20)!

LIVING IN GOD'S SHADOW

He who dwells in the secret place of the Most High
shall abide under the shadow of the Almighty.
I will say of the LORD, "He is my refuge and
my fortress; My God, in Him I will trust."
PSALM 91:1–2 NKJV

Ever heard the phrase "living in someone's shadow"? Maybe you have a sibling or friend or coworker who seems to outshine you no matter what you do, leaving you feeling a bit invisible. If you are thinking about this phrase in modern English, Psalm 91:1 sounds like a dubious blessing.

But consider Israel, the land of the psalm's original hearers—hot, arid, desert-like in places. On a blistering day, a traveler would see the shadow of a tall rock as a welcome place of rest and safety from the scorching sun. In the rest of this psalm's imagery, God presents Himself as a place of safety: Like a protective mother bird, He covers you with His feathers; as the deliverer He rescues you from traps and dangerous diseases; and His truth is a shield, knocking away the lies that your enemy Satan hurls at you.

So perhaps there's a person whose shadow you wouldn't mind living in—one who is ready and able to come to your aid, one who is ready to welcome you to hide yourself in Him.

Day 22

GETTING OUT OF THE DESERT

*He turned the desert into pools of water and
the parched ground into flowing springs.*
PSALM 107:35 NIV

Do you find yourself in the desert? Is life dry and boring? Are you parched from the sameness of it all? Look up! God is more than able to bring you out of that place. He can turn your desert into pools of water and bring new life to the lifeless.

Have you considered your gifts? What abilities or talents has God given you? Are you using them? Often when one becomes too self-focused or is not using her gifts, life becomes stagnant.

Maybe you are good with your hands. Could you volunteer with a local group that constructs homes for the poor? Or help with crafts in a kids' Sunday school class? Do you have musical ability? Nursing homes are always looking for someone to come and play an instrument or lead music for the residents. Or maybe your church's worship team needs help. These are just a few ideas. Get creative! Find a way to use a gift God has given you today.

When you are busy about God's work, you won't have as much time to feel bored with life. You will find that He can bring joy to replace sorrow, and a feeling of value that trumps that desert place every time!

Day 23

Your Heart's Desire

Souls who follow their hearts thrive;
fools bent on evil despise matters of soul.
PROVERBS 13:19 MSG

What does your heart desire? If you are walking with God, you should be paying attention to your heart's yearnings. That may be the very thing God has already gone ahead and prepared for you to do or be.

You were created with talents, preferences, and a personality unique to you. And God will direct your plans to follow where those things lead. Listen to what your heart hopes for. Test it and determine how and where God is using your heart messages to direct you.

Sometimes you may be unsure of what you want. You have been so busy taking care of others that you haven't stopped to consider what you desire. No worries. God knows the longings of your heart. Ask Him to clarify any dormant dreams or uncertainties.

Scripture promises that if you delight in the Lord, He will give you the desires of your heart (Psalm 37:4). Trusting God to do so might not seem reasonable or safe if you have had disappointments in the past. Yet God alone is worthy of your total confidence. Because He loves you like no other, you can trust Him. Have confidence in all He is doing in your life, as well as what He plans to do.

THE LORD HIMSELF
GOES BEFORE YOU

"The LORD himself goes before you and will be with you; he will never leave you nor forsake you. Do not be afraid; do not be discouraged."

DEUTERONOMY 31:8 NIV

How comforting and freeing when we allow God to go before us! Stop and consider that for a moment: you can relinquish control of your life and circumstances to the Lord Himself. Relax! His shoulders are big enough to carry all of your burdens.

The issue that has your stomach in knots right now? Ask the Lord to go before you. The problem that makes you wish you could hide under the covers and sleep until it's all over? Trust that God Himself will never leave you and that He is working everything out.

Joshua 1:9 (NIV) tells us to "be strong and courageous. Do not be afraid; do not be discouraged, for the LORD your God will be with you wherever you go." Be encouraged! Even when it feels like it, you are truly never alone. And never without access to God's power.

If you've trusted Christ as your savior, the Spirit of God Himself is alive and well and working inside you at all times. What an astounding miracle! The creator of the universe dwells within you and is available to encourage you and help you make right choices on a moment-by-moment basis.

Day 25

YOUR HEAVENLY FATHER

The LORD's love never ends; his mercies never stop.
They are new every morning; LORD, your loyalty is great.
LAMENTATIONS 3:22–23 NCV

Each year, in early June, a day is set aside to honor fathers. It is a complicated day for many. Because we live in a fallen world, relationships are far from perfect. Perhaps your relationship with your earthly father is wonderful, but it may be messy or fragmented. Make some time to celebrate your earthly father. Call your dad or, if you live nearby, spend some time with him. If it is within your power, seek to restore any brokenness in your relationship with your earthly father.

Regardless of your relationship with your earthly father, your heavenly Father loves you with an *unfailing* love. He is faithful to walk with you through the ups and downs of life. Remember that every day is a day to honor your heavenly Father. Begin and end today praising Him for who He is. Express thanksgiving. Present your requests to Him. Tell Him how much you love Him. God longs to be your Abba Father, a loving Daddy to you, His daughter!

Day 26

I Give Up

*Neither yield ye your members as instruments of
unrighteousness unto sin: but yield yourselves unto
God, as those that are alive from the dead, and your
members as instruments of righteousness unto God.*
ROMANS 6:13 KJV

God encourages us to surrender to Him. How does God expect us to do that? *Merriam-Webster* defines *surrender* as "to give (oneself) over to something (as an influence)." God has given us free will, so the choice becomes ours: to surrender or maintain total control.

When we make the decision to surrender, we give ourselves over to God and allow His authority in our lives. We place our hope in the God who runs the universe. Oswald Chambers said, "The choice is either to say, 'I will not surrender,' or to surrender, breaking the hard shell of individuality, which allows the spiritual life to emerge."

Isn't that an amazing thought? Our creator God cares enough about us to delve into our everyday lives and help us. Through the Holy Spirit within, God's gentle hand of direction will sustain each of us, enabling us to grow closer to our Father. The closer we grow, the more like Him we desire to be. Then His influence spreads through us to others. When we surrender, He is able to use our lives and enrich others. What a powerful message: Give up and give more!

Day 21

WHAT IF?

The LORD will keep you from all harm—
he will watch over your life.
PSALM 121:7 NIV

"Mommy, what if the sun falls down? What if an earthquake swallows our house? What if. . . ?" When the world appears scary to children, they run to their parents with questions. They look to their mothers and fathers for comfort, reassurance, and peace.

Grown-ups are no different. They run to Father God with their what-ifs. "What if I have cancer? What if I lose my job? What if there is a terrorist attack? What if. . . ?"

Psalm 46 provides the answer to all these questions. It says, "God is our refuge and strength, an ever-present help in trouble. Therefore we will not fear, though the earth give way and the mountains fall into the heart of the sea, though its waters roar and foam and the mountains quake with their surging. . . . The LORD Almighty is with us; the God of Jacob is our fortress" (verses 1–2, 7 NIV).

Feeling safe and secure rests not in the world or in other human beings but with God alone. He is a Christian's help and hope in every frightening situation. He promises to provide peace to all who put their faith and trust in Him.

What are you afraid of today? Allow God to encourage you. Trust Him to bring you through it and to give you peace.

Day 28

REFRESHED BY GOD

*A generous person will prosper; whoever
refreshes others will be refreshed.*

PROVERBS 11:25 NIV

Maybe you've hit a low point. Things aren't going as planned. You feel stuck at your job or stifled in a relationship. Maybe you're having a bad year. Or even just a bad day.

At any moment when you feel disappointed or unlucky or down, try this. Find someone who is in need—maybe someone who is also feeling knocked down—and do something for them. It doesn't have to be a big something. Give them a fountain drink, a small bouquet, a bar of chocolate, or a good book. Maybe just call and say hi or send a card.

The person doesn't even have to be someone you know. Go to a nursing home and read to someone who can't see anymore. Just spend some time listening to a person's story. Go to a bus stop and hand out free bottles of water. Go to the grocery store and offer people help with carrying groceries. Buy someone's coffee in the drive-through line at the coffee shop.

Once you've done some act of kindness or generosity, stop and take note of how you feel. Is life a little bit brighter? If it isn't, try again. If it is, try again. You will soon find that the more you give to others, the better you get at it, and the more you will feel refreshed by God.

Day 21

EVERYTHING WE NEED

*You can be sure that God will take care of
everything you need, his generosity exceeding
even yours in the glory that pours from Jesus.*
PHILIPPIANS 4:19 MSG

Have you ever gone through a period in your life when you were
completely dependent on God to supply everything for you? Perhaps
you lost your job or had an extended illness. It can be humbling to
be unable to provide for yourself and your family.

The Israelites faced similar circumstances when God freed them
from slavery in Egypt. As He led them through the desert toward
the promised land, He provided water and food in miraculous ways.
Every morning, one day's supply of manna would appear. Any
attempt to save it until the next day was futile; the manna would
rot. God wanted them to rely on Him daily for their provision.
Yet the Israelites' response wasn't to be grateful but to complain
they didn't have enough variety!

God often takes us through the desert before we get to the
promised land. It's in the desert that we learn the lessons we will
need to use in the promised land, most of which involve trusting
Him. It's in the desert that we learn God is who He says He is.
It's in the desert that we learn to obey Him, not because He says
to, but because it's what will ultimately give us the life we were
designed to live.

Day 30

THE BATTLE IS REAL, BUT SO IS OUR REFUGE

Keep me safe, O God, for I have come to you for refuge.
PSALM 16:1 NLT

Have you ever had days, weeks, or months when this was all you could pray? Or maybe in the heat of the battle, the intensity of the chase, the thought of running to Him for safety never even crossed your mind. Perhaps you believed this was a battle you could win on your own. Yet with each swing of your sword, you felt your strength fail.

Life is hard, and it's okay to admit that. The enemy we face on a daily basis is cunning and unrelenting. How wonderful it is that David looked to the Lord for his protection. And it wasn't protection in a spiritual sense—David's very life was at stake! He prayed to the Lord to keep him safe.

Maybe it feels like the Lord is far away—too intangible to be sought out for emotional strength, much less physical needs. My sister, He is never too far. He is an all-encompassing God who is able to keep you secure. He is ready and waiting to be your refuge. Whether your need is tangible or emotional, go to Him.

DRAW NEAR WITH CONFIDENCE

*So let us come boldly to the throne of our gracious
God. There we will receive his mercy, and we will
find grace to help us when we need it most.*
HEBREWS 4:16 NLT

In this verse you are told that you can approach God's throne with confidence. Why do you approach the throne? So that you can receive mercy and find grace to help in time of need.

Why would you need to receive mercy? Those who need mercy are those who have done something wrong and are therefore not in right standing with whomever they are asking mercy from. Inevitably you come before the throne of God with the baggage of your sin. Yet you are told to come with confidence before the throne of a holy God who hates sin. You don't need to be perfect or have your act together to come before God with confidence. You only need to be covered in Christ's blood.

This confidence with which you approach God's throne is not a self-confidence, but a God-confidence. It's a confidence that assures you that God is for you, that He loves you, and that He sees Christ in you. Your standing before God depends completely on His view of you and not on your own merit. He sees you as His beloved child. So go boldly to the foot of His throne, knowing that you will receive mercy and grace.

LEAVE YOUR CHAINS

*So Moses spoke thus to the children of Israel;
but they did not heed Moses, because of
anguish of spirit and cruel bondage.*
EXODUS 6:9 NKJV

His message was nothing but good news. The God of their fathers had heard their groaning! He was coming! He would rescue them and redeem them. They would be His people, and He would be their God.

But when Moses delivered this good news, the people couldn't hear it. They were so sunk down into pain and despair, so weighed down by their chains, they couldn't even imagine being anywhere else—much less having the God of heaven care about them.

The dying to self and loss of life that Jesus speaks of in Matthew 16:24–25 is not just aimed at those who are on top of the world and full of themselves. It's aimed at the lowest of the low as well. No matter where we are in our lives, we all have to be willing to set aside our cares, set aside the view that fills our sight, set aside the soundtracks that play over and over in our ears, and listen to the message of the Lord. We are sometimes like prisoners who have been given keys but won't leave our cells because we have grown so accustomed to our chains.

Leave your chains. Go out to what God has ready for you.

MIRACLE UPON MIRACLE

*"Go back and report to John what you have seen and
heard: The blind receive sight, the lame walk, those who
have leprosy are cleansed, the deaf hear, the dead are
raised, and the good news is proclaimed to the poor."*
LUKE 7:22 NIV

God's in the miracle working business, even today. How easily we
forget that all of creation serves as a daily reminder of this fact.
The same Creator who spoke mountains and rivers into existence
causes the sun to rise each morning and to cast its golden rays
over us as we journey from place to place.

There are miracles in a baby's smile, the wrinkled hand of an
elderly neighbor, the playful yap of a rowdy pup. There are supernatural reminders of God's grace in our bodies as well—a heart
that beats in steady rhythm, hands that bend and move, legs that
take us where we need to go.

May we never forget God started all of creation with just a
word. And, as we witness miracles in our lives, may we respond
with words of awe and wonder, praising our amazing Father for
all He continues to do.

Day 34

GO IN PEACE

The king's officer pleaded with Him, Sir, do come down at once before my little child is dead! Jesus answered him, Go in peace; your son will live! And the man put his trust in what Jesus said and started home.

JOHN 4:49–50 AMPC

A Roman official's son was near death. So the officer approached Jesus and begged Him to come home with him so He could put His hands on the child and heal him. But Jesus told the king's man not to be anxious, to go home in peace, because his son would indeed live.

At that very moment, the officer took Jesus at His word. He believed what Jesus said was reality. The man trusted Jesus and started back home. On his way there, his servants came to tell him the boy had indeed recovered—at the same moment that Jesus had told the man, "Go in peace; your son will live!"

Put no limits on what Jesus and His word can do in your life. There's no amount of time or space He cannot reach across with His power. Believe in His words, that things are indeed, just as He says they are. Trust what He tells you, then go in peace, knowing His truth is yours.

Yes, in Jesus

*For no matter how many promises God has made,
they are "Yes" in Christ. And so through him the
"Amen" is spoken by us to the glory of God.*
2 Corinthians 1:20 niv

Some have said that God's Word contains more than five thousand promises. It is encouraging to know He will provide and fight for you, give you strength, grant you wisdom, go before you, and never leave nor forsake you (Exodus 4:14; Isaiah 40:29; James 1:5; Deuteronomy 31:8). These promises are grounded in the ultimate proof of love displayed in Christ Jesus—the undeniable love of God for humanity. With His promises, God says "Yes! I love you." And in them, we grasp hold of the truth of His unfaltering affection and confidently respond with "Amen."

What does our expression of an "Amen" look like? An open heart. A willingness to let go of control. An attitude of hope. A trust that does not falter in the face of adversity.

You can trust God will fulfill every commitment He has made to you. Take courage in your loving God. Let His words strengthen your heart and give peace to your mind. God is more than capable of helping you today. Amen to that!

Day 36
NOT ONE MISSING

*Lift up your eyes and look to the heavens: Who created
all these? He who brings out the starry host one by one
and calls forth each of them by name. Because of his great
power and mighty strength, not one of them is missing.*
ISAIAH 40:26 NIV

Look up into the night sky and you will s ee stars too numerable
to count. Their presence demonstrates a beautiful truth for you to
hold on to. Their creator counts each one and calls them personally out by the name He has given them. Doesn't that sound like
a shepherd caring for his sheep? If God cares deeply about a ball
of fire, how much more does He care for you?

You are God's daughter made in His own image. He is aware
of your every detail and calls you by name. He hasn't lost a single
star in all the vast galaxies despite the black holes and endless
space. *Not one is missing!* You will certainly not be lost either. Because
of God's "great power and mighty strength," you can trust Him
with everything. You need not be afraid.

Is there something that terrifies you? Some fear for yourself
or a loved one that haunts you? Trust God to use His might and
power to keep you close and safe.

Day 31

GOD HEARS OUR CRIES

May the LORD answer you when you are in distress;
may the name of the God of Jacob protect you.
PSALM 20:1 NIV

We humans can be odd creatures. In all of nature, we're the only ones who hide our distress behind a smile. We hold our chins up and our shoulders back and press on, never letting on that behind our confident exterior, we're crumbling.

But God hears the cries of our hearts! He knows our suffering and feels our sorrow. When we call out to Him, even if through a silent seeping of our emotions, hidden behind the safety of our poised facade, He will answer! He loves us, and He will never leave us to trudge through troubled times alone.

There is never a need to hide our heartache from God. He sees us at our worst, and He thinks we are magnificent! He adores us. Whatever our source of distress, He knows. He cares. And He is there.

CRISIS COUNSELOR

*Offer unto God thanksgiving; and pay thy vows
unto the most High: and call upon me in the day of
trouble: I will deliver thee, and thou shalt glorify me.*

PSALM 50:14–15 KJV

We all experience moments of panic when we are almost overwhelmed with the need to talk to someone. Perhaps someone we know has developed a devastating illness, we've been in an accident, we experience the death of a friend or family member, or our character has been maligned. The pain is often so great that the only relief we can think of comes through sharing with someone we love or a confidant we feel can help us.

Often the person we want to talk to is not available. She or he may be busy, not at home, or it could be late in a different time zone. When that help or counselor is not available, discouragement or depression can result.

God is always there. He never sleeps; He's on call twenty-four hours a day, seven days a week. He is willing not only to listen but to give wise counsel. He gives peace beyond our understanding and joy in the midst of trials.

The next time you find yourself hurting or in a panic, call on God. Ask Him to listen and help you. You'll find He is the only counselor you need.

LIGHT IN THE DARKNESS

*"I will lead blind Israel down a new path, guiding them
along an unfamiliar way. I will brighten the darkness
before them and smooth out the road ahead of them."*
ISAIAH 42:16 NLT

In the dim moonlight, we can sometimes find our way in the darkness of our homes. In familiar places we know the lay of the land. At best we will make our way around the obstacles through memory and shadowy outline. At worst, we will lightly stumble into an armchair or a piano bench. When all else fails, we know where the light switch is and, blindly groping in the darkness, we can turn on the light to help us find our way.

But when we walk in the darkness of unfamiliar places, we may feel unsettled. Not sure of our bearings, not knowing where the light switch is, we become overwhelmed, afraid to step forward, afraid even to move. At those times, we need to remember that our God of light is always with us. Although we may not see Him, we can rest easy, knowing He is ever-present in the darkness of unknown places, opportunities, and challenges.

God will never leave us to find our way alone. Realize this truth and arm yourself with the knowledge that no matter what the situation, no matter what the trial, no matter how black the darkness, He is ever there, reaching out for us, helping us find our way. Switch on the light of His truth in your mind, and walk forward, knowing He is always within reach.

Day 40

SOUL SATISFACTION

*All my longings lie open before you, Lord; my sighing
is not hidden from you. . . . My soul thirsts for God.*
PSALM 38:9; 42:2 NIV

Trina found herself sighing again. She couldn't help it—it seemed
as if the weight of the world was on her shoulders, but she wasn't
able to pinpoint exactly what it was that troubled her so.

But God knew exactly what her sighs were all about. He knew
the weight on her heart. She couldn't verbalize it to anyone. These
deep longings pressed in on Trina as she tossed and turned at
night. She prayed that they'd subside or that God would provide
a distraction—or better yet, satisfy this longing deep within once
and for all, whatever it was.

Scripture guided Trina to the heart of the problem. "My
soul thirsts for God." She could think of several troubling issues
that worried her, and she had cried out to God to fix them—the
finances, the car, and broken relationships. But, really, she needed
more of Him—more of His presence, His Word, His consolation,
His hope. Nothing material or relational would fill the void—just
her living God, breathing fresh life into her aching soul.

Day 41

WHERE ARE YOU?

*Adam and his wife hid themselves from the
presence of the LORD God amongst the trees
of the garden. And the LORD God called unto
Adam, and said unto him, Where art thou?*
GENESIS 3:8–9 KJV

Throughout the Bible, God asks us questions, inviting us to dialogue with Him. The very first question God asked called Adam and Eve to self-awareness. *"Where are you?"* Of course God knew where the couple was that night. He asked to make them aware of where they were.

God waits for us at the appointed hour. He hovers over the latest Bible study guide and the beautifully illustrated prayer journal. He longs to listen to the words that pour out from our hearts. He remains eager to speak to us through His written Word and the Holy Spirit. But too many pages of the journal remain blank, and the Bible bookmark doesn't change places.

Today God still whispers, *"Where are you?"* God wants to spend time with us, but too often we hide among the trees of our gardens, the routines of everyday life. We have emails to answer, car repairs to see to, clothes to wash, phone calls to answer—and another appointment with God gets broken. The more appointments we break, the easier it becomes to forget.

Take a moment to answer God's question. He will meet you wherever you are.

Day 42

SLEEP WELL!

*It is vain for you to rise up early, to sit up late, to eat
the bread of sorrows: for so he giveth his beloved sleep.*
PSALM 127:2 KJV

We women are funny creatures.

If we are asked if we want God's blessings, we passionately
say, "Of course we do!"

Why then do we reject His gifts?

Psalm 127 says, for example, that sleep is a gift. Of all God's
gifts for health and prosperity that He wants to bestow on us, it's
the one modern women reject without a thought.

Thanks to the lightbulb, we have options. We don't have to
go to bed when the sun goes down. We can now sit up late doing
anything we want.

Ignoring sleep is faithlessness. Long nights of work show that
we don't trust God to provide our needs. He says, "Sleep, and I
will take care of you."

Not only will God take care of us when we sleep, but He also
promises new mercies each morning (Lamentations 3:23). Waking
renewed is one such mercy.

Instead of vainly burning the midnight oil, be blessed: Go
to bed.

Day 43

A PERFECT FIT

You were bought at a price.
1 CORINTHIANS 6:20 NIV

Sometimes life can feel like a huge puzzle, and we're constantly trying to figure out how our piece of life fits into the big picture. We all have a desire to belong to something special—someone important. Surprisingly, we can overlook the most important connection we have: We belong to God.

No matter where you've been or what you've done, God has accepted you. He is all about your future, and that includes spending eternity with Him. He shaped you to the perfect size to fit into His purpose and plan. And no matter what road you take, He has made a place for you. He purchased you with the price of His own Son's life. And He gave you everything you need to be accepted as a joint heir with Jesus.

When it seems others do not want you on their team or you find you're having a hard time fitting in, remember you are part of God's family—born of the household of faith. He created you and formed you to be a perfect fit.

Day 44

GOD IS OUR EVERYTHING

My body and my heart may grow weak. God, you give
strength to my heart. You are everything I will ever need.
PSALM 73:26 NIRV

You may not have heard of Asaph. He is the man who wrote
Psalm 73. Asaph was David's music director and author of twelve
of the psalms.

In Psalm 73, Asaph wonders, *If God is good, then why do*
the righteous suffer and the wicked prosper? He says, "Did I keep
my heart pure for nothing? Did I keep myself innocent for no
reason? I get nothing but trouble all day long; every morning
brings me pain" (verses 13–14 NLT). Asaph confesses that he
sometimes feels like giving up and joining the wicked (verses 2–3).

In desperation, Asaph seeks God in His sanctuary. There he
realizes that while the wicked might prosper for a season, God will
defeat them in His own way and in His own time. Asaph ends up
praising God, "How good it is to be near You! You are all I will
ever need" (verse 28 NIV).

When our bodies are tired and sick, when we feel as if we
can't go on, Psalm 73:28 reminds us that God is our everything.

GOD IS PATIENT

The LORD is slow to anger but great in power;
the LORD will not leave the guilty unpunished.
His way is in the whirlwind and the storm,
and clouds are the dust of his feet.

NAHUM 1:3 NIV

Clouds always point to God's power. He created the clouds. God resides within and beyond the heavens. As this verse tells us, the Lord is so huge, the clouds are merely the dust of His feet.

By watching clouds, we see hints of God's presence. We see God as creator when we imagine the different shapes of clouds to resemble animals, funny faces, and flocks of sheep.

Storm clouds remind us that God is also powerful. During the raging winds, crashing thunder, and startling lightning, our fear grows. The devastating violence of a storm can obliterate everything in its path. Is this the same playful God we remember on fair-weather days?

But God is very patient. He waits in His unhurried way for us to acknowledge Him as our King and Savior. He welcomes us back into His arms. He invites us to look up at the clouds in His heaven and understand His many sides—powerful, creative, and loving.

Day 46

GOD RESCUES HIS BELOVED

*He reached down from on high and took hold of
me; he drew me out of deep waters. He rescued me
from my powerful enemy, from my foes, who were
too strong for me. They confronted me in the day
of my disaster, but the LORD was my support.*

PSALM 18:16–18 NIV

David wrote this psalm at a time when he was being pursued by Saul. Imagine David's terror as he and his band of loyal followers clung within the concealing walls of caves for shelter while Saul sought to slaughter him. During this time of desperation, David learned to lean on God's power, convinced in his heart that He alone could rescue him from harm.

Have you ever known such desperation? A time when even the ground beneath you seemed unable to support you? Perhaps you were exactly where God wanted you, just as David was, and yet untold trials and tribulations were heaped on you anyway. Did you doubt God's presence? Did you realize that He could act in your behalf, despite the obvious circumstances?

The very nature and character of God demands that He rescue those whom He loves. When confronted with a crisis, like David, you can put your life in His hands.

Day 41

YOUR DAYS ARE GOD'S

In the third year of the reign of King Cyrus of Persia,
Daniel (also known as Belteshazzar) had another vision.
He understood that the vision concerned events certain to
happen in the future—times of war and great hardship.
DANIEL 10:1 NLT

Daniel was given several glimpses into the future. He saw things that probably perplexed and even terrified him. (There's nothing like having the veil peeled back for a peek at what's coming.)

Maybe there have been times in your life when you've wished you could see into the future. Will you get that job you've been hoping for? Will you live in a fine house? Will your children grow up happy and healthy? How many grandchildren and great-grandchildren will you have? Whether you're propelled by worry or joy, there are things you'd like to know.

The future is filled with unknown variables, but it's best you find out as you go along in life. There are probably things you couldn't bear to see now, so asking for a glimpse beyond the present time isn't to your advantage. Because, as He did the manna, God gives you what you need for each day, no more, no less.

Instead of worrying about the future, give it to the Lord. All your days are His, after all.

Day 48

WHAT GROWS FROM GRIEF

*Those who plant in tears will
harvest with shouts of joy.*
PSALM 126:5 NLT

You are crushed. All your hopes for your future, that beautiful dream of a life you had painted in your mind, have blurred—like a chalk drawing washed away by a storm. Maybe it was a lost job, a lost friend, or a lost romance—but something significant has changed in your life, and the disappointment threatens to tear you apart.

The people of Israel knew sorrow and disappointment. So many times, either through their own wrong actions or the actions of others, their lives were thrown into turmoil. And suddenly the promised land seemed too far to reach, or the temple crumbled, or the enemies appeared on every side—and there was no way out.

But God always came back for them, and as the psalmist records here, He brought them home to Jerusalem.

God will remember you too. So start again. Take up the faith of the farmer and plant your seeds, watering them with tears. Trust in the one who can make anything grow—even in the wilderness of grief.

Day 41

BANISH FEAR

When I saw him, I fell at his feet as if I were dead.
But he laid his right hand on me and said, "Don't
be afraid! I am the First and the Last. I am the
living one. I died, but look—I am alive forever and
ever! And I hold the keys of death and the grave."
REVELATION 1:17–18 NLT

Fear can cling to you like a shadow. It is always lurking, following at your heels. Your daily life may be filled with fears both great and small—some suppressed and some rising to the surface to churn in your stomach. You may experience the fear of never belonging, of failure, of loss, of the unknown, or of death. These can be debilitating, stealing your joy and hope.

But when John saw the Lord and collapsed at His feet, Jesus placed His hand on His servant and told him not to fear. For though Jesus endured the wrath of God and death, He now lives forever and ever. It's impossible to fathom the breadth of eternity, but Christ will fill it. And He holds the keys of death and the grave. He has mastered them, and He promises that neither of them shall take you captive. He has rescued you.

Although there are many fearful things on this forsaken earth, remember that nothing can usurp Christ's rightful rule.

Day 50

HANNAH'S PRAYER

"The eyes of the LORD search the whole earth in order to strengthen those whose hearts are fully committed to him."
2 CHRONICLES 16:9 NLT

There are many great prayers in the Bible. There are prayers for wisdom and for unity, prayers of repentance and negotiation with God. Hannah's was an anguished prayer for a child.

Hannah was barren. She prayed before God with a broken heart and promised God that if He gave her a child, she would commit him to the Lord all the days of his life. God heard and answered her prayer.

Does God always answer every prayer for a child in this way? No, He doesn't. There are women whom God loves deeply and unconditionally who will not bear a child in this life. But in this case, God granted Hannah a male child whom she named Samuel. She only had Samuel for a short time before she took him to Eli, the priest. Samuel was not an ordinary child. He heard the voice of God at a very young age. He grew up to become a judge and prophet that could not be matched in all of Israel's history.

God is looking for ordinary people whose prayers reflect hearts completely committed to Him. He found such commitment in Hannah, and He answered her prayer. He will answer your humble, faithful prayers too—in His own perfect way and time.

Day 51

ON THE RUN — WITH GOD

*O God, You are my God, earnestly will I seek You; my
inner self thirsts for You, my flesh longs and is faint
for You, in a dry and weary land where no water is.*

PSALM 63:1 AMPC

Absalom, King David's son, was attempting to overthrow his
father. So David fled his palace, his comforts, his people. Cursed,
then pelted with stones and dirt, this weary and beleaguered king
wrote Psalm 63 in the wilderness of Judah.

There David remembered God's power and glory. He recalled
His loving-kindness, knowing that is more precious than life itself.
And in spite of all that was happening in his life, David told God,
"So will I bless You while I live; I will lift up my hands in Your
name" (verse 4 AMPC).

Even though David was on the run once again, even though
he was out of his comfort zone, he hadn't forgotten the most
important thing: his love, worship, and pursuit of God.

When all seems lost in your life, when those who once loved
you now curse you, when you are relegated to a barren wasteland,
remember Psalm 63. Know that the most important thing you
have—faith in God—is there for you to cling to and rejoice in.
He is all the comfort you need, no matter where you are.

Day 52

LET GOD TAKE CARE OF YOU

"Consider how the wild flowers grow. They do not labor or spin. Yet I tell you, not even Solomon in all his splendor was dressed like one of these. If that is how God clothes the grass of the field, which is here today, and tomorrow is thrown into the fire, how much more will he clothe you—you of little faith!"

LUKE 12:27–28 NIV

Take a look at God's creation. He has created this world with such intricate detail. He designed every tree, the majestic mountains, a glorious sun, and a mysterious moon. Each animal has been given unique markings, parts, and sounds. Consider the long-necked giraffe, the massive elephant, the graceful swan, and the perfectly striped zebra!

If God makes the flowers, each type unique and beautiful, and if He sends the rain and sun to meet their needs, will He not care for you as well?

He made you. What the Father makes, He loves. And that which He loves, He cares for. We were made in His image. Humans are dearer to God than any of His other creations. Rest in Him. Trust Him. Just as He cares for the birds of the air and the flowers of the meadows, God is in the business of taking care of His sons and daughters. Let Him take care of you.

GOD OF MIRACLES

*He listened to Paul as he was speaking. Paul
looked directly at him, saw that he had faith to
be healed and called out, "Stand up on your feet!"
At that, the man jumped up and began to walk.*

ACTS 14:9–10 NIV

Paul and Barnabas were traveling around, sharing the gospel message. They preached it boldly. Many accepted, while others rejected their message. When they were in Lystra, Paul was given power by the Lord to heal a lame man, a man who had never walked—until now! Through the power of the Holy Spirit, Paul healed him, and scripture reveals to us why this man was selected: when Paul looked at the man, he could see "that he had faith to be healed."

Do you believe as this man did? Do you wake up each day expecting the Lord to do great things? Or have you given up and laid to rest a big dream in your life?

You serve a God who is powerful enough to make a lame man stand up and walk! Believe in Jesus. He's above and beyond all you can imagine. He can bring beauty from ashes in your life. He can make dry bones live again.

EVEN NOW

"Even now," declares the LORD, "return to me
with all your heart, with fasting and weeping and
mourning." Rend your heart and not your garments.
Return to the LORD your God, for he is gracious
and compassionate, slow to anger and abounding
in love, and he relents from sending calamity.

JOEL 2:12–13 NIV

The Israelites had periods of great rebellion against God. They turned to terrible pagan idols made of wood and stone. They ignored God's laws and no longer relied on Him. They forgot they were God's treasured possession, holy among the nations.

Like Israel, we have all rebelled against the Lord at some point in life. We have strayed far from home. And when we look over our shoulder to see how far we have gone, we often tell ourselves that it's too late to turn back. We've done too much. Wandered too far. Surely if we went home, God's gates would be firmly shut, barring our entry.

But God says, "Even now return to me." Even after all you have done—after all the idols you have pursued, and all the commandments you have broken—come back home. All He requires is your whole heart, brimming with repentance. A heart that has been torn by the remembrance of the depth of your depravity and your deep, deep need for a Savior.

Like Israel, you also are God's treasured possession, His precious child. His gates remain open, anticipating your return.

EVEN TO OLD AGE

"Even to your old age and gray hairs I am he, I am he who will sustain you. I have made you and I will carry you; I will sustain you and I will rescue you."

ISAIAH 46:4 NIV

No doubt you have looked in the mirror day after day, year after year, and noted the changes that come with the passage of time. Much to our chagrin, age brings with it some not-so-subtle differences of which you may not be a fan. Perhaps a few wrinkles emerge, or gray hairs, or less energy. Father Time does indeed make his mark.

Regardless of these physical changes, God promises He will always be there to support us and carry us through the hard times. Remember the beautiful poem "Footprints in the Sand" by Mary Stevenson? In the memorable last lines, God reminds us: "The years when you have seen only one set of footprints, my child, is when I carried you."

Through the journey of life, even through old age, God reminds us that He will always be there. Our job is simply to believe Him.

Day 56

FULLNESS

*I pray that you, being rooted and established in
love, may have power. . .to know this love that
surpasses knowledge—that you may be filled
to the measure of all the fullness of God.*
EPHESIANS 3:17–19 NIV

When you understand how deeply you are loved, God's fullness infuses you to the brim.

What keeps you from accepting God's love? Perhaps feelings of unworthiness and guilt block your heart. Or the shame of secret sins isolates you. Yet the one who knows you best accepts you the most completely. Christ's blood was more than sufficient, and you stand before God faultless and beloved. Let go of any thought that you must earn the affection that God pours into you freely.

The fullness of God is like the deep pool at the base of a mountain waterfall, deep enough for you to plunge into, laughing with joy. Immerse yourself in the great incomprehensible mystery of who God is—an all-knowing and all-powerful being who chooses friendship with you. He is enduringly faithful but forgives all of your unfaithfulness. He is God the mighty warrior of the Old Testament and Christ the gentle lamb of the New.

Though God is unfathomable, He delights in revealing Himself to you so that you may be filled to the brim with the fullness of God.

Day 51

RELAX, RELY, REJOICE

David. . .said: The Lord is my Rock [of escape from
Saul] and my Fortress [in the wilderness] and
my Deliverer. . . . As for God, His way is perfect;
the word of the Lord is tried. He is a Shield to
all those who trust and take refuge in Him.

2 SAMUEL 22:1–2, 31 AMPC

Both Saul and David were the Lord's anointed. And that's where
the similarity ends. For Saul never really and truly put his trust in
God. Instead, he put his trust in himself and those around him.
He feared the opinion and power of people more than he feared
God and His law. That is why Saul's kingdom was torn from his
hands, why he felt threatened by and so chased David, and why
he, at the end, consulted the witch of Endor instead of God.

And then there was David, the man after God's own heart.
Although he made mistakes, he was quick to confess to and humble
himself before God. Because he trusted God, God became his
shield and refuge. Because David trusted the word and promises
of God, God continually delivered him in the wilderness.

When you trust and take shelter in God your Rock, He will
become your impenetrable shield. And in following His word,
you'll find your way perfect. Relax. Rely. Rejoice in the Rock that
is your God.

GOD LOVES FIRST

We love because he first loved us.
1 JOHN 4:19 NIV

Where does love begin? Love—that unselfish and unconditional emotion that drives us to our knees in worship, to forgiveness when broken, and to give to others beyond where common sense ends.

The Bible tells us we love because God loves first. Our love flows from God's bottomless well of devotion for us. He initiates the relationship He wants with us, drenching us with His love as He adopts us as His children.

We worry when we can't love others as He told us in the greatest commandment—to love Him and to love others. We can't do this on our own. But God loves with an everlasting love.

The power of His love within us fuels our love when human love is running on empty. He plants His love within our hearts so we can share Him with others. We draw from His endless supply.

Love starts with God. God continues to provide His love to nourish us. God surrounds us with His love. We live in hope and draw from His strength, all because He first loved us.

WITH GOD, ALL THINGS ARE POSSIBLE

*Jesus looked at them and said, "With man this is
impossible, but with God all things are possible."*
MATTHEW 19:26 NIV

The rich young ruler's conversation with Jesus had not gone as
expected. Instead of learning that he had fulfilled all the requirements of the law—which he thought would admit him to heaven—
the young man was told to sell his possessions and give to the
poor. Dejected, he gave up and went home.

This turn of events prompted much discussion between Jesus
and His disciples, centering on the difficulties of being admitted
to heaven. Frustrated with the impossible scenario Jesus was
painting, complete with camels going through the eye of a needle,
the disciples finally asked: "Who then can be saved?" (19:25 NIV).

With the question finally asked, Jesus zeroed in on the heart
of the matter: No one can be saved by their own efforts! The rich
young ruler had tried everything humanly possible and still he
came up short. Man's greatest efforts pale in comparison to the
requirements of a holy God.

But grace, freely offered by God and accepted by individuals,
will admit us to heaven. With God, all things *are* possible: especially enabling forgiven sinners to live eternally. Realizing we can
do nothing is the key to gaining everything.

Day 60

MUCH, MUCH MORE

With God's power working in us, God can do much, much more than anything we can ask or imagine. To him be glory in the church and in Christ Jesus for all time, forever and ever. Amen.
EPHESIANS 3:20–21 NCV

Think back to a time when something happened in your life that you never saw coming. Something that happened out of the blue, was not on your radar, and absolutely amazed you. When God's power is at work within you, the possibilities are beyond your imagination

The New International Version of the Bible says that He can do "immeasurably more" than what you could imagine. Whatever problem you are facing right now—big or small—God cares. As you pray about it and seek God's will, don't put Him in a box thinking that there's no way out or that there is only one right answer. His response just might be beyond your understanding and your wildest imagination.

Remember that things aren't always what they seem. When you feel disappointed in God's answers to your prayers, look outside the box. God is always, always working everything out for your good. God sees all. What may feel like the best answer may be totally destructive to you or someone you love. Trust that God can do much more than anything you could ever ask or imagine!

Day 61

BEGIN AGAIN

*I am not writing you a new command but one
we have had from the beginning. I ask that
we love one another. And this is love: that
we walk in obedience to his commands.*

2 JOHN 5–6 NIV

Most people start off the new year with the best of intentions. "This year will be different. This year will be better. *I* will be better."

But somewhere along the way, you get distracted. You get tired. You lose ground. You forget. You fail.

Why not begin again?

You don't have to wait for the next New Year's Day. You don't have to wait for permission to be reborn. Every day can be your spring.

All you have to do is decide. Decide to be obedient to what God has told you to do from the beginning. Decide to be honest with yourself. Decide to stay on the path. Decide to love. Decide to walk.

Examine your failures. Take note of your distractions and temptations. Plan strategies that will lead to healthy relationships, a healthy lifestyle, a balanced work life, and a devoted spiritual life.

There is nothing all that special or magical about New Year's Day. It's just a day. And today is just a day too. It won't be easy, whatever it is. Every good work requires effort. But you don't have to wait until you're perfect. In fact, you shouldn't. Begin again today.

Day 62

A Shelter from the Storm

"This is what the Sovereign LORD says: I will take a branch from the top of a tall cedar, and I will plant it on the top of Israel's highest mountain. It will become a majestic cedar, sending forth its branches and producing seed. Birds of every sort will nest in it, finding shelter in the shade of its branches."

EZEKIEL 17:22–23 NLT

What a lovely passage from the book of Ezekiel. It paints a brilliant picture, with images of birds finding shelter in the branches of a majestic cedar. Clearly, God has always cared about serving as our shelter during a storm.

Perhaps you've experienced that firsthand. God has given you rest, not only on weekends and vacations but even in the middle of the storms you've faced.

Think of a time when God spread Himself out over your situation in much the same way the branches of that cedar tree were spread to welcome the birds. He's not a discriminator. The passage assures us that "birds of every sort" are welcome.

What sort of bird are you? Are you ready to fly into God's arms today for some much-needed rest?

Day 63

KEEP YOUR EYES ON GOD

For we have no might to stand against this great company that is coming against us. We do not know what to do, but our eyes are upon You. . . . The Lord says this to you: Be not afraid or dismayed at this great multitude; for the battle is not yours, but God's.

2 CHRONICLES 20:12, 15 AMPC

One of the best and most inspirational stories in the Bible is found in 2 Chronicles 20. There we find Judah's King Jehoshaphat being told that a huge army is coming to attack him and his people. Immediately after hearing this news, Jehoshaphat sets himself to seek God. He tells Him what's happening, then lets God know that although Judah doesn't have the strength to stand against these enemy armies, and although he and his people don't know what to do, their eyes are on God.

Hearing these words from Jehoshaphat, God tells him not to be worried or afraid of this great mass of warriors at Judah's gate for this battle is His. All His people need to do is "take your positions, stand still, and see the deliverance of the Lord [Who is] with you" (2 Chronicles 20:17 AMPC).

When you find yourself about to panic, stop. Let God know your situation. Then, with your eyes on Him and your faith in Him, stand still and witness the victory.

Day 64

WILDERNESS DAYS

*So he said, "I have been very zealous for the
LORD God of hosts; for the children of Israel
have forsaken Your covenant, torn down Your
altars, and killed Your prophets with the sword.
I alone am left; and they seek to take my life."*

1 KINGS 19:10 NKJV

After the Lord's triumph at Mount Carmel, Elijah spent forty days
in the wilderness, despondent beyond belief, thinking he would
soon die at the wicked hands of Ahab and Jezebel. Despite all of
his work for God, all Elijah saw was the death of God's prophets,
and God's people going more wayward. He cried out, "It is enough!
Now, LORD, take my life, for I am no better than my fathers!"
(1 Kings 19:4 NKJV).

Instead of God giving Elijah a pep talk—"Remember all
My miracles? My ravens feeding you by the brook? Get back in
the game, Elijah!"—He sent an angel to sustain him in his grief.
At the end of the forty days, God showed his servant His near-
ness in the still, small voice after the earthquakes and the wind
and fire.

Maybe you have beaten yourself up for not doing more or
being more for God. Or maybe you feel like your efforts go
unseen or your resources are exhausted. But during your wilderness days, your compassionate God is by your side too and He
always has more grace than you expect.

COMFORT FOR COMFORT

*For this reason Jesus had to be made like his brothers
and sisters in every way so he could be their merciful
and faithful high priest in service to God. Then
Jesus could die in their place to take away their
sins. And now he can help those who are tempted,
because he himself suffered and was tempted.*

HEBREWS 2:17–18 NCV

God chose to come to earth in human form to be made like us.
To understand what it's like to be human. To be able to fully take
our place and remove our sins. Because He was fully human while
being fully God, He can help. He can comfort. The Bible says that
He "comforts us in all our troubles, so that we can comfort those
in any trouble with the comfort we ourselves have received from
God" (2 Corinthians 1:4 NIV).

It's so encouraging that Jesus was just like us! Our God is
not one who wants to remain as a distant high king, out of touch
with the commoners. He wants a very personal relationship with
each one of us. He lowered Himself to our level so that we could
have personal and continual access to Him. His glory knows no
bounds, yet He desires to be our friend. Take great comfort in that.

And then when people around you are troubled, you can step
in. You can wrap your arms around someone else who needs a
friend because of what Jesus has done for you.

BLESSABLE

*Love the LORD your God and. . .serve him with
all your heart and with all your soul—then I
will send rain on your land in its season.*
DEUTERONOMY 11:13–14 NIV

We all want God's blessings. We want it to rain on our crops; we want the sun to shine on our picnics; and we want a gentle breeze to relieve us from summer's scorch. We want job security and bigger paychecks.

Though God allows some blessings to grace every person in the human race, there are some keys to receiving more of God's goodness. If we want God's blessings, we must be blessable.

So how do we become blessable? We must love God. And we must serve Him with all our hearts.

Loving God is the easy part. But the evidence of that love comes through our service to Him, and that's a little harder.

When we love God, we serve Him by loving others. We serve Him by taking the time to mow the widow's lawn or prepare a meal for someone who's ill or provide a coat for someone who's cold. We serve Him by offering a hand of friendship to the friendless or by saying something positive about the victim of gossip.

When we love God and our actions show evidence of that love, we become blessable. That's when God will pour out His goodness on us in ways we could never imagine.

Day 61

GOD IS IN CONTROL

"The foundations of law and order have collapsed.
What can the righteous do?" But the LORD is in his
holy Temple; the LORD still rules from heaven.

PSALM 11:3–4 NLT

What does daily life look like when an earthquake rocks a third-world country, killing hundreds of thousands and leaving an already-desolate nation in ruins? When a tsunami sweeps away entire villages? When a hurricane flattens all within a one-hundred-mile radius of the shore?

Law and order collapse when natural disasters strike. The struggle for basic survival eclipses all else and creates a tremendous need for strong leadership. All too often, corrupt or inept governments are unable to meet the needs of their citizens when a catastrophe strikes.

Where is God when it hurts? Where is God in the midst of injustice? Does God care? These timeless questions never lose their relevance. The entire book of Job wrestles with these questions. The psalmist also picks up the lament, and only responds that God is still on the throne.

We may never understand why bad things happen, or why God seems to be silent. But we can know that regardless of the way things appear, our loving God is still in control—even when things appear to be spiraling out of control. How will you trust God today?

Day 68

YOU WILL BE COMFORTED

"Blessed are those who mourn, for they will be comforted."
MATTHEW 5:4 NIV

Jesus began His Sermon on the Mount with nine blessings, or "Beatitudes." The Amplified Version suggests that blessed means "enviably happy [with a happiness produced by the experience of God's favor and especially conditioned by the revelation of His matchless grace]" (Matthew 5:4 AMPC).

Apparently Jesus' interpretation of happiness doesn't match ours: Happy are the poor? The hungry and thirsty? The persecuted? Happy are those who *mourn*?

Yes, for they will be comforted.

The psalmist frequently praised God as the source of comfort (71:21; 23:4; 86:17). Isaiah commanded the mountains to burst into song because of the Lord's comfort (49:13). Even Jeremiah, the weeping prophet, called God "my Comforter in sorrow" (8:18 NIV). In Jesus, Christians receive comfort "in all our troubles" (2 Corinthians 1:3–4 NIV).

The earth will experience the final fulfillment of that promise in heaven, when "God will wipe away every tear from their eyes" (Revelation 7:17 NIV).

In this life, tears will come—but so will God's comfort.

GOD, THE RESCUER

*But when the people of Israel cried out to the LORD
for help, the LORD raised up a rescuer to save them.
His name was Othniel, the son of Caleb's younger
brother, Kenaz. The Spirit of the LORD came upon
him, and he became Israel's judge. He went to
war against King Cushan-rishathaim of Aram,
and the LORD gave Othniel victory over him.*

JUDGES 3:9–10 NLT

God has always been in the business of rescuing people—from calamities, from each other, from illness, from breakdowns in relationships, from unforeseen weather events, from starvation, and sometimes even from themselves.

Take a look at the motivational statement at the beginning of this verse: "when the people of Israel cried out to the LORD for help." That's where it starts. God hears the cries, the prayers, the pleas of His people and raises up a rescuer.

Over two thousand years ago, God heard the cries of His people and sent His Son, Jesus, as the ultimate rescuer. He did what none of the former "gods" could do—He offered eternal rescue to all who would place their trust in Him.

Today, when you cry out to God, trust that He will hear your prayer. Know that Jesus will rescue you from whatever's coming against you. For that's His business today, tomorrow, and forever.

Day 10

GOD ALWAYS COMES THROUGH

The jar of meal was not spent nor did the
bottle of oil fail, according to the word
which the Lord spoke through Elijah.
1 KINGS 17:16 AMPC

God rewards you when you have faith in Him and His Word, no matter how far-fetched His commands seem. Case in point: Elijah and the widow.

God told Elijah to go to Zarephath because He'd commanded a widow there to provide for him (1 Kings 17:9). So, the ever-obedient Elijah goes to Zarephath. There he sees a widow gathering sticks. He asks her to bring him some water and bread. Imagine Elijah's surprise when she tells him she has nothing but a "handful of meal in the jar and a little oil in the bottle" (1 Kings 17:12 AMPC) and was now gathering sticks to make herself and her son a last meal.

Yet Elijah knows his God is a god of His word, a doer of the seemingly impossible. He tells the widow not to fear but to make him a cake and *then* prepare some for her and her son. Because God has said that during the famine, the widow's jar of meal and her bottle of oil would not run out! So the widow followed Elijah's advice and found God was true to His word.

Just as God came through for the widow of Zarephath, God will come through for you. *Simply believe!*

Day 11

A HEALTHY FEAR

*To fear the LORD is to hate evil; I hate pride
and arrogance, evil behavior and perverse speech.*
PROVERBS 8:13 NIV

When we think about our fears, our minds and bodies almost always tense. Whether it's a fear of heights, spiders, public speaking, failure, or being alone, everyone has fears. In fact, it's considered perfectly natural to avoid what we fear.

So why does the Bible say we should "fear" God? In reality, to fear God is not the same as fearing the creepy-crawly spider inching up the living room wall. Instead, we fear God when we have a deep respect and reverence for Him.

Imagine that the president of the United States was paying your home a visit. The house would be extra clean, the laundry would be washed and put away, and the children would be instructed to be on their best behavior. Why? Because the visitor deserves respect.

Our lives should reflect a similar reverence for our heavenly Father every day—our souls scrubbed extra clean, sin eliminated, and love for our creator bursting forth in joy. God wants speech and actions to match. Take time today to stand in awe of the one who deserves our greatest respect and love.

Day 12

A RIVER OF HEALING

He asked me, "Have you been watching, son of man?" Then he led me back along the riverbank. When I returned, I was surprised by the sight of many trees growing on both sides of the river.
EZEKIEL 47:6–7 NLT

If you've ever been through a drought, you know the kind of damage it can do—to your grass, your crops, even your attitude. When the land around you dries up, it can even cause your soul to get dry and cracked.

Picture a river running through that field of dried grass. The moment the water spills over its banks and onto the parched, dry land, everything changes. The river brings life! Before long, trees are growing, life is returning.

Jesus is the river of life! He's come to split the dry, parched areas of your life wide open and to pour His living water over it all so that life might return.

What dried-out areas can you turn over to God today? Picture Him soaking those areas with holy water. How amazing, to watch them spring to life once more!

IN THE MIDST OF TROUBLE

*Though I am surrounded by troubles, you will protect
me. . . . The LORD will work out his plans for my
life—for your faithful love, O LORD, endures forever.*
PSALM 138:7–8 NLT

Sometimes when we feel the walls of a tough situation closing in
on us, we lose sight of God. We fail to see that He is with us absolutely everywhere—no matter what situation we find ourselves in or
put ourselves in—and He never stops intervening in our lives.
David expressed wonder at the thought, saying, "You know everything I do. . . . You go before me and follow me. You place your
hand of blessing on my head. Such knowledge is too wonderful
for me, too great for me to understand!" (Psalm 139:3, 5–6 NLT).

David could go no place where God wasn't already present,
waiting to shepherd him. "Where can I go from your Spirit?
Where can I flee from your presence?" David asked. "If I rise on
the wings of the dawn, if I settle on the far side of the sea, even
there your hand will guide me, your right hand will hold me fast"
(Psalm 138:7, 9–10 NIV).

Are troubles making you claustrophobic? Shift your focus to
the one who is ever present, ever faithful, and ever working out
His plans for you.

Day 14

IN ALL THINGS

We know that in all things God works for
the good of those who love him, who have
been called according to his purpose.

ROMANS 8:28 NIV

Through the traffic-snarled highway home and on the quiet path through peaceful parkland; in the tense, executive office conference and it the chatty cafeteria atmosphere; on the phone with distant relatives or sitting together around a family campfire—God can work in all kinds of places and circumstances for the good of those who love Him.

You may think about God working only when you are sitting in a worship service or reading the Bible or on a prayer retreat. Or maybe you think about Him working only when something good happens—when a prayer is answered, a relationship mended, or a crisis averted.

But God is always at work. He doesn't take vacation days. He doesn't ever stop knitting you together and unfolding His grand story. Even at the times when you feel your weakest, when you don't even know what to pray for and can't find the words to say, the Spirit helps you and speaks for you. No matter how you feel, where you are, what you are doing, or who you are with—God is working for your good.

LEADING A LAMB TO SAFETY

But [God] led His own people forth like sheep
and guided them [with a shepherd's care] like
a flock in the wilderness. And He led them on
safely and in confident trust, so that they feared
not; but the sea overwhelmed their enemies.

PSALM 78:52–53 AMPC

Some days you may feel as if you are being squeezed, wrung out, hung out to dry. You mind is so scattered, your being so anxious, that no solutions come to mind. Any relief on the horizon appears distant, at best. It seems as if you have one problem coming from behind and nothing but a nameless dark out in front of you, keeping you from moving forward.

This is when it's good to remember God. How He led His people to safety over and over again. When you remember the plagues of Egypt, the parting of the Red Sea, the water gushing from a rock in the wilderness, the manna coming down from heaven, the water turned into wine, the waking and walking of the dead, the calming of a storm, then you realize you're safe in God's hands. You can move forward in confident trust. You can have the courage you need to let God shepherd you out of your wilderness and into His light.

Day 16

GOD'S WAY IS PERFECT

*As for God, his way is perfect: the LORD's word is
flawless; he shields all who take refuge in him.*
PSALM 18:30 NIV

God's way is perfect. That sounds nice. . .but it also sounds a little
cliché, especially when we're in the throes of heartache and despair.
If God's way is perfect, why does it hurt so much? Is God cruel?
Doesn't He care about us?

God's way is without flaw. . .but life has plenty of imperfections
and shortcomings. As long as we're on this earth, we will have
trouble. Didn't He say as much?

But when we run to Him in that trouble, He is a shield. He
is a refuge. He is our safe place. When we run to Him, He will
love us, comfort us, and protect us. Life may not be perfect, but
God always is.

CONTAGIOUS LAUGHTER

*And Sarah said, "God has made me laugh,
and all who hear will laugh with me."*
GENESIS 21:6 NKJV

Nothing brings more joy to our hearts than when God blesses our lives. Like Sarah, we may at first laugh with disbelief when God promises us our heart's desire. For some reason, we doubt that He can do what we deem impossible. Yet God asks us, as He did Sarah, "Is any thing too hard for the LORD?" (Genesis 18:14 NKJV).

Then when the blessings shower down upon us, we overflow with joy. Everything seems bright and right with the world. With God, the impossible has become a reality. We bubble over with laughter, and when we laugh, the world laughs with us! It's contagious!

When Satan bombards us with lies—"God's not real"; "You'll never get that job"; "Mr. Right? He'll never come along"—it's time to look back at God's Word and remember Sarah. Imbed in your mind the truth that with God, nothing is impossible (Matthew 19:26). And then, in the midst of the storm, in the darkness of night, in the crux of the trial, laugh, letting the joy of God's truth be your strength.

CHOOSE TO FOLLOW JESUS

*"On your way," said Jesus. "Your faith has saved
and healed you." In that very instant he recovered
his sight and followed Jesus down the road.*

MARK 10:52 MSG

Jesus spent time in Jericho and was leaving town with His disciples. On His way, a blind beggar named Bartimaeus cried out to Him. The beggar needed God's grace and mercy for he was unable to see. So Jesus called the man over and asked him what he wanted. Bartimaeus replied, "I want to see" (Mark 10:51 MSG). Jesus said, "On your way. . .Your faith has saved and healed you" (Mark 10:52 MSG). His sight restored, Bartimaeus "followed Jesus down the road."

As you consider all of the ways in which life can bring you down—health issues, job losses, the death of friends or family members, the suffering of children—it may take a lot of effort to look up to God, to cry out for His unmerited favor and mercy, to throw off whatever may be hindering you, to run after the Lord, and to put your most fervent and heartfelt desire into words.

So, sister, today, even if it physically or emotionally hurts, pick your head up. Literally cry out to God for what you need most. Then, by faith, whether you receive an instant healing or complete silence, choose to follow Jesus.

SPOT FREE

If we confess our sins, he is faithful and just and will
forgive us our sins and purify us from all unrighteousness.
1 JOHN 1:9 NIV

Have you ever had a stain on a blouse that wouldn't come out?
Maybe you massaged detergent into it and then washed it over
and over again, all in hopes that you could make the errant spot
go away. In the end, you tossed the blouse in the trash, unable to
wear it because it made you look (or feel) less than perfect.

Sin is the same way. It leaves a spot—an indelible mark—on
us. We can't hide it. We can't scrub it away. We can't disguise it
with a lovely scarf. It marks us for life. Until Jesus.

When we encounter Jesus, when we take Him at His word and
ask for His forgiveness, He performs in an instant what we could
not perform in years of trying. The sin—all that ugliness of the
past—is gone. *Poof.* No guilt. No condemnation. No doubt. When
we make Him Lord of our lives, we get the best "laundering" job
of our lives. What a joy, to be spot free!

Day 80

GOD USES OUR EVERY EFFORT

*Always work enthusiastically for the Lord, for you
know that nothing you do for the Lord is ever useless.*
1 CORINTHIANS 15:58 NLT

Martin Luther was a devout monk whose love for the Word of God brought us the Protestant Reformation. Luther didn't always want to be a monk, however. He started out as a brilliant lawyer. But in a moment of fear, he vowed to become a monk if he survived a dangerous lightning storm. Despite his father's disappointment, Luther dedicated himself to the church.

Martin Luther's father felt his son's talents were being wasted, completely unaware that he would change the world forever.

Nothing we give to God is wasted, whether for praise, worship, or works of the kingdom. Sometimes that offering is in the form of sacrifice. Elisabeth Elliot and her husband, Jim, faced cannibals to spread the gospel. Years after Jim's violent death, Elizabeth wrote, "I will offer to God both my tears and my exultation. Nothing we offer to Him will be lost." God has kept every tear in a bottle, and He knows their price (Psalm 56:8).

God has promised that when we give ourselves for His sake, He will return "pressed down, shaken together, and running over" (Luke 6:38 NKJV). Whether our reward is in this life or the next, God's promise has been and will always be faithful.

THE LORD'S PLANS

Commit your actions to the LORD,
and your plans will succeed.
PROVERBS 16:3 NLT

At an early age, an ambitious woman planned her entire life. She determined she would earn her law degree by age twenty-five, marry by twenty-eight, become a partner in her law firm by thirty-five, and retire at fifty. She was quite disappointed when her plan failed.

Do you have any plans for your life?

The Lord desires that we have plans for our lives. He encourages us to have aspirations, goals, and hopes; however, He provides a framework for developing and implementing those plans. God wants us to develop them in cooperation with His will for us. Those plans should be in line with His plan; His overall purpose for our lives; our spiritual gifts, abilities, interests, and talents; and His perfect timing.

God requires us not to hold on too tight to the plan, but rather to commit or entrust it to Him. When we surrender it to the Lord, He will secure, or "make firm," the plan. God's will cannot be thwarted; therefore, God's purpose, plan, and work will be established. There is no need to worry—just commit your plans to the Lord.

Day 82

GOD'S FOREVER BRIDE

"I will betroth you to me forever; I will betroth you in righteousness and justice, in love and compassion. I will betroth you in faithfulness, and you will acknowledge the Lord."
HOSEA 2:19–20 NIV

Throughout the book of Hosea, God speaks to Israel, His chosen people, who have fallen away and worshipped other gods. They were unfaithful, breaking the covenant God made with them. The Lord continually compares Israel to a straying wife committing adultery against Him. But despite Israel's rebellion, God still promises to restore her.

These verses may seem distant and irrelevant in the modern world. But as a Christian, you have been adopted into God's nation. You are one of His people, a citizen in His kingdom. When you bow before idols—which can be anything from money to relationships—it grieves the Lord. He is a jealous God, desiring your undivided attention.

But the most astonishing thing is that you are also betrothed to Him to be His bride—beautiful, pure, honored, and cherished. God offers to purify those who enter into a covenant with Him. His wedding gift to you is righteousness, justice, love, compassion, and faithfulness. In all of these things, He never fails or falters.

Rejoice! For you are God's forever bride.

INTO HIS PRESENCE

*Let us come before him with thanksgiving
and extol him with music and song.*
PSALM 95:2 NIV

If God is everywhere, how is it possible to come *into* His presence? While it's true that God is ever-present, His children are given a special invitation to draw near to Him. Yes, He may be at the banquet, but *we* can occupy the seat of honor right next to Him.

The way we draw near to God is through a beautiful, balanced combination of reverence and excitement. While our respect for God requires a measure of solemnity, God is no fuddy-duddy. He wants us to be happy and joyful in His presence. He longs to hear a simple, sincere, excited "thank You" from His children, for all the things He's done in the past. He longs to see us sing and dance in His presence and tell Him how much we love Him.

When God feels distant, we can remember our special invitation to join Him in intimate conversation. He will welcome us into His arms when we fall before Him, give excited thanks, and sing joyful songs of love and praise.

Day 84

REMEMBER THE GREATNESS OF GOD

*"He performs wonders that cannot be fathomed,
miracles that cannot be counted."*
JOB 5:9 NIV

In Job 5, Job's friend Eliphaz tries to put in plain words the reason for Job's suffering. In his opinion, Job must have done something sinful to be in such a dreadful state. Eliphaz tells Job what he would do if he were suffering because of his sins. He would appeal to God. He would confess his sins and hope for God's mercy. After all, God "performs wonders that cannot be fathomed, miracles that cannot be counted."

In other words, Eliphaz says Job should seek God's justice, because God is greater than anyone can imagine. He alone is the one who forgives our sinfulness and heals our suffering.

Job's afflictions were not due to anything that he had done, but Eliphaz's instructions to him would have been good *if* he had sinned. We see them again in 1 John 1:9 (NIV), "If we confess our sins, he is faithful and just and will forgive us our sins and purify us from all unrighteousness."

Are you feeling guilty about some sin in your life? Remember the greatness of God. Romans 10:13 (NIV) says: "Everyone who calls on the name of the Lord will be saved."

GOD CARES ABOUT YOU

*The LORD is close to the brokenhearted and
saves those who are crushed in spirit.*
PSALM 34:18 NIV

Some versions of the Bible provide a clue about when this psalm was written. They begin with an introduction: "A Psalm of David when he feigned madness before Abimelech, who drove him away and he departed" (NASB). You can read more about this time in David's life in 1 Samuel 21.

Psalm 34 is an acrostic poem. When written in Hebrew, the verses begin with the successive letters of the Hebrew alphabet. It is David's song of praise and thanksgiving for God's redemption. In some ways, it is like the book of Proverbs, because it teaches the reader about the character of God.

"The LORD is close to the brokenhearted and saves those who are crushed in spirit" (verse 18). This reassuring verse guarantees that God is close to us when we are sad. It promises to save us from despair.

Jesus restated these words in His Sermon on the Mount: "Blessed are the poor in spirit: for theirs is the kingdom of heaven. Blessed are they that mourn: for they shall be comforted" (Matthew 5:3–4 KJV).

Are you brokenhearted today? Is your spirit packed down with despair? Then meditate on Psalm 34:18. Ask God for help. He cares about you! (1 Peter 5:7).

JESUS' BIRTH GIVES HOPE

And there were shepherds living out in the fields nearby, keeping watch over their flocks at night. An angel of the Lord appeared to them, and the glory of the Lord shone around them, and they were terrified. But the angel said to them, "Do not be afraid. I bring you good news that will cause great joy for all the people. Today in the town of David a Savior has been born to you; he is the Messiah, the Lord. This will be a sign to you: You will find a baby wrapped in cloths and lying in a manger."

LUKE 2:8–12 NIV

The holidays can be a time when fear creeps up on us unexpectedly. We can fear for our country, fear the family conflicts that may surface over holiday dinners, fear the state of our finances and relationships. . .the fear list can be long.

What the angel said to the shepherds applies to us now and always. "Do not be afraid. I bring you good news that will cause great joy for all the people." This Christmas, let your focus be on that joyful news. Jesus' birth gives us hope. We don't have to fear.

First John 4:18 tells us that perfect love casts out fear. Perfect love was born on Christmas day. Let that perfect love fill your heart with joy, hope, and peace. Then there will be no room in your heart for fear.

Day 87

FLOWERS FALL

*"The grass withers and the flowers fall,
but the word of the Lord endures forever."*
1 PETER 1:24–25 NIV

It's funny how people try to make things last that were never meant to do so. For example, we hold on to mementos of special occasions, sometimes keeping the flowers that were worn on the day or that decorated the scene. We will press flowers, dry them, and preserve them in various ways. When that isn't enough, we have silk renditions created. Or we take photographs and hold on to those instead.

We want good things to last. We want people to live long lives and relationships to endure hardships. We root for the longsuffering hero who finally wins in the end. We hold detailed ceremonies to remember those we have lost.

Though these bodies of ours were not meant to continue forever, when we have accepted Jesus as our Savior and Redeemer, we become "born again, not of perishable seed, but of imperishable, through the living and enduring word of God" (1 Peter 1:23 NIV).

It's this contradiction—forever souls bound in temporary houses—that makes us long for all good things to never die. But peace and contentment—a cure of sorts for that longing—can be found in the enduring Word of God. The more time we spend there, the more we realize we have all the time in the world.

BE STILL

"Be still, and know that I am God."
PSALM 46:10 NIV

From the minute the alarm clock goes off in the morning, we are busy. Many women rush off to work or begin their tasks around the house without even eating breakfast. Most of us keep hectic schedules, and it is easy to let the day pass by without a moment of peace and quiet.

In Psalm 46:10 the command to be still is coupled with the result of knowing that He is God. Could it be that in order to truly recognize God's presence in our lives, we must make time to quiet ourselves before Him?

Sitting quietly before the Lord is a discipline that requires practice. Just as in our earthly relationships, learning to be a good listener as we converse with our heavenly Father is important. If prayer remains one-sided, we will miss out on what He has to say to us.

Although God may not speak to us in an audible voice, He will direct our thinking and speak to our hearts. Stillness allows us to dwell on God's sovereignty, His goodness, and His deep love for us. He wants us to remember that He is God and that He is in control, regardless of our circumstances.

Be still. . .and know that He is God.

WHEN GOD'S PEOPLE PRAY

Pray for the peace of Jerusalem:
"May those who love you be secure."
PSALM 122:6 NIV

When it comes to making a difference in this world, it's easy to feel helpless. Wars are being fought on the other side of the world. People are starving, suffering, hurting. As much as we'd like to help, there's not much we can do, right?

Except, there is something we can do. It's the most powerful thing anyone can do—we can pray. God, in all His power, has invited us to come alongside Him. He's asked us to join Him in His work by praying for each other.

For centuries, God's people have been treated unfairly and unjustly. Yet we've survived, when other groups haven't. The reason we've survived when so many have sought to silence us is because we have something our enemies don't have. We have the power of God behind us.

When we pray, we call upon every resource available to us, as the children of God. We call upon His strength, His compassion, His ferocity, His mercy, His love, and His justice. We have the ability to extend God's reach to the other side of our town or the other side of the world, all because we pray.

Day 10

SIDE BY SIDE

Have no fear of sudden disaster or of the ruin that overtakes the wicked, for the LORD will be at your side and will keep your foot from being snared.
PROVERBS 3:25–26 NIV

Our world today is crammed with grim news. Television and internet reports blast us with every detail of a disaster, often filling our hearts with dread. From the pulpit we hear "perfect love casts out fear." However, we frequently remain apprehensive. There are things of which we must be aware, but we do not need to become overtaken with fear and worry. For the Lord our God has given us a promise in His Word. He is at our side.

The Lord sees the concerns and dreads of His children and has surrounded us with His love. When we gaze into His face and seek His presence, the light of His love will flood any dark corners, dispelling the anxious thoughts and scary shadows. His hand is there to hold us close, allowing us to feel His heartbeat.

As a boat casts off its tether from the dock, we need to cast off the ties to fear and worry and drift upon the sea of peace offered by our heavenly Father. He is at our side and will keep us safe, for He is true love.

Day 11

FRAGRANCE

May my prayer be set before you like incense; may the lifting up of my hands be like the evening sacrifice.
PSALM 141:2 NIV

Have you ever wondered if your little prayers for help are irritating to God? Do you hesitate asking Him for directions in recovering lost keys or finding a parking spot? Don't. Because God actually loves it when you turn to Him for anything, big or small. He breathes in your prayers as fragrant incense. So you are never, ever a bother to Him.

God looks at you with eyes of love. Every one of your prayers—long or short, frantic or calm—are a joy. He also gathers up and takes pleasure in all your "popcorn prayers"—little trusting thoughts that you send His way.

God is even more delighted when you offer Him your lifted hands, which is your way of expressing that He is your sovereign, almighty King and you are His loyal and loving servant.

So pray away today. And perhaps try worshipping God with your hands raised in adoration. It will lift your heart as well as His.

Day 12

JUST AS YOU ARE

*It is through Him that we have received grace
(God's unmerited favor) and [our] apostleship to
promote obedience to the faith and make disciples
for His name's sake. . .and this includes you, called of
Jesus Christ and invited [as you are] to belong to Him.*
ROMANS 1:5–6 AMPC

There's nothing you can do to earn God's grace. It's a free gift He gives to you, wanting nothing but love and obedience in return. Yet even then you may feel as if you're falling short. But not to worry. You have and are called by and invited to belong to Jesus Christ—*just as you are!* In other words, God had you at "hello."

When a woman gets pregnant, people might say she and her husband are "expecting." And that's true. They're expecting a child. Yet they do not know who that child will look like or how he or she will behave. And even when that child does appear, even when it's birthed or adopted into a (hopefully) loving family, how it will someday "turn out" is a mystery to everyone but God!

Just like that expected child, you too are no mystery to God. He has called you, invited you, to take this life journey with Him—*just as you are.* So stop striving and begin thriving. God's got you. Your job is to simply "get" Him.

Day 13

GOD'S PLANS ARE BEST

"When your days are over and you go to be with your ancestors, I will raise up your offspring to succeed you, one of your own sons, and I will establish his kingdom. He is the one who will build a house for me, and I will establish his throne forever."

1 CHRONICLES 17:11–12 NIV

David wanted to build a temple to house the ark of the covenant. He felt guilty that he was living in a fine home built of cedar and that the ark had no home. His heart was in the right place. But God had other plans.

The prophet Nathan delivered God's word to King David that his son Solomon was the one God would allow to build the temple. God wanted a man of peace to construct it. Although the message wasn't exactly what David expected, it pleased him nonetheless. The warrior David accepted Nathan's news and was beyond thankful to the Lord for establishing his family to be used in God's service.

Even if you feel your plans are God-centered and for His glory, He may have His reasons for thwarting them. So if something isn't going the way you had envisioned, resist the urge to blame God. Trust Him. He will use you as He sees fit. His choices and His timing are always perfect.

Day 14

NO GUILT, JUST GRACE

*Yet the news about him spread all the more,
so that crowds of people came to hear him and
to be healed of their sicknesses. But Jesus often
withdrew to lonely places and prayed.*
LUKE 5:15–16 NIV

"You make time for things that are important to you." Do you immediately feel guilty when you read that adage? *I know, I know. I should make sure I get family time, prayer time, and gym time, but I'm beyond stressed even thinking about trying to add one more thing to my schedule!*

You're not alone. You know, Jesus probably felt pressures in His work too. As His fame spread, actual multitudes of people came to Him to be healed. Showing compassion, Jesus healed their diseases and preached God's good news. But we also see He "withdrew to lonely places" to pray. Jesus, fully God, was also fully human—He got hungry, tired, and probably emotionally drained from witnessing the brokenness in His creation firsthand. He met with the Father for rest and strength so He could be prepared to help those who needed Him.

Get out from under the guilt and lean into His grace: God invites you to come to Him—no matter where you are or what you're doing in your day—to exchange your cares for His strength, peace, and joy. He will meet you where you are.

Abide in the Vine

"I am the vine; you are the branches. If you remain in me and I in you, you will bear much fruit; apart from me you can do nothing."

John 15:5 niv

Fruit is the tangible evidence of life. Only live plants can produce fruit. Nourishment travels from the roots to the branches, sustaining the fruit.

Jesus refers to Himself as the vine and to us as branches. Unless we are attached to the vine, we are not receiving spiritual nourishment. We become grafted into the vine by faith in Jesus Christ as Lord and Savior. His power then flows through us, producing spiritual fruit.

The fruit we bear is consistent with His character. Just as apple trees bear apples, we bear spiritual fruit that reflects Him. Spiritual fruit consists of God's qualities: love, joy, peace, patience, kindness, goodness, faithfulness, gentleness, and self-control. The fruit of the spirit cannot be grown by our own efforts. We must remain in the vine.

How do we abide in Him? We acknowledge that our spiritual sustenance comes from the Lord. We spend time with Him. We seek His will and wisdom. We are obedient and follow where He leads. When we remain attached to Him, spiritual fruit will be the evidence of His life within us. Abide in the vine and be fruitful!

Day 16

GOD IS OUR DWELLING PLACE

He that dwelleth in the secret place of the Most High
shall abide under the shadow of the Almighty.
PSALM 91:1 KJV

What a wonderful promise! God will cover—in a cloud of glory and protection—anyone who enters into His presence and stays in continual communion with Him. Under the old covenant, this applied only to the high priest entering into the Holy of Holies. But under the new covenant, all Christians can enter into God's presence through the blood of Jesus Christ.

As we daily abide in the scriptures and come into God's presence, He assures our safety and security no matter the circumstances. The word *shadow* indicates a shelter, covering, or protection from the heat and storms of life. Just as a tree's looming branches shield us from the hot sun, God provides refuge and protection wherever we are and whatever challenges we encounter.

The names given to God in this verse define the various aspects of His loving protection and care. "Most High" means that He is greater than any threat or problem we face, and "Almighty" emphasizes His power and majesty.

In another verse the psalmist wrote, "God is our refuge and strength, a very present help in trouble" (Psalm 46:1 KJV). The Lord is present at all times to help and protect us. He *is* our dwelling place.

Day 11

SERENITY

"They will be like a tree planted by the water that sends out its roots by the stream. It does not fear when heat comes; its leaves are always green. It has no worries in a year of drought and never fails to bear fruit."
JEREMIAH 17:8 NIV

Jeremiah paints a beautiful picture with his words. He describes what life is like for those whose trust is in the Lord, those who have full confidence in Him. This idyllic scene brings comfort and hope to the reader. It is a message of peace and serenity. A tree planted by water will never thirst; it will never fear excessive heat because it remains hydrated. No matter what, it will always bear fruit and thrive.

You will be like that tree if you trust in the Lord fully, knowing He will always care for you and meet your needs. Thus, you need not stress.

Psalm 1:3 contains similar words to those of Jeremiah 17:8, saying that those who delight in and meditate on God's law are "like a tree planted by streams of water, which yields its fruit in season and whose leaf does not wither—whatever they do prospers" (NIV).

Fully trust in God, live in His Word, and then revel in His peace. Ah. . .that's better.

Day 18

TALK TO THE ONE WHO CAN HELP

*Give all your worries and cares
to God, for he cares about you.*
1 PETER 5:7 NLT

A lot of people today say they pray, especially when someone is sick or there has been some kind of tragedy—but prayer is more than a good luck wish or an emergency contact number. Prayer is the channel through which we interact with our heavenly Father; it is the way we process the events and emotions of our lives and how we can see His will come to pass in our families.

Prayer is your lifeline. It is the vital connection that keeps you in touch with the Father. Imagine being disconnected from your devices all day, every day, for a week. At the end of that time, you would feel uninformed and shut out, cut off from the people who are most important to you. Perhaps God feels a little bit like that when we keep the channel of prayer closed on an ongoing basis. For, at its simplest, prayer is talking to Him. And when we don't talk to Him, we shut Him out of the details of our lives. Of course, being omniscient, He is aware of what is going on anyway, but He wants us to invite Him in, to want to share our days with Him.

Have you prayed today? Don't see it as an obligation or a guilt inducer but as a chance to communicate with the one who loves you more than anyone else and who can do more about your situation than anyone else.

Day 11

GRACE GIVEN AND RECEIVED

So the last shall be first, and the first last:
for many be called, but few chosen.
MATTHEW 20:16 KJV

Is receiving grace a hard concept for you to accept from God? Often it may be easier to extend grace to another person as opposed to extending it to yourself or receiving grace from another.

You might follow all of the commandments (Exodus 20:3–17) or sing praises to the Lord (Psalm 30), but you still feel like something isn't right between you and God. Could it be that something is holding you captive? Enslaving you to the point where there is a figurative barricade between you and God?

The parable of the workers in the vineyard, found in Matthew 20:1–16, is about God's grace in your life. Sometimes it doesn't feel fair when grace is given to others. You might want justice. Yet when the tables are turned, it may be hard for you to receive unmerited favor.

Why some people are given their fair share, others less, and some more doesn't always seem to make sense. What is clear is that God loves you no matter what! Even when circumstances in your life don't make sense, abide in Him. As you do, watch the barricade in your life come tumbling down because you are open to the grace He gives.

GOD IS FAITHFUL

But then I recall all you have done, O LORD;
I remember your wonderful deeds of long ago.
PSALM 77:11 NLT

The psalmist cries out in this chapter, feeling abandoned by God. Has God stopped loving him? Have His promises failed? Before you judge this lack of faith, look to your own. Have you doubted God, felt like He has forgotten you?

God's Word points again and again to His faithfulness. Recall the Bible stories. Consider Noah hammering the final nail into a massive ark while there was not a cloud in the sky, and Abraham climbing the mountain with his beloved Isaac. Imagine the emotions of Christ's disciples those three long days between His death and resurrection. And yet each time God came through.

God is as faithful today as He was in the past. He provides. He sustains. He shows up.

When you question your Father's love, look back. Recall altars of remembrance in your own life, those constructed at places of His provision. Can you see them in your mind's eye? They are there, standing as strong as the stone monuments by which the Israelites remembered Him.

Thank God in your weakest hour for the way He came through the last time, and the time before. He is the God who sees you (Genesis 16:13), who never changes (James 1:17), the one whose faithfulness to you endures forever.

Day 101

BOUNDARY LINES

*You have set a boundary that they may not pass
over, that they may not return to cover the earth.*
PSALM 104:9 NKJV

God is the creator and ruler of the earth. At the sound of His voice, mountains tremble. At His command, storms begin and end. He is so powerful that the human mind cannot begin to comprehend His strength.

God, at one time, flooded the entire earth because it was evil. He saved only one man and his family and two of each animal. After the flood, God put a rainbow in the sky as a promise. He made a covenant with humans that He would never again flood the earth. He told the waves they would never come forth with such a vengeance again.

God sets forth boundaries in your life as well. Those "boundary lines" fall for you in "pleasant places" (Psalm 16:6 NIV). Even if you are facing your own "flood" in life—unemployment, loss, disappointment, or depression—God is your portion. Your joy is found in Him, not your circumstances. He will never give you more than you can bear and will draw the lines for you. He is always with you and always has your best interest at heart.

VENTURE WITH GOD

*Elisha said to her, What shall I do for you? Tell
me, what have you [of sale value] in the house?
She said, Your handmaid has nothing in the house
except a jar of oil. Then he said, Go around and
borrow. . .empty vessels—and not a few.*
2 KINGS 4:2–3 AMPC

A widow had lost her God-fearing husband. Now creditors were
coming to take her two sons to be slaves. So she went to Elisha
for help. And he asked what Jesus often asked His followers:
"What shall I do for you?" His immediate follow-up question was,
"What do you have?"

That's when the widow looked around, saw what she had,
and offered this one asset—a jar of oil—to Elisha. He told her
to borrow vessels from all her neighbors—and not just a few. In
other words, to see plenty in this venture. Then she was to go
into her house with her sons, shut the door, and start pouring
the little oil she had into the other jars. She ended up filling
all the vessels, selling the oil, paying off her debt, and living off
the rest with her sons.

When you're in dire straits, tell God about it. Tell Him what
you'd like Him to do for you and what you have on hand. Then
follow His directions, seeing plenty in your venture, trusting that
under His directions, all will come out well.

POWER UP

The Spirit of God, who raised
Jesus from the dead, lives in you.
ROMANS 8:11 NLT

God is the same yesterday, today, and forever. His strength does not diminish over time. That same mountain-moving power you read about in the lives of people from the Old and New Testaments still exists today. The same power that caused the walls of Jericho to fall, an ax to float, and a dead girl to live again is still available today. The force of God that formed the world, brought the dry land above the waters of the sea, and raised Jesus from the dead is available to work out the details of your life.

It's natural to want to do things on our own. We all want to be independent and strong. When faced with a challenge, the first thing we do is try to work it out in our own skill and ability—within our own power. But there's another way.

We don't have to go it alone. Our heavenly Father wants to help. All we have to do is ask. He has already made His power available to His children. Whatever we face—wherever we go—whatever dreams we have for our lives, take courage and know that anything is possible when we draw on the power of God.

NO FEAR OF BAD NEWS

*They will have no fear of bad news; their
hearts are steadfast, trusting in the LORD.*
PSALM 112:7 NIV

Have you ever waited in a doctor's office to discuss results of a
blood test or biopsy? Waiting is hard, particularly when there's a
good chance you may receive bad news.

The Bible tells us that those who walk with God need not fear
bad news. Nothing can touch a believer's life that has not been
filtered through the fingers of a loving God.

God is good—all the time. Not just on the days when the
college acceptance letter shows up in your mailbox or the love of
your life proposes marriage. He's just as good on the day that the
doctor says the C word or you stand at the graveside of one you
cherished.

Scripture does not say you will not face trouble. It does not
claim that bad—really bad—things cannot touch your life. What
it does promise is that you, Christian sister, will never go it alone.
God is at—and on—your side.

Stay true to Him. Put your faith in the One who will hold
you tight and walk with you when bad news does come. Trust He
knows what's best for you. He's got this.

GOD'S GOT THIS

*"Look at the nations and watch—and be utterly
amazed. For I am going to do something in your days
that you would not believe, even if you were told."*
HABAKKUK 1:5 NIV

The prophet Habakkuk cried out to God, "Our LORD, how long
must I beg for your help before you listen? How long before you
save us from all this violence? Why do you make me watch such
terrible injustice? Why do you allow violence, lawlessness, crime,
and cruelty to spread everywhere? Laws cannot be enforced; justice
is always the loser, criminals crowd out honest people and twist
the laws around" (Habakkuk 1:2–4 CEV).

Do Habakkuk's words sound familiar? They were written
about twenty-six hundred years ago, yet they echo the cries of
Christians today. "Lord, why won't You do something about the
injustice and violence in the world?"

God answered Habakkuk, "If I told you how I'm going to fix
this, you wouldn't believe Me." Then God allowed an evil army
to cause even greater injustice and violence, but He promised to
punish them in the end. This was not the answer that Habakkuk
expected—or wanted.

When you become discouraged with the state of the world,
meditate on Habakkuk 1:5. God is in control. He works all things
together for the good of His people (Romans 8:28).

REFRESHMENT IN DRY TIMES

"The grass withers and the flowers fall,
but the word of our God endures forever."
ISAIAH 40:8 NIV

The grass was lifeless, crunchy, and brown. The trees had already started to lose their leaves, and it was only August. Flowers wilted, and the ground was nothing but dry dirt. The previous winter was unseasonably warm with very little snow. Spring had been practically nonexistent, and summer was day after day of relentless, scorching heat with very little rain. It was a drought with no change in sight.

Sometimes our lives feel just like the grass—dry and listless. Maybe we're in a season where things seem to stand still, and we've tried everything to change our circumstances for the better to no avail. It is during those times that we need to remember the faithfulness of God and the permanence of His Word. His promises to us are many and true! God will never leave us or forsake us; and He will provide for, love, and protect us. And, just like the drought, eventually our personal dry times will give way to a time of growth, refreshment, and beauty.

LIKE A LILY

*And why take ye thought for raiment? Consider the
lilies of the field, how they grow; they toil not, neither
do they spin: And yet I say unto you, That even Solomon
in all his glory was not arrayed like one of these.*
MATTHEW 6:28–29 KJV

In this sermon, Jesus wasn't specifically talking to women; rather, He was addressing people who didn't have many resources but had many needs. His message was to trust God for food and clothing and shelter. How can we apply what He said to our concerns today?

Some would feel the message is that we shouldn't really care about what we wear; that as long as it's decent and serviceable, we should be content. There is a measure of truth to that when one considers the millions around the world who live in poverty. Yet God created women to care about beauty and to be His beauty-bearers to the world. It is a natural thing for women to desire to be beautiful. The trouble comes when our caring turns to comparing.

Jesus used the lilies of the field to demonstrate how the Father provides. He doesn't compare one to another; He created them all and delights in the beauty of each. How foolish it would be for the flowers to measure themselves against each other! After all, the field isn't theirs and the glory isn't their own. It all belongs to Him. Today, let's trust the divine gardener and His individualized care. The lilies do.

Day 108

GOD DELIGHTS IN YOU

*"The LORD your God will delight in you if you obey
his voice and keep the commands and decrees written
in this Book of Instruction, and if you turn to the
LORD your God with all your heart and soul."*
DEUTERONOMY 30:10 NLT

No doubt the Israelites were intrigued to hear that God actually took delight in them, especially after all of their mess-ups. Like any good father, His heart warmed at the sight of His children, no matter how naughty they'd been. They gave Him that wonderful fuzzy feeling that all parents get when they watch their little ones do the simplest things.

Did you know that God delights in you too? It's true! You bring such joy to your Daddy-God's heart.

For some women, that might be hard to hear. . .or believe. Many are convinced that they are a disappointment to the Lord, that their mistakes have somehow separated them from Him. Nothing could be further from the truth. Today and every day, turn to God and see that He has a sparkle in His eye and hands extended. You're His daughter, and you bring Him such joy!

ANCHOR OF THE SOUL

*This hope we have as an anchor of the soul, both
sure and steadfast, and which enters the Presence
behind the veil, where the forerunner has entered
for us, even Jesus, having become High Priest
forever according to the order of Melchizedek.*

HEBREWS 6:19–20 NKJV

We *have* this hope, not "we will" or "we had." As children of God, we possess Christ as the anchor of our souls. The "veil" referred to was a physical, thick curtain that separated the holy of holies from the rest of the tabernacle. Only once a year could the high priest enter after being cleansed. But Jesus tore that veil in two with His sinless life, death, and resurrection. He opened the gates to a relationship with His Father.

This is the good news that we now have a Redeemer who has brought us in relationship with the Father. Not a relationship that brings superhuman powers, but the defeat of sin. We can now enter the Lord's presence and, because of Christ, be seen as blameless. No human being has ever led a blameless life, which is why God sent His Son to do so for us. The debt that God demanded He also paid. What wondrous love is this that He would pay what we owe!

In Christ, we face each day redeemed. What peace this truth should bring to our hearts.

CALMER OF STORMS AND SOULS

*[Jesus' disciples in the boat] all saw Him and were
agitated (troubled and filled with fear and dread).
But immediately He talked with them and said,
Take heart! I Am! Stop being alarmed and afraid.*
MARK 6:50 AMPC

After feeding five thousand men with five loaves and two fishes,
Jesus told His disciples to get into a boat and sail ahead of Him
to Bethsaida. Meanwhile, Jesus sent the crowd of people away,
then went off by Himself to pray. When evening came, a storm
rose up on the sea.

With the wind against them, the disciples had trouble rowing.
Jesus, seeing their futile efforts, walked on the turbulent sea toward
them, then acted as if He were going to pass them by. The fright-
ened disciples thought they were seeing a ghost! To ease their fear,
Jesus spoke, knowing His followers would recognize His voice.
He identified Himself and encouraged them to stop being afraid.
Once He got into their boat, the wind ceased.

Remember who Jesus is and the amazing things He has done
for you. Never think He's overlooking you. Take courage that you
will recognize His voice, His presence, and His power when He
is near. Be assured He's looking out for you. He will never pass
you by. He has words to calm your spirit. He's ready to get into
your boat and still your storms. Simply allow Him into your vessel.

Day 111

LOST AND FOUND

"And the one who sent me is with me—he has not deserted me. For I always do what pleases him."
JOHN 8:29 NLT

We lose things on a daily basis. Each year we probably spend hours looking for things—keys, sunglasses, lipstick, or even the saltshaker that normally rests next to the stove. We know these items don't sprout wings and walk off but have been set somewhere and forgotten by you or someone you know.

You are God's most prized possession, and while He'll never forget where you are, sometimes we walk off from Him. We lose ourselves in the things we need to do, the places we need to go, and the people we need to see. Our calendars fill up with commitments we're obligated to keep. We often commit to too many things and exhaust ourselves trying to stay ahead of our schedules.

The further we displace ourselves from God—not necessarily on purpose—the more we become lost in our own space. While we're doing life on our own, we can forget that He is standing there waiting to do life every day with us. If you feel distant from Him today, look up. He's waiting for you to find your rightful place with Him.

Day 112

HANG IN THERE

*Let perseverance finish its work so that you may
be mature and complete, not lacking anything.*
JAMES 1:4 NIV

Perseverance can't be rushed. The only way to develop perseverance is to endure pressure, over a long period of time. A weight lifter must gradually add more weight if he wants to build up his muscles. A runner must run farther and farther, pushing past what is comfortable. If these athletes want to grow and improve, they must persevere through pressure, over time.

The same is true for our faith. If we want to grow as Christians, we have to endure pressure. God allows difficult things into our lives to help build our strength and endurance. Just as the athlete who gives up at the first sign of hardship will never improve at her sport, the Christian who abandons her faith during times of distress will never reach maturity.

No one ever said the Christian life was an easy one. In fact, Christ told us we'd endure hardships of many kinds. But He also said not to get discouraged. When we stick it out and follow Him no matter what, we will become mature and complete, perfectly fulfilling God's plan for our lives.

LOVE WITHOUT LIMITS

Your love, LORD, reaches to the heavens,
your faithfulness to the skies.
PSALM 36:5 NIV

God's love and faithfulness have no bounds. They reach to the heavens. They stretch to the skies and beyond.

This is hard for us to understand. As humans, even our very best attempts at love and faithfulness are limited. God's love is limitless. When He created you, knit you together in your mother's womb, and brought you into this world, He loved you. He loves you just as much today as He did when you were an innocent babe. He is incapable of loving you any less or any more than He already does. God's love is not based on what you do or don't do. It is not here today and gone tomorrow due to any mistake or failure in your life. He is faithful even when we are faithless.

If it seems that you are not close to God as you once were, He is not the one who moved. Draw close to your heavenly Father. You will find that He is there, faithful and true, ready to receive you back unto Himself. Thank the Lord today for an unfailing, unfathomable sort of love. What a blessing is the love of our faithful God!

BOLDLY COME

*God's free gift leads to our being made right with
God, even though we are guilty of many sins.*
ROMANS 5:16 NLT

Why do you think it is that as a general population, we often
assume that God is out to get us? We tend to jump immediately to the notion that God is angry with us and ready to bring
down the hammer. We become afraid to go to church or read the
Bible—thinking that as soon as we enter the building or crack the
cover, we will drown in waves of guilt and condemnation.

We even become too afraid to pray.

This must be one of the devil's most effective schemes—to
convince us to fear talking with God—when talking with God
is what will ultimately transform us from the inside out. Indeed,
prayer is what we were created for. We were created for a relationship with Him—the entire Bible is the story of our being restored
to that relationship.

The next time you are afraid to pray, refuse the fear. Know in
confidence that, unlike the devil, you are covered by the blood of
the Lamb and can enter freely into His presence.

Day 115

STANDING STRONG

Finally, be strong in the Lord and in his mighty power. Put on the full armor of God, so that you can take your stand against the devil's schemes.
EPHESIANS 6:10–11 NIV

Are you a member of the Fraidy Cat Club, one who cringes over dark places, loud noises, or hostile environments? Many people are. But the truth is that God is the one who fights for you (Exodus 14:14; Deuteronomy 1:30; 3:22; 20:4). Trusting in Him, you can stand strong behind His armor and in His strength. Put on all that God has provided to defend against the devil's attempts to confuse, manipulate, and scare you.

What schemes does the enemy use against you? Satan loves to batter you with shame that you haven't done enough or the idea that God can't possibly forgive you again. The enemy takes pleasure in making you doubt your salvation or in making you think that God could never love someone like you. The enemy wants to trick you into losing the peace and joy of abundance in Christ.

No worries. Your God-given armor has you covered. It's your task to put each piece on with focus, understanding that the battle has already been won. Stand strong. God's power looks mighty good on you.

PROVIDING IT ALL

*For God so greatly loved and dearly prized the world
that He [even] gave up His only begotten (unique)
Son, so that whoever believes in (trusts in, clings to,
relies on) Him shall not perish (come to destruction,
be lost) but have eternal (everlasting) life.*
JOHN 3:16 AMPC

Beginning with Adam, God provided for His loved ones: a ram
for Abraham to spare his son, manna for the wandering Jewish
people. The Bible resonates with the provisions of a mighty God.
And the Word says our God is the same today as He was then.
So we know He will provide for our needs. True is love reflected
by His care for us every day.

His provision is not just for our material needs, but more
importantly He extends us unmerited favor and grace when we
least deserve it. He provides us with an all-encompassing love once
we accept it. And He seals His promises with the gift of the Holy
Spirit making us heirs to the throne. When we realize the depth
of care we've received from our heavenly Father, it is breathtaking.

Always a step ahead, He made provision before any need
existed. God gave us His all, His best, when He gave us His Son.
He provided it all. We serve a glorious and mighty God.

Day 117

GOD OF YOUR UPS AND DOWNS

*Hallelujah! You who serve GOD, praise GOD! Just to speak
his name is praise! Just to remember GOD is a blessing—
now and tomorrow and always. From east to west, from
dawn to dusk, keep lifting all your praises to GOD!*
PSALM 113:1–3 MSG

As you read through the psalms, you gain a glimpse of the highs
and lows from the writer's soul. In the lowest points of his life
journey, he pours out his heart, hopeless and distressed, maybe
even feeling disconnected from God, thirsting for His presence.

Yet, through prayer, the writer finds comfort in God for his
brokenness and pain. He reminds himself of God's faithfulness and
unfailing love, and how it refreshes his spirit. Then he pulls himself
up, encourages himself in the Lord, and becomes determined to
experience the joy that only God can give. He rises again through
faith in God, climbing ever higher with praise and thanksgiving.

Like the psalmist, you too can trust God with your ups and
downs. Allow Him to go with you to the mountaintops and back
down into the valleys. Wherever you are in your journey, you can
safely and freely bare your soul to the God who listens and knows
you like no other.

PATHWAY TO GOD'S HEART

The LORD is my rock, my fortress and my deliverer;
my God is my rock, in whom I take refuge.
PSALM 18:2 NIV

Despite being blessed by God, Hezekiah's life was anything but smooth. In 2 Kings 18, the Assyrian envoy Rabshakeh speaks out against Hezekiah's leadership, telling the people not to listen to Hezekiah's teachings that the Lord will save them. Hezekiah understandably reacts strongly to Rabshakeh's speech. He tears his clothes and puts on sackcloth. But instead of wallowing in self-pity, Hezekiah goes straight to the house of the Lord and sends a message to God's prophet Isaiah.

Isaiah's response to Hezekiah regarding this threatening situation is, "Do not be afraid of what you have heard" (2 Kings 19:6 NIV). The prophet then tells Hezekiah how the Lord will take care of the situation. Hezekiah seeks the Lord in prayer *again*. And the response he receives is that the Lord has heard his prayers, and deliverance does come, just as the Lord promised.

Hezekiah, with the kingdom at stake, sought the one, true, holy God on bended knee. He knew prayer was the pathway to the heart of God, and God blessed him.

GOD IS SINGING YOUR SONG

*"The LORD your God is with you, the mighty
Warrior who saves. He will take great delight
in you, in his love he will no longer rebuke you,
but will rejoice over you with singing."*

ZEPHANIAH 3:17 NIV

God's passion for His people shows itself in many ways.

His mighty power saves us. He delights in us. His love brings peace and quietness to our hearts. And His pleasure is revealed as He rejoices over us with singing.

Angels sang the night Jesus was born (Luke 2:13–14). The psalms are full of lyrics people have used to praise God over the centuries. And Revelation 5:11–12 paints a glorious picture of heaven, complete with continual songs of praise.

But there is a song that's been written just for you. It has your name as its title. And the composer, God Himself, sings your song over you as you go about life here on earth.

Close your eyes. Listen carefully. Do you hear God's melodious voice? He's singing your song. Raise your voice and join Him in the heavenly music!

Day 120

JUST BELIEVE

While Jesus was still speaking, some people came from the house of Jairus, the synagogue ruler. "Your daughter is dead," they said. "Why bother the teacher anymore?"

MARK 5:35 NIV

What hopelessness. Jairus, a synagogue ruler, pleaded with Jesus to heal his sick child. Jesus was en route to the man's home when they got the news that the child had died. Why trouble the Galilean teacher further? It was kind of Him to come, but there's nothing He can do now, the naysayers thought. Yet Jesus' response was one of encouragement and hope, "Don't be afraid; just believe" (Mark 5:36 NIV).

When Jesus entered Jairus' home, he heard the crying. "Why all this commotion and wailing? The child is not dead but asleep," He said. But they laughed. After removing the doubters, Jesus took the child by her hand and said, "Little girl, I say to you, get up!" and the child was brought back to life (Mark 5:39–42 NIV).

When the odds are stacked against us and circumstances riddle us with hopelessness, our tendency is to manage our burdens as well as we can and stop praying. Doubtful, we wonder: *Can God restore an unhappy marriage? Can He heal cancer? Can He deliver me from financial ruin?* Will *He?*

Jesus knows the way out. Only believe; have faith in Him and never lose hope.

Day 121

TRIALS HAVE A PURPOSE

*Then Joseph said to his brothers, "Please come closer
to me." And they came closer. And he said, "I am your
brother Joseph, whom you sold into Egypt. Now do not
be grieved or angry with yourselves because you sold me
here, for God sent me ahead of you to preserve lives."*

GENESIS 45:4–5 NASB

How many of us could forgive as Joseph did? His jealous siblings
had kidnapped him, thrown him into a pit, and then allowed him to
be sold into slavery. Yet Joseph trusted that from God's perspective,
not his own, his trials had a purpose.

Joseph walked through his humiliating ordeal with his eyes
focused on the Lord. He continued not only to love his brothers
but to find forgiveness in his heart for them. Studying his life will
help us to look at our own situations differently: God can accomplish miracles in the midst of trials.

Is there a hurt so deep inside that you have never shared it with
another human being? Perhaps someone in your own family has
rejected or betrayed you. Remember the pain suffered by Joseph;
remember the anguish of Jesus Christ, who was betrayed by one
as close as a brother, Judas Iscariot. God knows your pain, and He
is strong enough to remove any burden.

Day 122

WHERE TO FIND REST

> *"On that day offerings of purification will be made for you, and you will be purified in the LORD's presence from all your sins. It will be a Sabbath day of complete rest for you, and you must deny yourselves. This is a permanent law for you."*
>
> LEVITICUS 16:30–31 NLT

The day of atonement bore much significance and put much weight on Moses' and Aaron's shoulders, as well as on the Israelite community. Afterward, after being purified in the Lord's presence from all sins, there would be a time of rest.

As a woman of God, you too might feel like you carry a lot of weight on your shoulders. Family, work, and church responsibilities can be a lot to manage. Then there's trying to eat well, getting in daily exercise, and the list goes on and on. A woman might wonder *Where is the rest in all of that?*

The most important thing you will ever do throughout your daily routine is spend time with your heavenly Father and Creator. Without staying in line with the one who knitted you together and knows your every thought and feeling, how can you keep a good attitude through it all? You can't. But with God's help, you can.

So take five minutes to breathe deeply and talk to God. He wants to hear from you.

WHEN YOU'RE DEEP IN THE PIT

*But I called on your name, LORD, from deep within
the pit. You heard me when I cried, "Listen to my
pleading! Hear my cry for help!" Yes, you came
when I called; you told me, "Do not fear."*

LAMENTATIONS 3:55–57 NLT

Maybe you've heard the old expression "He has to hit rock bottom before he'll come to God." It's true! Many people won't turn their eyes to Jesus until they're in such a deep, dark place that they have no other choice.

The book of Lamentations focuses on the people of God in deep torment, lamenting to the Lord about their troubles. Some situations were so painful, some pits were so deep, God's children may have felt they'd never escape them.

Perhaps you can relate to the people of God who'd hit rock bottom, as revealed in today's verses. Yet hope remains, for these verses also show that God hears our cries, no matter how low we've fallen. His response to us, even while we're sinking deep in our sin? "Do not fear!"

Isn't that the most gracious thing you could say to a person who's buried in a pit, terrified she will stay there forever? God, the rescuer, comes to save even the ones most hopeless. What a wonderful Father!

Day 124

FLIP YOUR REACTION

"Absolute futility," says the Teacher. "Everything is futile."
ECCLESIASTES 12:8 HCSB

"Everything is futile." What a downer. Much of Ecclesiastes is about the ways this life is pointless. Solomon ("the Teacher") observed the goings-on of the world, and he tested various pursuits. In the end, he concluded all of it was vanity, like chasing after the wind. "It's all smoke, nothing but smoke" (12:8 MSG).

Considering his less than glowing review, Solomon's response isn't the downer you might expect. "I recommend having fun, because there is nothing better for people in this world than to eat, drink, and enjoy life. That way they will experience some happiness along with all the hard work God gives them under the sun" (8:15 NLT). Again Solomon urges, "Seize life! Eat bread with gusto, drink wine with a robust heart. Oh yes—God takes pleasure in your pleasure! . . . Each day is God's gift. It's all you get in exchange for the hard work of staying alive. Make the most of each one!" (9:7, 9–10 MSG).

What an upside-downer! Even though life won't change—it will still be messy and messed up—we can flip our reaction to life. Rather than bemoaning all that's wrong, we can rejoice and be glad in the days that our Lord has made (Psalm 118:24).

Day 125

HELP IN DOUBT

*For the LORD is great and greatly to be
praised; He is to be feared above all gods.*
PSALM 96:4 NKJV

When the widow's son was brought back to life, she declared to Elijah, "Now by this I know that you are a man of God, and that the word of the LORD in your mouth is the truth" (1 Kings 17:24 NKJV).

It's interesting that she didn't say this after Elijah showed her the miracle of the flour and oil. Perhaps she'd wondered, *Was that really the God of Israel who rescued us from starving?* Maybe it was one of the local gods. But she put her full trust in Jehovah when her son was restored to her; no other god could reverse death's curse.

Maybe pain is running rampant in your life or you are looking at what's happening in the world and wondering where God even is. But He's here, and He's powerful—the God who brought the widow's boy back from the dead also raised your Savior. . . and resurrected your heart to new life.

When doubt strikes and death seems triumphant, immerse yourself in His truth. Don't fear your doubt, for God doesn't; abiding in Christ sometimes looks more like clawing to catch hold of Him. Seek Him; He will show you the truth the widow knew—that He is present and mighty—and fill your heart with what it needs.

Day 126

GOD IS ALWAYS
THINKING ABOUT YOU

You saw me before I was born. Every day of my life
was recorded in your book. Every moment was laid out
before a single day had passed. How precious are your
thoughts about me, O God. They cannot be numbered!
PSALM 139:16–17 NLT

The words "I'm thinking of you," often bring comfort in the midst of a personal struggle or family crisis. It's soothing to know someone cares—and that you are in his or her thoughts.

Have you ever wondered what *God* thinks about you? Not a moment passes that you are not in His thoughts. From the very beginning of time, your Father's thoughts for you compelled Him to send His Son, Jesus, to the cross so you could have an eternal relationship with Him. Even amid the most trying personal crisis of Jesus' life—while hanging on the cross—you were on the heart of the Father.

What a powerful revelation to know you are on God's mind. Take time today to contemplate this news from a novel perspective. Let this truth sink into your heart as you begin to understand how God thinks about you.

TALK TO YOUR BEST FRIEND

God is faithful, who has called you into
fellowship with his Son, Jesus Christ our Lord.
1 CORINTHIANS 1:9 NIV

When do you pray? How often do you call on God? Where do you talk to Him?

Just as we converse with our spouse or best friend about what's happening in our lives, the Lord expects and anticipates conversations with us too.

Yes, He knows all about us, but He desires our fellowship one-on-one. Jesus chose twelve disciples with whom to fellowship, teach, and carry His gospel to every nation. They lived and ate with Jesus; they knew Him personally; they were His best friends. In the same manner, God gives us the divine privilege to know Him on a personal level through our relationship with Christ.

When, where, or how we talk to God is of little importance to the Savior. We can converse with the Lord while driving down the street, walking through the park, or standing at the kitchen sink. We can ask for His help in the seemingly insignificant or in bigger decisions. Our concerns are His concerns too and He desires for us to share our heartfelt thoughts with Him.

Fellowshipping with God is talking to our best Friend, knowing He understands and provides help and wisdom along life's journey. It's demonstrating our faith and trust in the one who knows us better than anyone.

Day 128

REST FOR YOUR SOUL

"Come to me, all you who are weary and burdened,
and I will give you rest. Take my yoke upon you
and learn from me, for I am gentle and humble
in heart, and you will find rest for your souls.
For my yoke is easy and my burden is light."
MATTHEW 11:28–30 NIV

Jesus says, "Come to me." Just as He invited the little children to come to Him, Jesus calls us to come to Him and bring all of our burdens and lay them at His feet. He wants to help. He wants to relieve the load we're carrying.

A yoke is a harness placed over an animal or set of animals for the purpose of dragging something or carrying heavy equipment. Jesus liked to use visual imagery to get His meaning across. Can't you just picture all of the burdens you are carrying right now strapped to your back like an ox plowing a field? Now imagine yourself unloading each one onto Jesus' shoulders instead. Take a deep breath.

Jesus tells us many times throughout the Gospels not to worry. Worrying about something will never help you. Worry makes things worse and burdens seem larger. Worry clutters up your soul. Jesus wants us to find rest in Him. Hear His gentle words rush over you—"Come to me." Find rest for your soul.

Day 121

CAST YOUR BURDEN

Cast your burden upon the LORD and He will sustain you; He will never allow the righteous to be shaken.
PSALM 55:22 NASB

This verse assumes and acknowledges that you have a burden. Everyone has burdens. It's okay to admit that you are carrying around concerns, responsibilities, and emotional baggage that is heavy and often overwhelming. You especially should admit this to God. There is no reason to hide from God the strength-depleting and sometimes crushing burden that you are carrying. He knows all about it anyway. There is *every* reason to come to Him with it.

He asks you to give Him your burden. Just think about it. Wouldn't you be thrilled if someone came along and asked you to let go of whatever it is you're carrying and hand it over to them so that you can stand upright and use your energy in other ways, free from the heaviness of your burden? This is exactly what God is asking of you. But He is perfectly capable of carrying it. In fact, He's more capable than you are of dealing with whatever hardships you're facing. You can trust Him with your burden.

When you cast your burden on God, He will sustain you and not allow you to be shaken. What an awesome God you serve, that He would desire to come alongside you, carry your heavy load, and walk with you through life to strengthen and protect you.

SUCCESSFUL IN EVERYTHING

*Whatever mission Saul sent him on, David was
so successful that Saul gave him a high rank in
the army. This pleased all the troops, and Saul's
officers as well. . . . In everything he did he had
great success, because the LORD was with him.*

1 SAMUEL 18:5, 14 NIV

What made David successful was not just that Yahweh—the
God of all creation, the God of the Exodus, the God whose
name was not to be spoken—was with him. What made him
successful was that David was *conscious* of Yahweh being with him.
Yahweh permeated his very being. David tapped into the Lord's
wisdom, knowledge, and power. David stayed connected through
peacetime and battles. He wrote poems about Yahweh, how He
was his shepherd, protecting him, leading him, anointing him,
blessing him.

The same thing that made David successful will make you
successful. No matter where you go, no matter where you are
sent, be conscious of the God who walks with you. Consult His
knowledge and wisdom. Spend time in prayer, asking for guidance and protection. Be assured that He is within, spreading His
light upon your path. Trusting Him with all, you can then go
forward in confidence, knowing He will make you successful for
His name and glory.

Day 131

NEW THINGS

"See, I am doing a new thing! Now it springs up;
do you not perceive it? I am making a way in the
wilderness and streams in the wasteland."

ISAIAH 43:19 NIV

God is not limited as you are. He makes new paths for you where you see none. He provides refreshing streams where there were none. When your way seems blocked and circumstances distressing, look for God to surprise you with an unexpected solution. God is constantly moving you forward in life. New things will appear on the horizon.

Do you struggle with change? Do transitions leave you anxious? Trust that God's plans for you are good and that His heart is loving. God will not give you more than you can handle.

Do not focus on previous years or past hurts. Be available for what God has for you today. Look attentively for what may seem like a small trickle. Be ready for that trickle to turn into a spring and then a river. Prepare to get wet as you wade into your future personally designed by God with you in mind. He knows you better than you know yourself. Celebrate new life in abundance without looking back to the solid shore of your past.

Go have your adventure with God at your side.

Day 132

JOY IN THE RIDE

*Yes, there will be an abundance of
flowers and singing and joy!*
ISAIAH 35:2 NLT

What if we viewed life as an adventurous bicycle ride? With our destination in focus, we would pedal forward, but not so swiftly as to overlook the beauty and experiences that God planted along the way.

We would note the tenacity of a wildflower in bloom despite its unlikely location for growth. We would contemplate God's mercy and savor the brilliance of a rainbow that illuminated a once-blackened sky.

At our halfway point, we would relax from the journey, finding a spot in life's shade to refresh and replenish ourselves for the return trip. We wouldn't just ride; we would explore, pausing along the way to inhale the fresh air and scent of wildflowers.

In life, however, sometimes the road gets rough, and we are forced to take sharp turns. When that happens, we miss the beauty that surrounds us. But if we savor the ride and keep moving forward despite the bumps in the road, then "flowers and singing and joy" will follow.

So when your legs grow weary and your pathway seems long, brace yourself, board your bike, and keep on pedaling. Joy awaits you just around the bend.

Day 133

WOMEN DISCIPLES

*He went throughout every city and village, preaching
and shewing the glad tidings of the kingdom of God:
and the twelve were with him, and certain women,
which had been healed of evil spirits and infirmities.*
LUKE 8:1–2 KJV

Women, along with the twelve disciples, accompanied Jesus as He built the kingdom of God.

Luke lists Mary Magdalene, from whom Jesus exorcised seven evil spirits; Joanna, the wife of Chuza, King Herod's household manager; and Susanna, as well as many others. Jesus healed these women and met their needs, and they supported His ministry with their own money—a risky business, as women could not generate much income at that time.

The women also endured the inconvenience and outright danger shared by His other disciples. Perhaps rumors about the women's relationships with Jesus or the men in their party generated criticism, threatening their reputations and even their marriages. Still they chose to sit directly under His teaching. And despite the political implications, these brave women stayed with Jesus while He died on the cross. Some, including Mary Magdalene and Joanna, were among the first to see Jesus after His resurrection.

What an encouragement these verses give to women everywhere! Jesus loved and honored His women disciples. When we choose to devote our lives to Him today, He welcomes our love with all His heart.

Day 134

EXCEEDING EXPECTATIONS

"Here is a boy with five small barley loaves and two small fish, but how far will they go among so many?"
JOHN 6:9 NIV

So often in life we want to know the whole plan up front. And if God doesn't give us the plan, we start making it up on our own. We get ten steps down the road and decide what can and can't be done. We think we are limited by our resources of time, talent, and finances.

But as today's verse shows, Jesus simply needs us to trust Him with a little and then let Him work. He doesn't need us to do His work, but He allows us to be part of His process. In the story, not only was there plenty to eat, but there were leftovers besides. These people had a physical need for food, and He gave them spiritual food as well.

Spiritually, Jesus gives us everything we need to be satisfied and then even more, so it spills over onto others. When we seek God and put His kingdom first, He provides for our physical and spiritual needs. He is our satisfaction. He is the ultimate answer.

Surrender to Him and see how He works beyond your limited thinking. He always exceeds our expectations.

YOU ARE A WOMAN OF WORTH

*A wife of noble character who can find? She is
worth far more than rubies. Her husband has full
confidence in her and lacks nothing of value. She
brings him good, not harm, all the days of her life.*

PROVERBS 31:10–12 NIV

Are you the woman of worth that Jesus intends you to be? We
often don't think we are. Between running a household, rushing
to work, taking care of the children, volunteering for worthwhile
activities, and still being a role model for our families, we think
we've failed miserably. There just isn't any way we can be that
perfect Proverbs 31 woman!

Sometimes we don't fully realize that learning to be a noble
woman of character takes time. We learn many valuable lessons
through our family experiences, from time management to fiscal
responsibility to diplomacy. Our experiences can be offered to
another generation seeking wisdom from others who have "been
there." You are a woman of worth. God said so!

Day 136

A WORSHIP OFFERING

*"Then he must remove all the sheep's fat, just as he does
with the fat of a sheep presented as a peace offering.
He will burn the fat on the altar on top of the special
gifts presented to the LORD. Through this process, the
priest will purify the people from their sin, making
them right with the LORD, and they will be forgiven."*
LEVITICUS 4:35 NLT

Burnt offering. Grain offering. Peace offering. Sin offering. So
many details to remember.

Perhaps the laundry list of instructions found in Leviticus 1–4
seems a bit overwhelming, daunting, and rather confusing. But if
you look upward and ask God for His perspective, you'll realize
that many of the Levitical rules and rituals can be translated into
worship offerings. Those people in the Old Testament who cared
enough to follow all of God's laws and decrees obviously loved
God enough, wanted to obey Him, and took Him at His word.

Thankfully, because of what Jesus did on the cross, you don't
have to follow a thousand different rules! You don't have to walk
through a series of steps just to make your sins right with God.
That means you can enjoy reading the book of Leviticus and worship Him with gratitude as you do so.

LOVE MADE PERFECT

*There is no fear in love. But perfect love drives
out fear, because fear has to do with punishment.
The one who fears is not made perfect in
love. We love because he first loved us.*

1 JOHN 4:18–19 NIV

It's good to fear God, isn't it? God is awesome and fierce in His power. Yet, while we need to have a healthy respect for God, we don't need to be terrified of Him. At least, not if we really love Him.

Those who truly love God with all their hearts and souls have nothing to fear, for we know He loves us even more. We know that although He may allow us to walk through some difficult things, His plans for us are always good. When we love God, His love is made perfect in us. Our love for God causes His love for us to reign.

It's only when we choose not to love God that we need to fear Him, for though God's patience is long, He is a just God. He will not let the guilty go unpunished. When we love God with our lives, there's no need for punishment. When we love God with our lives, we love others and put their needs ahead of our own. And that, dear friends, is how His love is made perfect in us.

RUN TO JESUS

*Then he got up and rebuked the winds
and the waves, and it was completely calm.*
MATTHEW 8:26 NIV

Sailing on a large sea can be a little scary, even in the best weather. Sailing in the midst of a furious storm can be terrifying.

But for a storm to frighten the disciples of Jesus—some of whom were experienced fishermen—it must have been severe. The story from Matthew 8 tells us that the storm came up suddenly, and waves swept over the sides of the boat. The disciples ran to wake up Jesus, who was calmly sleeping through the event.

Before we go further, realize this: they ran to Jesus. Jesus wondered why they would come to Him, and yet be so panicked. But at least they came to Him. They knew He would be able to help.

What kind of crisis are you in right now? Maybe you are in a situation that feels just as stressful and overwhelming as that which the disciples faced.

Run to Jesus. He's in charge. Even the wind and waves know they've done wrong when Jesus comes to yell at them.

GOD'S LIGHT FOR OUR PATH

*So the cloud of the LORD was over the tabernacle by
day, and fire was in the cloud by night, in the sight
of all the house of Israel during all their travels.*
EXODUS 40:38 NIV

Have you ever been forced to choose between "good" and "best"?
When life presents us with more than one great opportunity, it can
be hard to decide what to do. The path we should take depends
on many different factors, and the road may not be clear at first.

How do we determine God's will? It's an age-old question,
and to be sure, discovering God's choice for us is not easy. But it
is simple.

First, we must pray for God's guidance. He promises to give us
wisdom when we ask for it. Second, we need to search His Word
and make sure our potential decision lines up with scripture. Third,
we should ask for counsel from godly advisers. And fourth, we
must search our hearts to see if the opportunity fits well with the
personality, talents, and priorities God has given us.

Rest assured, God will shine His light on the right path, just
as He led the Israelites with a cloud by day and a fire by night.
And when it comes, His guidance will be accompanied with peace,
joy, and a certainty that we have followed one who has our (and
His) best interests at heart.

Day 140

THE END OF YOUR ROPE

*Do not be far from me, for trouble
is near and there is no one to help.*
PSALM 22:11 NIV

You can feel the desperation in David's prayer as you read Psalm 22. He feels utterly rejected and alone as he cries out to God.

Have you been there? Have you ever felt so alone and helpless that you are sure no one is there for you? Jesus meets us in those dark places of hopelessness. He calls to us and says, "Do not let your hearts be troubled and do not be afraid" (John 14:27 NIV). "Never will I leave you; never will I forsake you" (Hebrews 13:5 NIV). You are never alone.

The late youth evangelist Dave Busby said, "The end of your rope is God's permanent address." Jesus reaches down and wraps you in His loving arms when you call to Him for help. The Bible tells us that He is close to the brokenhearted (Psalm 34:18).

We may not have the answers we are looking for here in this life, but we can be sure of this: God sees your pain and loves you desperately. Call to Him in times of trouble. If you feel that you're at the end of your rope, look up! His mighty hand is reaching toward you.

THE GIFT THAT KEEPS ON GIVING

*Just as people are destined to die once, and after
that to face judgment, so Christ was sacrificed
once to take away the sins of many; and he will
appear a second time, not to bear sin, but to bring
salvation to those who are waiting for him.*
HEBREWS 9:27–28 NIV

After we've been Christians awhile and traveled down the road
of our spiritual journey, it's easy to lose sight of what started us
on our way. Christ's blood paid the price for our sins and is the
cost of our spiritual journey. From His death, we receive several
benefits.

We get forgiveness of sins. Not only did Jesus pay the
price for everything we ever have done or ever will do wrong,
but God annuls our sins. He treats them as if they never happened. This means we are rescued from the judgment we deserve for
our sinful rebellion. In addition, we are brought into God's family.

After Jesus rose from the dead, He made a promise to return
and give us a permanent place in heaven. He sent the Holy Spirit
to live inside us and to act as the deposit on the contract that He
will return one day to fulfill.

The journey of faith is not free, but Jesus has paid the price.
We receive freedom now and hope for the future.

Day 142

WRESTLING MATCH

*For we do not wrestle against flesh and blood,
but against principalities, against powers, against
the rulers of the darkness of this age, against spiritual
hosts of wickedness in the heavenly places.*

EPHESIANS 6:12 NKJV

You struggle all day—from whacking the alarm button in the morning, to unwinding yourself from the covers, to pushing yourself out of bed. You yank out some clothes and shove your body into them. You tug on your socks and shoes and stretch your weary muscles. You grab a water bottle and force yourself out the door.

Some days, every minute of the day, from before sunrise until that moment you drag yourself to bed, feels like one big wrestling match—and that's even when no other person is around! You fight against fatigue. You argue with your wants. You shout down the negative voices in your mind. You battle against irritation, impatience, and selfishness. It's a battle of the wills—and good will is losing.

It's vital to remember, on days like these, that God is not against us. Nor is every other person we meet our enemy. Rather, we are fighting against unseen forces—twisted thoughts and disturbing dreams and whispered lies that wrap around our hearts and minds.

But we have the armor of God and, backed by the one who defeated even death, we can win this match any day!

THE FEAR OF GOD

"And I will make an everlasting covenant with them, that I will not turn away from doing them good; but I will put My fear in their hearts so that they will not depart from Me."

JEREMIAH 32:40 NKJV

The fear of God is not the kind of fear that causes nightmares or that jumps out at you from a dark corner.

The fear that God wants to put in our hearts is the healthy, life-giving, transformational reverence and awe of Him. It is the feeling of wonder that comes when we know the Creator of the universe knows our names. It is the position of humility we take before the throne of the King of kings. It is the dazzling of our senses that occurs when we try to imagine His eternal glory. It is the absolute astonishment at being loved so fully, so fiercely, and so faithfully by our perfect Father in heaven.

This fear may well take our breath away. It may freeze us in our tracks or shock us into silence. But it will also fill us up, encourage our spirits, and speak to our hearts. It will cause us to stay, instead of run away. It will make the impossible, possible.

Day 144

CALLED TO REST

But Jesus often withdrew to lonely places and prayed.
LUKE 5:16 NIV

Christians often make the mistake of believing the Lord wants us to be busy about His work constantly. We sign up for everything and feel guilty saying no to anything that is asked of us. This is perhaps especially true of women. We feel it is our duty to serve.

Certainly, we are called to be about God's work. We are His hands and feet in this world, and He can use us in mighty ways. But we are also called to rest and pray. Jesus put a priority on this, frequently leaving the crowd to seek solitude. He encouraged His followers to do the same. One day when they had been busy meeting the needs of people all day, Christ insisted that the disciples come away with Him to rest and to nourish themselves.

There is no denying that our lives are busy. All sorts of demands are placed on women today. You may find yourself in a station in life that pulls at you from every angle. Make time to rest. Find a place that is quiet where you can pray. Jesus modeled this for us. He wants us to find rest in Him.

ENCOURAGE YOURSELF

David encouraged himself in the LORD his God.
1 SAMUEL 30:6 KJV

David and his army went off to fight, leaving their families behind in Ziklag. While they were gone, their enemy the Amalekites raided the city, burned it, and captured the women and children. When the men returned, they found just a smoking pile of rubble. Enraged and weeping uncontrollably, some blamed David and wanted him killed. What did David do when no one was around to encourage him? He encouraged himself in the Lord (1 Samuel 30:1–6).

David had a personal relationship with God. He knew the scriptures, and he relied on God's promises. Instead of giving in to discouragement, he applied those promises to his own situation and found strength. David relied on God to build him up. Many believe that he wrote these words in Psalm 119:15–16: "I will study your commandments and reflect on your ways. I will delight in your decrees and not forget your word" (NLT). *I will delight myself in Your decrees.* In the middle of his grief and loneliness, David delighted himself in the Lord.

Christians never have to face discouragement alone. As they trust God, they can also recall past times when He brought them success. They can communicate with Him through prayer and find support in His Word.

Remember, God is always on your side, always there, and always ready to lift you up.

Day 146

GOD NEVER FORGETS US

"See, I have engraved you on the palms of my hands."
ISAIAH 49:16 NIV

Have you ever had a bad day turn into a bad week. . .turn into a bad month. . .turn into a bad year? Judah was in the middle of one of those times. The storm clouds of impending judgment had begun to gather, and God was preparing to hold His people accountable for forsaking Him. Assyria and Babylon were growing in power, and it wouldn't be long before living in exile became the new reality for God's people.

In the middle of tumultuous times, it's tempting to proclaim that God has forgotten us. Both Israel and Judah struggled with the idea that God had abandoned them. But God took steps to contradict this notion. In an image that prefigures Jesus' crucifixion, God boldly proclaimed that His children were engraved on the palms of His hands. The nail-scarred hands that His Son would endure bear the engraved names of all of us who call upon Him as Savior and Lord.

God does not forget us in the midst of our troubles! It is His nail-scarred hand that reaches down and holds our own.

Day 147

SURROUNDED — FOR GOOD

"Do not be afraid, for those who are with us are more than those who are with them." Then Elisha prayed and said, "O LORD, please open his eyes that he may see." So the LORD opened the eyes of the young man, and he saw.
2 KINGS 6:16–17 ESV

The prophet Elisha's servant had gotten up early one morning. He headed outside, when he was stunned by the sight of the Syrian army with its horses and chariots surrounding the city! Panicked, he yelled to Elisha, "Alas, my master! What shall we do?" (2 Kings 6:15 ESV).

Elisha told his servant not to fear because the heavenly agents with them were way more numerous than the earthly army beyond their door. Elisha then prayed and asked God to open his servant's eyes so he could see God's army surrounding them!

As the Syrians approached, Elisha prayed for God to blind the soldiers. "So He struck them with blindness, according to Elisha's word" (2 Kings 6:18 HCSB). And Elisha led the temporarily God-blind army back to Samaria.

As a servant of God, you need never fear for God is with you—*all the time*. No matter what you do or where you go, God is there. And so is His army, His angels, His heavenly host—whether you see them or not.

ATTITUDE MAKES THE DIFFERENCE

*I will sing to the LORD all my life; I will
sing praise to my God as long as I live.*
PSALM 104:33 NIV

Have you ever noticed a difference among elderly individuals?
Some seem depressed. They go through their days focusing on their
ailments and woes. Others are bright and happy with cheerful spirits
and never a word of complaint. Are the chipper seniors healthier?
Have they been spared arthritis, diabetes, heart issues, and digestion
troubles? Not at all! The difference lies in a little thing that makes
a big difference—the attitude they choose to take.

If you determine to sing to the Lord all the days of your life,
as the psalmist did, you will have a hard time listing off all your
troubles to everyone who will listen. It's pretty tough to sing praises
to Jesus while whining about what aches.

Happiness is a choice. If you have the joy of the Lord planted
deep within your soul, you will be able to shine for Him, regardless
of your circumstances. Commit today to praise Him all the days
of your life. It will make all the difference in the world!

Day 149

DELIGHTFULLY YOU

*You [Judah] shall no more be termed Forsaken,
nor shall your land be called Desolate any more.
But you shall be called Hephzibah [My delight is
in her], and your land be called Beulah [married];
for the Lord delights in you, and your land shall
be married [owned and protected by the Lord].*
ISAIAH 62:4 AMPC

Your name at birth is the first gift from your parents and your first identity. But no matter how you have been labeled until now, your God has given you a new name.

The terms Forsaken and Desolate call forth images of a dry, deserted, barren land where nothing grows or flourishes. But "My Delight" is the new name God gives you. Captivated by you, He adores spending time with you. He awakens you with a brilliant sunrise and lulls you to sleep with a glowing moon and twinkling stars, heavenly displays that show how much pleasure He takes in you.

Let go of the other names you have accumulated: Too Heavy, Too Tall, Not Smart Enough, Not Pretty Enough, Too Much Trouble. You are enough. . .and not too much. God is not seeking perfection, beauty, or grace. He is seeking you. Bloom in the love of a Father who has renamed you His Delight.

HE HEARS YOU AND
SEES YOUR TEARS

*"Return and tell Hezekiah the leader of My
people, 'Thus says the LORD, the God of David
your father: "I have heard your prayer, I have
seen your tears; surely I will heal you."'"*

2 KINGS 20:4–5 NKJV

Hezekiah was one of the most faithful kings of Judah. His faith
and prayer made a difference in his own life, his family, and in the
lives of the people of God he led.

When Hezekiah became very ill, the prophet Isaiah gave
him a message from the Lord instructing him to put his things
in order because he was going to die. What a horrible message
to receive! Imagine the emotions he must have felt. Immediately
Hezekiah prayed, reminding the Lord of his faithfulness and
devotion to Him. The scripture says, "Hezekiah wept bitterly"
(2 Kings 20:3 NKJV).

But God.

Before Isaiah even made it out of the palace, the Lord instructed
to him to go back to Hezekiah with another message: "I have heard
your prayer, I have seen your tears; surely I will heal you."

God looked upon His child and loved him, just like He looks
upon you and is moved with compassion about the things that
concern you.

WALKING IN TRUTH

I have no greater joy than to hear that
my children are walking in the truth.
3 JOHN 4 NIV

If the apostle John delighted in seeing his spiritual children walk in truth, how much more must God appreciate those who devotedly follow Him! He too wants those who love Him to walk in His ways.

Wouldn't all Christians naturally follow close on Jesus' heels? After all, doesn't the same salvation affect them all? Would anyone want to be a hair's breadth farther from Jesus than she need be?

In an ideal Christian world, that would be true—and it will be so in eternity. But while we remain on earth, sin easily tempts us. Our hearts are more prone to wander than we'd like to admit. Unfortunately, sin often sticks to us and holds us back from God.

That's just why believers must continually resist sin's hold and draw near to Jesus. He has opened the doors of forgiveness for every believer who habitually confesses the sticky sin that pulls her or him away from God. Again and again, we can turn to our Lord for a new lease on the new life.

As we habitually turn to God, sin's grip loosens. The goop sticks less, and God sticks more.

DON'T SWEAT THE SMALL STUFF

*I consider that our present sufferings are not worth
comparing with the glory that will be revealed in us.*
ROMANS 8:18 NIV

When a woman gives birth, the time she spends in pregnancy
and labor can seem like an eternity. She's uncomfortable. She's
nauseous. She's swollen. And it all leads up to hours, maybe even
days of painful labor and suffering.

But then she holds that beautiful son or daughter in her arms,
and the memory of any pain fades so far to the background, it's
not even worth considering. The joy of seeing the one she loves
face-to-face fills up her heart and mind so completely, it wipes away
any shadow of discomfort and suffering. Plus, the years of joy and
fulfillment that child brings are much longer than the months of
pregnancy or the hours of labor.

That's how heaven will be for us. Life is like pregnancy and
labor. This life isn't the completion, it's the preparation! Our
years here are just a moment compared to eternity. When life is
difficult, don't sweat it. It won't last forever. One day we will leave
it all behind to be flooded with His complete, perfect love and
acceptance. All the pain of this life will be lost in comparison to
the complete peace we'll experience, forever and ever.

ENCOURAGEMENT FROM THE SCRIPTURES

For everything that was written in the past was written to teach us, so that through the endurance taught in the Scriptures and the encouragement they provide we might have hope.

ROMANS 15:4 NIV

You know those days when nothing goes right? Sometimes those days stretch into weeks and months. You don't get the promotion. Your car breaks down. Someone you love gets sick. Disappointment settles in and brings its brother, Discouragement. Things are not going according to your plan, and you may wonder if God even hears your prayers.

Looking at the heroes of the Old Testament, you'll see that God's plan for those people wasn't smooth sailing either. Joseph was sold into slavery, falsely accused by Potiphar's wife, and unjustly imprisoned. Moses tended flocks in the wilderness for forty years after murdering a man and before leading God's people out of slavery. David was anointed king but had to run for his life and wait fifteen years before actually sitting on the throne.

Those stories give us hope and encouragement. Our plans are quite different from God's plans, and His ways of doing things are quite different from what we would often choose. We see how things worked out for the people of the Old Testament. We can take encouragement from the fact that the same God is at work in our lives.

HE WON'T LET YOU DOWN

*I tell you that Christ has become a servant of the
Jews on behalf of God's truth, so that the promises
made to the patriarchs might be confirmed.*
ROMANS 15:8 NIV

Everyone has been hurt at one time or another by a broken promise. When that happens, it is best to forgive and go on. People are
just people. They mess up. But there is one who will never break
His promises to us—our heavenly Father. We can safely place our
hope in Him.

Hebrews 11 lists biblical characters who placed their trust
and hope in God and weren't let down. Do you think Noah was
excited about building an ark? Surely Sarah and Abraham hadn't
planned on parenting at their ages. Daniel faced the lion's den
knowing his God would care for him. We can find encouragement
from their examples, knowing that their faith in the God who'd
come through for them time and again wasn't misplaced. They
did not grow weary and lose heart. They knew He was always
faithful.

Today we choose to place our hope in God's promises. We
won't be discouraged by time—God's timing is always perfect.
We won't be discouraged by circumstances—God can change
everything in a heartbeat. We will keep our hearts in God's hand.
For we know He is faithful.

AN EVER-FLOWING SPRING

"The LORD will guide you continually, giving you water when you are dry and restoring your strength. You will be like a well-watered garden, like an ever-flowing spring."
ISAIAH 58:11 NLT

It's easy to fall into the trap of looking to earthly things to restore us. Instead of immediately looking to the one who made us and knows every detail of what we need, we often look other places. The Lord is our water when we are dry. He restores our strength. As we look to Him, we will become like a lush, well-watered garden. Fruitful. Energetic. Growing.

This is one of those verses to keep close to your heart during a busy season. When it feels like your next day of rest is far off, this is a promise to cling to and draw strength from. Every day, as often as you can, make space for quiet moments with the Lord. A few moments can give you everything you need. Even as you fall asleep at night, this passage can be one you recite to bring you into a peaceful rest.

The Lord will restore you as you choose to take time to meditate on His Word and sit in His presence. When you are seeking out the right source, you will find you can make it through even the most rigorous of weeks.

THE GOD OF HOPE

May the God of hope fill you with all joy and peace
as you trust in him, so that you may overflow
with hope by the power of the Holy Spirit.
ROMANS 15:13 NIV

Hope is something that can easily be marred and destroyed. It seems almost like a childlike, naive concept. In the harsh world we live in, we quickly learn to not hope for things so that we won't end up disappointed.

This verse is a prayer that you would *overflow* with hope. What an interesting concept—to be surrounded by, filled up with, and buoyed by hope. The biblical concept of hope is a steadfast confidence that something *will* happen in the future. So what can you possibly hope for that you can be confident will come to pass?

You can hope for an eternity spent illumined by the light of your heavenly Father. You can hope for the time when God will wipe every tear from your eye. You can hope for the time when you will be reunited with all God's children who have gone before you. You can hope in a God who will never leave you and never forsake you through life on this earth and even through death. You can hope in a joyful welcome home at the end of this life. You can hope in the fact that God works everything according to His will for the good of His children.

God truly is the God of hope.

Day 151

GUILT-FREE

"In those days, at that time," declares the LORD,
"search will be made for Israel's guilt, but there will
be none, and for the sins of Judah, but none will be
found, for I will forgive the remnant I spare."
JEREMIAH 50:20 NIV

People experience guilt for many reasons. Some have guilt from years ago. Others pick up a fresh load of guilt on a daily basis. The problem is that guilt is a powerful thing and can be debilitating. But take heart! God wants you to live guilt-free because He forgives you.

To the survivors of Israel and Judah, God declares there will be no guilt and no regret. The people are to look forward not back. Yesterday is done, and if you strayed from God's path, ask His divine forgiveness and move on. He will gladly grant it. Once forgiven, forget it. Don't let guilt be a weight that drags you down into the depths of regret. If God forgives you, why not forgive yourself?

Each day, God gives you a new page to write the next chapter of your life. So learn from your mistakes, but don't get lost in them. Just as God gifted Israel and Judah with a guilt-free life, He will do the same for you.

PRAY WITHOUT CEASING

Pray without ceasing. In every thing give thanks:
for this is the will of God in Christ Jesus concerning you.
1 THESSALONIANS 5:17–18 KJV

Pray without ceasing. Pray continually. Never stop praying. Pray all the time. Regardless which translation of the Bible you choose, the command is the same. It seems impossible! How can one pray all the time?

Consider this. You are young and in love. You must go to school and work. You may be separated by a great distance from your beloved. And yet, every moment of every day, that person is on your mind. You talk on the phone and text constantly. His name is always on your lips. So much so that some of your friends find it annoying.

Is your relationship with Jesus like the one described here? He wants to be the name on your mind when you are daydreaming. He wants to be the first one you chat with each morning and the last one you confide in each night. He wants you to be so utterly absorbed in Him that it begins to annoy some of your friends!

Pray without ceasing. Love Jesus with all your heart. He is crazy about *you.*

"Daughter"

He said to her, "Daughter, your faith has healed you.
Go in peace and be freed from your suffering."
MARK 5:34 NIV

The woman in this passage had suffered greatly from an affliction that made her ceremonially unclean; she was an outcast, not able to participate in society. In an act of desperation, she pushed through the thick crowd to Jesus and touched His garments. When Jesus turned around and asked who had touched Him, she fell in fear and trembling at His feet and told her whole story. This woman had probably been in shameful hiding for many years and now, in front of a large crowd, recounted her humiliating story. Probably some of the spectators were repulsed by her story, and yet Jesus, in front of the whole crowd, called her "daughter." Can you imagine how it must have felt to this rejected and shamed woman to hear herself called "daughter"—a term of belonging and love?

You also have been adopted and called a daughter of God. Don't hide your shame and struggles from Him. In circumstances where you can hardly stand up under the weight of your burden, fall at His feet as this woman did. You will not be rejected or shamed by Him. He calls you "daughter." He loves you and is able to heal you.

Day 160

DECISIONS, DECISIONS

*And they prayed and said, You, Lord, Who know
all hearts (their thoughts, passions, desires, appetites,
purposes, and endeavors), indicate to us which one
of these two You have chosen to take the place in this
ministry and receive the position of an apostle.*

ACTS 1:24–25 AMPC

Decisions, decisions. It's sometimes hard to know what to do in certain situations. Or who would be best suited for various scenarios. In Acts 1, the apostles were "[waiting together] with the women and Mary the mother of Jesus, and with His brothers" in the upper room in Jerusalem where they "devoted themselves steadfastly to prayer" (Acts 1:14 AMPC). And while they were waiting, Peter suggested they find someone to take the place of the now-dead traitor Judas. Not knowing whom to pick, they asked God to tell them whom *He* chose.

God knows all about each one of us. And because He sees what we cannot, there's no limit to His depth of knowledge about us and our circumstances.

Confused? Go to God. Ask Him for His advice. Know that He knows everyone's circumstances and thoughts, that He can fit anyone to do what He has purposed them to do. Your only job is to ask His choice and trust that He knows best.

FINDING REAL REST

And I said, Oh that I had wings like a dove!
for then would I fly away, and be at rest.
PSALM 55:6 KJV

There are days. . .

when the family gets sick and the dog disappears,

when the phone doesn't stop ringing,

when your favorite sweater ends up in the dryer,

when your boss takes his frustration out on you,

when you think things can't get any worse, but they do.

There are days.

On such days, it's tempting to wish for an easy way out. If only you could get away from phones and responsibilities and people who want more of you than you have to give.

If only you could fly away! Then you could be at rest.

Really?

It takes more than a quiet place or a time away to bring true rest. Often, even if we go away from the noise and demands of family, we find ourselves thinking of the very ones we wanted to leave. Instead of being at peace, we're full of guilt and regret.

Instead of flying away, we must jump into God's everlasting arms and dive into His Word. Rest is found in knowing Christ and understanding that through His sacrifice, we are at peace.

As we allow God's peace to fill us, we will find real rest.

REJOICE!

Rejoice in the Lord always. I will say it again: Rejoice!
PHILIPPIANS 4:4 NIV

Paul wrote these words from prison. Considering his circumstances, it doesn't seem like he had much reason to rejoice. Yet, he knew what many of us forget: when we have the Lord on our side, we always have reason to rejoice.

He didn't say, "Rejoice in your circumstances." He told us to rejoice in the Lord. When we're feeling depressed, anxious, or lost in despair, we can think of our Lord. We can remind ourselves that we are so very loved. We are special to God. He adores us, and in His heart, each of us is irreplaceable.

Perhaps the reason we lose our joy sometimes is because we've let the wrong things be the source of our joy. If our joy is in our finances, our jobs, or our relationships, what happens when those things fall through? Our joy is lost.

But when God is the source of our joy, we will never lose that joy. Circumstances may frustrate us and break our hearts. But God is able to supply all our needs. He is able to restore broken relationships. He can give us a new job or help us to succeed at our current job. Through it all, despite it all, we can rejoice in knowing that we are God's, and He loves us.

FROM PERSONAL EXPERIENCE

*And they shall know [from personal experience]
that I am the Lord their God, Who brought
them forth out of the land of Egypt that I might
dwell among them; I am the Lord their God.*
EXODUS 29:46 AMPC

We all have personal experiences that point to our Creator—times when we know God intervened. Take a moment to recall those moments when you knew He was the reason for your bravery, strength, wisdom, peace, or joy. Seasons you knew there was divine intervention on your behalf. Maybe you had the motivation to forgive someone you thought was unforgivable. Or you found the ability to love someone many considered unlovable. Maybe a broken marriage was fixed or an unexplained illness healed. Or maybe your heart was filled with confidence and courage at just the right moment. Chances are you have a storehouse full of personal experiences, courtesy of your heavenly Father.

It's important to remember God has a perfect track record in your life. You need to know He is real, alive, and active today. And it's vital that you can look back and recall those times He showed up, because it reminds you that if He's done it once, He will do it again. It's called hope.

Day 164

THE-GOD-WHO-SEES

*Now the Angel of the LORD found her. . .[and] said
to her, "Return to your mistress, and submit yourself
under her hand". . . . Then she called the name of the
LORD who spoke to her, You-Are-the-God-Who-Sees.*
GENESIS 16:7, 9, 13 NKJV

Hagar ran away from her circumstances: Sarai, an abusive mistress.
Part of Hagar's trouble had been caused by her own actions. For
having become pregnant by Abram, she had begun disrespect-
ing the childless Sarai.

We too sometimes think we can run from our troubles. But
when we come to the end of ourselves, God is there, ready to
give us the wisdom we need but may not want. He may ask us to
go back, telling us how to "be" in our circumstances: submissive,
obedient, loving. He had a vision for Hagar that she would be the
mother of a son and have many descendants.

Even today, this God-Who-Sees sees you and your situation.
He is ready to reveal Himself to you and share His wisdom. He
may not remove you from your circumstances, but He will give
you the word you need to get through them. Afterward, you'll
see your situation in a new light, with a new hope for your future,
step by step.

RELEASE YOUR BURDEN

*"I removed the burden from their shoulders;
their hands were set free from the basket."*
PSALM 81:6 NIV

God reached down and saved the Israelite people from slavery in Egypt. He led them out of the land when the time was right. The Exodus began with Him, through Moses, instructing the people in some strange ways. Following His directions, they smeared the blood of a Passover lamb around their doorframes. They prepared unleavened bread. They walked right up to the edge of a raging sea and passed through on dry land. They looked back over their shoulders to see their pursuers swallowed up by that same great body of water.

Your God is a burden remover. He does not desire for you to remain enslaved to addiction or abuse. He wants to part the waters before you and provide safe passage. He may calm the storm and beckon you to walk on the water, or He may hold you close and calm you in spite of the storm that causes destruction all around you.

If you are downcast, look up today! Find God there, ready to call you His child, ready to loose the chains of that which binds you. Find Him faithful. Release your burden to the one who has the power to cast it out of your life.

Day 166

LAUGH AT THE DAYS TO COME

She is clothed with strength and dignity;
she can laugh at the days to come.
PROVERBS 31:25 NIV

The only way a woman can be clothed in strength and dignity and laugh at the future is to know the one who longs to hold her future in His hands.

The Lord is the only one who can provide the Proverbs 31 promises mentioned. He is the only one who deserves your faith. Trusting in the Lord with all your heart is the only right way to live. So what does that kind of passionate faith look like? It turns your wringing hands into praising hands—not because you naturally rise every morning feeling perky and carefree, but because deep down you choose to believe worry is worthless and praise is priceless.

If you trust in God, He will indeed work all things for your good (Romans 8:28). You can count on it. As a Christian, you should count on it! That kind of trust—which is so very counter to what the world preaches—releases you from a life without hope. And it gives you the freedom to know joy—even amid earthly sorrows.

GOD MAKES US BEAUTIFUL

*For the LORD takes pleasure in his people; he
will beautify the humble with salvation.*
PSALM 149:4 NKJV

Standing in front of a magazine rack can be depressing if you believe everything on the covers. Women in skimpy clothes with long, flowing locks and perfect figures adorn most magazines. The article titles are just as daunting: "How to Have the Body of Your Dreams in 30 Days," "What Men Really Want in a Woman," and "Lose 10 Pounds in a Week." Their information on how to be beautiful or be the perfect woman tempts a lot of us into buying the latest issue, thinking it will solve our problems.

The world's definition of beauty is a far cry from God's. We were created in His image; made in His likeness. There's nothing wrong with trying to lose weight, buying a new dress, or getting our hair cut. We all want to look and feel our best—but not by the world's standard. Trying to measure up to others leads to disappointment and low self-esteem.

As God's children, we are made beautiful through Him. It's not a physical beauty like the world lauds. It's an inner loveliness that comes through knowing Christ. We take on a beauty the world can't understand or achieve. To those who know us and love us, we are beautiful women because of God's Spirit within us, radiating a beauty beyond human imagination.

WITH US

All this took place to fulfill what the Lord had said through the prophet: "The virgin will conceive and give birth to a son, and they will call him Immanuel" (which means "God with us").

MATTHEW 1:22–23 NIV

Since before the beginning of time, God has had us in mind. He created a world designed just for us. He placed us in it, and walked with us. And even though we disobeyed, He had a plan for that too. He never wanted to leave us. He has written a story that from beginning to end, and all the parts in the middle, points to one conclusion: "God with us."

Mary didn't know what part in this story she was playing. She didn't know God had been planning for this moment from the time He said, "Let there be light" (Genesis 1:3 NIV). She didn't know this baby she was about to carry would be called the Light of the world.

But Mary believed. She believed the words of the angel, as did Joseph, a son from the line of the king of God's people. Mary and Joseph believed and obeyed. And that's how they became part of the story.

What part does God have for you to play? Believe what He says to you. Obey. And He will be with you every step of the way.

LIVE FREE

*Now the Lord is the Spirit, and where the
Spirit of the Lord is, there is freedom.*
2 CORINTHIANS 3:17 NIV

The sun rises and sets daily, and no one attempts to alter its course.
The waves of the ocean come and go on the sandy shore, too
powerful to be deterred. So it is with the Spirit of the Lord. He is
powerful and free. And with His power, He has set you free. This
means you are not under the burden of striving. You can simply
be who Christ made you to be. You are free to enjoy life without
pressure to be who someone thinks you should be.

God loves you and has given you the freedom to live each day
loving Him, yourself, and others. He's given you the freedom to
make the best choices. You are not restricted to living in a small
and painful world but have been set free to celebrate being alive.

Christ fulfilled the law so that you don't have to. You can eat
the foods you prefer, sing the songs you chose, dress in your own
style, read what interests you, and attend church where you like.

Ask yourself what Christ wants you to enjoy today. Listen
for His Spirit's promptings. Be free to enjoy the day He created.

Day 170

BEHIND THE SCENES

*Now faith is confidence in what we hope for
and assurance about what we do not see.*
HEBREWS 11:1 NIV

Movies, theater, and sports productions all require people working behind the scenes. The audience very seldom sees what it takes to bring the final product together. Hours of preparation, planning, and technical assimilation come together before an audience sees a single performance—the outcome of the production company's hard work.

In the same way, your faith works behind the scenes of your life to produce a God-inspired outcome to situations you face. What you see is *not* what you get when you walk by faith.

Be encouraged today that no matter what takes place in the natural—what you see with your eyes—it doesn't have to be the final outcome of your situation. If you've asked God for something, then you can trust that He is working out all the details behind the scenes.

What you see right now, how you feel, is not a picture of what your faith is producing. Your faith is active, and God is busy working to make all things come together and benefit you.

Day 171

STAYING CLOSE

"Be strong and courageous. Do not be afraid;
do not be discouraged, for the LORD your God
will be with you wherever you go."
JOSHUA 1:9 NIV

It's easy to tell others not to worry. It's easy to remind our friends that God is with them and He's got everything under control. And it's easy to remind ourselves of that, when everything's going smoothly.

But when life sails us into rough waters, our natural instinct is to be afraid. We worry and fret. We cry out, not knowing how we will pay the bills or how we will face the cancer or how we will deal with whatever stormy waves crash around us. When life is scary, we get scared.

And believe it or not, that's a good thing. Because when we are afraid, when we are overwhelmed, when we realize that our circumstances are bigger than we are, that's when we're in the perfect place for God to pour out His comfort and assurance on us.

He never leaves us, but sometimes when life is good, we get distracted by other things and don't enjoy His presence as we should. When we feel afraid, we are drawn back to our heavenly Father's arms. And right in His arms is exactly where He wants us to be.

FULLY EQUIPPED

His divine power has given us everything we need for a godly life through our knowledge of him who called us by his own glory and goodness. Through these he has given us his very great and precious promises, so that through them you may participate in the divine nature, having escaped the corruption in the world caused by evil desires.

2 PETER 1:3–4 NIV

As Christians, we are fully equipped to live a godly life on earth. We don't have to live in a state of constant confusion. We don't have to stress about what to do or how to live. God has given us everything we need to be able to follow Him daily.

Second Corinthians 1:21–22 (NIV) tells us, "He anointed us, set his seal of ownership on us, and put his Spirit in our hearts as a deposit, guaranteeing what is to come." When we accept Christ as our Savior and Lord of our life, God gives us *His Spirit*! He places His very own Spirit in *our* hearts! Isn't that amazing? Take some time to fully reflect on that.

John 15:26 (NCV) calls the Holy Spirit our "Helper." We are never alone. God's Spirit is right there with us as we make decisions, as we go about our day, as we face trials, and as we enjoy His blessings. We have a constant Helper everywhere we go.

DUST

As a father has compassion on his children, so the LORD has compassion on those who fear him; for he knows how we are formed, he remembers that we are dust.

PSALM 103:13–14 NIV

Do you ever feel weak or inconsequential, like the slightest wind of difficulty could just blow you away? These verses tell you that you are but dust and that God is aware of that. That doesn't sound very encouraging, does it? But in actuality, great strength can be gleaned from this truth.

The Lord knows your frame. He knows that at times you are prone to weakness and worry and lack the strength to continue. So if you are harboring guilt that you have not lived up to some heavenly standard that you feel God has placed on you, release that guilt. He is mindful of what you are capable of and doesn't ask that you be some kind of superwoman. This is not an excuse for complacency or laziness, but an encouragement that your efforts are recognized and smiled on by God.

Even though you are but a speck of dust in the history of the universe, God has compassion on you and knows you as a father knows his child. How stunning! It doesn't matter that you sometimes feel weak and inconsequential—the Most High God knows and loves you. In that truth resides all the strength and value you need.

BRINGING US TO COMPLETION

*Being confident of this, that he who began
a good work in you will carry it on to
completion until the day of Christ Jesus.*
PHILIPPIANS 1:6 NIV

Remember the old saying, "If at first you don't succeed, try, try again"? That's an encouraging statement. But it doesn't tell us how many times we should try. It doesn't tell us when we should throw in the towel and give up.

While there may be an appropriate time to give up on a certain skill or project, we should never give up on people. We should continue to hope, continue to pray, continue to love them. After all, that's what God does for us.

No matter how many times we fail, no matter how many times we mess up, we know God hasn't written us off. He's still working on us. He still loves us. He knows our potential, because He created us, and He won't stop moving us forward until His plan is completed.

Those of us who have been adopted into God's family through believing in His Son, Jesus Christ, can be confident that God won't give up on us. No matter how messed up our lives may seem, He will continue working in us until His plan is fulfilled, and we stand before Him, perfect and complete.

THE ULTIMATE SECURITY

"You will know at last that I, the LORD, am your
Savior and your Redeemer, the Mighty One of Israel."
ISAIAH 60:16 NLT

Do you ever wonder what life would be like if we *knew* that the Lord was our Savior and Redeemer, the Mighty One of Israel? What would our lives look like if we believed this with every fiber of our being? Take a moment to think about that. How would your attitude about today change? This passage goes on to say, "I will make peace your leader and righteousness your ruler" (Isaiah 60:17 NLT).

It is a worthy goal to seek the Lord in everything we do, to get to know Him better with each passing day. What would our lives look like if we knew, really *knew*, that He alone is our Savior and Redeemer? Fear would be far from us, for we would understand that even mountains tremble before our God. Worry would drain away as we understood that He is the one who provides for every one of our needs.

Even in the face of death, if that was what the Lord willed, we would be at peace, for then we would be even closer to meeting Him face-to-face. We would move forward in every opportunity with confidence. We would battle with courage, knowing our ultimate security is in God.

Day 176

YOU ARE FORGIVEN

*So now there is no condemnation
for those who belong to Christ Jesus.*
ROMANS 8:1 NLT

There is no condemnation for those who are in Christ Jesus. This means there is no room for guilt or blame in your life. Even when you do things that make you feel like you have failed God, yourself, or others, your standing before God does not change. When you are in Christ, you are clothed in the clean, holy robes of God's Son. When God looks at you, He doesn't see the sins you've committed or the things you haven't done; He sees His holy, blameless Son.

How is this possible? It's possible because Christ died in your place. The sins that would have condemned you in God's holy court were placed on Christ's shoulders and buried with Him. They have no hold over you anymore. So let go of your guilt and regret.

Acknowledge that Christ's work on the cross was enough to cleanse and purify you before a holy God. Live in the freedom of the knowledge that no one and nothing can condemn you. Christ has stood in your place so that you can come boldly before the Father in the clean robes that have been washed in the blood of the Lamb. Ask for His forgiveness and claim His forgiveness in your life.

PERFECT LOVE

*There is no fear in love. But perfect love drives
out fear, because fear has to do with punishment.
The one who fears is not made perfect in love.*

1 JOHN 4:18 NIV

In this fallen world, love can be a dangerous game. You will face rejection and betrayal. You might place your hopes and trust in someone who isn't worthy of them. Eventually the people you love will let you down. All too often, the love that others exhibit is fickle and selfish. But love wasn't meant to break hearts.

God designed you to experience perfect love. This kind of love fortifies and sustains. It places you on solid ground. It surrounds you and fills you up. And it sets you free from fear. Can you fathom a love so whole, so pure? It might be difficult for you to imagine such a perfect love because no one has ever offered it to you—except for the one who laid down His life for yours, who shouldered God's wrath in order to spare you. His love is perfect and utterly selfless. In it there is no fear of condemnation. No fear of unfaithfulness. No fear of separation. Death's sting has been erased.

The power of Christ's perfect love has broken your chains. You are free.

HE MAKES ALL THINGS NEW

*Create in me a pure heart, O God, and renew
a steadfast spirit within me. Do not cast me
from your presence or take your Holy Spirit from
me. Restore to me the joy of your salvation and
grant me a willing spirit, to sustain me.*
PSALM 51:10–12 NIV

King David committed adultery and had the woman's husband killed in battle (Psalm 51). Talk about guilt! Yet the Bible says David was a man after God's own heart. David truly loved God—but being a king with power, he messed up royally.

David had faith in God's goodness. He was truly repentant and expected to be restored to God's presence. He could not stand to be separated from God. He recognized that he must become clean again through the power of forgiveness.

Perhaps there have been times when you felt distant from God because of choices you made. There is no sin that is too big for God to cover or too small to bother Him with. He is willing to forgive, and He forgets when you ask Him. He expects you to do the same.

God sent Jesus to the cross for you to restore you to relationship with Himself.

Day 177

LOVING OURSELVES

For the whole law is fulfilled in one word:
"You shall love your neighbor as yourself." But
if you bite and devour one another, watch out
that you are not consumed by one another.
GALATIANS 5:14–15 ESV

Some of the most difficult people to be around are people who don't like themselves. Oh, it may seem like they love themselves and dislike everyone else, but that's not usually the case. When we don't like the person we see in the mirror each morning, we usually don't care much for anyone else either.

When we're commanded to love others as we love ourselves, it's a given that we actually love ourselves. God wants us to take care of our needs, show kindness to ourselves, and be gentle with our thoughts about ourselves. And He wants us to treat others that way as well.

When we love ourselves the way God loves us, and we love others in the same way—by taking care of their needs and showing kindness, gentleness, and respect—our relationships become healthy and fulfilling.

THE LORD IS OUR PORTION

I say to myself, "The LORD is my portion;
therefore I will wait for him."
LAMENTATIONS 3:24 NIV

For the Israelites, the word *portion* held multiple meanings. It could refer to a piece of land or an inheritance. Portions could also imply the necessities of life like daily food, water, and clothing. Old Testament writings often designate the kind of life one was born into and the family one was raised in as our portion in life.

In this verse, the writer declares that the Lord is his portion. He states clearly that he inherited the right to worship God, and that God provides the essentials to support his life. He is also welcomed to be a part of the family of God.

The Lord is our portion too. But when will we fully receive this inheritance and celebrate with Him? We know it is coming, but it's difficult to wait.

Hope gives us strength as we anticipate our return to God. We belong to God and know someday we will worship Him face-to-face in His presence. Knowing God will keep his promise, we can say with confidence, "The Lord is my portion; therefore I will wait."

Day 181

GOODBYE, DEATH

O LORD, you are my God; I will exalt you; I will praise your name, for you have done wonderful things, plans formed of old, faithful and sure.

ISAIAH 25:1 ESV

Young or old. Man or woman. Across classes, continents. . .you name it, death touches us. Since that day in the garden of Eden when death entered the world, death hasn't left. It has spread far and wide—everywhere, in fact, because everyone sins, and the two (death and sin) go hand in hand. Sin's stiff payment is death, and death costs us dearly. We feel it deep down at the funeral. We could fear it down deep all our days.

But. . .

God has a remedy for death: life through Him. God will surely punish sinners—reading about His wrath can be grim!—but God will just as surely pardon those who believe in His Son. He has had a grip on death always, and He will get rid of death before long. Depend upon it. Praise Him for it:

He will destroy death forever. The Lord GOD will wipe away the tears from every face. . .for the LORD has spoken. On that day it will be said, "Look, this is our God; we have waited for Him, and He has saved us. This is the LORD; we have waited for Him. Let us rejoice and be glad in His salvation."

ISAIAH 25:8–9 HCSB

THE ONE YOU CAN COUNT ON

*Blessed be the LORD my Rock, who trains my
hands for war, and my fingers for battle—my
lovingkindness and my fortress, my high tower
and my deliverer, my shield and the One in whom
I take refuge, who subdues my people under me.*
PSALM 144:1–2 NKJV

David learned at an early age that he could count on God. Although small in stature, he killed a lion and a bear, protecting his father's sheep from certain death. His courage and boldness came from within, from strength in his relationship with God.

His brothers, onlookers, and especially his enemy, the Philistine giant Goliath, laughed at him when he stood before them declaring he would take down Israel's enemy. He knew he could count on God. He had faith that God would go before him and give him victory in the battles he faced.

God has been with you and prepared you for what lies before you. You don't have to go into battle alone. When you know God as the one you can always count on, you can stand in the face of the giants in your life and come out of your battle a giant-slayer!

WORKING OUT

*It pays to take life seriously; things work
out when you trust in GOD.*
PROVERBS 16:20 MSG

Today's verse reads like a contradiction: The first part says, take life seriously. Concentrate without frills or fun. The second, it will all work out. Don't worry, be happy. What goes around comes around.

Although the two statements seem to collide, God's Word is true and does not lie. Things work out for those who take life seriously.

Taking life seriously doesn't mean it depends on you. You are strongest when you are weak. The outcome is up to Christ.

It doesn't involve working harder, twenty-five hours out of every twenty-four. If you are focused on work only, your life is out of balance.

A serious life may include working hard, being concerned about the future, and maintaining a savings account, but only because your life is balanced, centered on God's will. As the second part of the verse states, "trust in GOD." Or as other translations put it, heed God's Word and listen to His instructions.

Live deliberately. Live consistently. Listen for God's instructions before you act.

When you live as God directs, both vertically and horizontally, things will work out for you. You can count on it.

HE CARES FOR YOU

*"You yourselves have seen what I did to Egypt, and how
I carried you on eagles' wings and brought you to myself."*
EXODUS 19:4 NIV

Often we feel deserted. As though God doesn't hear our prayers. And we wait. When Moses led the children of Israel out of Egypt toward the promised land, he did not take them on the shortest route. God directed him to go the distant way, lest the people turn back quickly when things became difficult. God led them by day with a pillar of clouds and by night with a pillar of fire. How clearly He showed Himself to His children! The people placed their hope in an almighty God and followed His lead. When they thirsted, God gave water. When they hungered, He sent manna. No need was unmet.

The amount of food and water needed for the group was unimaginable. But each day, Moses depended upon God. He believed God would care for them.

If God can do this for so many, you can rest assured that He will care for you. He knows your needs before you even ask. Place your hope and trust in Him. He is able. He's proven Himself, over and over. Read the scriptures and pray to the one who loves you. His care is infinite. . .and He will never disappoint you.

STRENGTH TO STRENGTH

*Blessed (happy, fortunate, to be envied) is the man
whose strength is in You. . . . They go from strength
to strength [increasing in victorious power]. . . .
O Lord of hosts, blessed (happy, fortunate, to be
envied) is the man who trusts in You [leaning and
believing on You, committing all and confidently
looking to You, and that without fear or misgiving]!*
PSALM 84:5, 7, 12 AMPC

What joy there is for the woman who looks to God for her strength. Looking to Him isn't something she is forced to do but *pleased*— in fact eager—to do. God builds up not only her joy in Him, but her strength, increasing her power.

The key is trust. That's what brings a woman such joy, gives her such strength. She trusts God's watching out for her, watching over her. She stops along the way and waits until He turns her tears of sorrow and bitterness into a place of springs and replenishing rain. She cannot help but smile as she looks at God, seeing Him as her "Sun and Shield" (Psalm 84:11 AMPC), her light and protection. And she doesn't just slightly trust but commits everything to Him with confidence.

Trust God to take you from strength to strength.

Day 186

JUST BE

God is our refuge and strength, a very present help in trouble. Therefore we will not fear. . . . Be still, and know that I am God.
PSALM 46:1–2, 10 NKJV

Women, born nurturers, are constantly looking to fulfill the needs of others. We are usually the ones who not only plan the meals but also write up the grocery list, do the shopping, then cook them. We are usually the main caregivers, from children to aging parents. In our families, we are usually the go-to person—for missing socks, lost homework or car keys, a ride to soccer practice, whatever. Then there are our coworkers who know we pride ourselves on multitasking, taking on big projects while also attending to the details no one else seems to be concerned about.

In all these areas, we are running around *doing* and, as a result, can *do* ourselves right into the ground. But God wants us to first and foremost just *be*. He reminds us that because His presence and strength are all we need, fear has no place in our lives. When we believe in those facts, when we trust in Him with all we love, have, and are, we can relax.

Be still. Rest in the silence of His presence. So forget about planning tomorrow. Instead, just *be* in today, knowing He's got it all under control.

GOD NEVER SLUMBERS

He will not let your foot slip—he who
watches over you will not slumber.
PSALM 121:3 NIV

Ever stayed up all night studying for a major test, waiting for a loved one to come home, or rocking a sick child? The next day or two your mushy brain barely functions, and your body, drained of all energy, finds it difficult to focus even on the most important decisions.

You'll regain your balance and energy only after several nights of refreshing sleep. The human body requires regular periods of rest in order to thrive.

The psalms tell us that God does *not* sleep. He watches over us, never once averting His eyes even for a few quick moments of rest. God guards our every moment.

The Lord stays up all night, looking after us as we sleep. He patiently keeps His eyes on us even when we roam. He constantly comforts when fear or illness make us toss and turn.

Like a caring parent who tiptoes into a sleeping child's room, God surrounds us even when we don't realize it.

We can sleep because God never slumbers.

GOD WANTS TO HEAR FROM YOU

"And when you are praying, do not use thoughtless repetition as the Gentiles do, for they suppose that they will be heard for their many words."
MATTHEW 6:7 NASB

Remember kneeling beside your bed and praying when you were a kid? Why did it all seem so simple then? We just talked to God like He was really there and kept our requests short and simple.

Then, as you got older, the lengthy and spiritual prayers of the "older saints" became intimidating. So where's the balance? Reading a little further in this passage from Matthew, at verse 9, Jesus gives us His own example for prayer. If you can remember the acrostic ACTS, you'll have an excellent formula for prayer: Adoration, Confession, Thanksgiving, and Supplication.

As we come before the Lord we first need to honor Him as Creator, Master, Savior, and Lord. Reflect on who He is and praise Him. And because we're human we need to confess and repent of our daily sins. Following this we should be in a mode of thanksgiving. Finally, our prayer requests should be upheld. Keeping a prayer journal allows for a written record of God's answers.

Your prayers certainly don't have to be elaborate or polished. God does not judge your way with words. He knows your heart. He wants to hear from You.

Day 187

LET GOD FIGHT FOR YOU

*The Lord will fight for you, and you shall
hold your peace and remain at rest.*
EXODUS 14:14 AMPC

Letting God fight for us can be a tall order because we're capable women, ready and able to handle what comes our way. It may not be pretty, but we get the job done. We are moms and wives, company owners and shift managers, coaches and teachers, and everything in between. And when we're standing in God's strength and wisdom, we're a force to be reckoned with. Amen?

Yet there are times we're to let God fight for us. We're to take a step back and trust as He handles the situation. We're to wait on His timing and plan, even when it seems there's no movement whatsoever. And instead of jumping in and trying to make everything come together, we're to take a seat. We're to let God be God.

What makes that hard for you? Are you more comfortable in the driver's seat? Do you feel better when you're calling the shots? Is it easiest when you get to control all interactions and outcomes?

God is asking you to trust Him enough to surrender your game plan to His. And when you do, you'll find peace.

OBEDIENCE BRINGS BLESSING

"If you fully obey the LORD your God and carefully keep all his commands that I am giving you today, the LORD your God will set you high above all the nations of the world."

DEUTERONOMY 28:1 NLT

We often ask God to elevate us. We look for higher positions at work, greater favor with our bosses, even higher status with our friends. We take on positions of leadership with the Parent Teacher Organization, the garden club, the women's Bible study group. . .all sorts of things.

Oh, how we love to rise to the top. It's interesting though to think that God's elevation plan begins with our submission. *Ouch.* In fact, His plan hinges on one simple word: *obedience.* If you obey Him, then you free His hands to bless you.

What have you set your sights on? What area of your life are you hoping to elevate? Ask God to show you if there are any areas where you need to buckle down and obey Him. Perhaps that simple act of obedience will open the door to that next big thing.

GOD MEETS NEEDS

"But the mountains of Israel will produce heavy crops of fruit for my people—for they will be coming home again soon! See, I care about you, and I will pay attention to you. Your ground will be plowed and your crops planted."
EZEKIEL 36:8–9 NLT

It's fascinating to see how God always made provision for His people in Old Testament times. He fed them manna in the desert, quail from the heavens, and provided heavy crops of fruit when they reached the promised land.

Why did God so often prove Himself through food and daily provisions? Because the Israelites saw the meeting of their daily needs as a sign of love and care from their creator.

Would a mother hold back daily provision from her child? No! On the contrary, she would do anything she could to make sure that child had everything he needed—food, clothing, shelter, water—all of the basic necessities of life.

God wants to meet your needs too. So whatever you're lacking, whatever you're afraid you'll have to do without, lift that need to the Lord. . .and wait with expectation for His provision.

EVERLASTING LIFE AND LOVE

*They sang responsively, praising and giving thanks
to the Lord, saying, For He is good, for His mercy
and loving-kindness endure forever toward Israel.
And all the people shouted with a great shout when
they praised the Lord, because the foundation
of the house of the Lord was laid!*

EZRA 3:11 AMPC

What a celebration Israel held after beginning the restoration of temple worship. Trumpets sounded, cymbals crashed, voices raised in song. Most shouted for joy. Some wept, remembering the glory of Solomon's temple, destroyed during the exile of the Israelites.

Solomon's temple had replaced the tabernacle built under Moses's direction. And the offerings God commanded for Moses' tabernacle pointed back to the offerings made by Cain (given out of obligation) and Abel (given out of love), and the difference between them.

God has always weighed the heart of the giver more than the offering. The temple offered hope of forgiveness and redemption, but it was only temporary. A permanent change of heart was needed.

Fast forward to the final sacrifice, given once for all: Jesus' death on the cross. His blood covers our sin and runs through our hearts, rejuvenating, renewing, giving new life. "God demonstrates his own love for us in this: While we were still sinners, Christ died for us" (Romans 5:8 NIV).

That's a love story for the ages. That's a reason to celebrate!

WALKING SECURELY

Whoever walks in integrity walks securely,
but whoever takes crooked paths will be found out.
PROVERBS 10:9 NIV

Shortcuts can be tempting, and certainly, they do sometimes save time. But cutting moral corners almost always ends in someone, or someone's reputation, getting hurt.

Crooked paths often take you off the main course. They may lead to unwelcome and unexpected obstacles. They may be dangerous—not well lit or smoothly paved. And if you fall and get hurt, you won't be able to tell anyone where you are! The problem is, all these stresses and trials leave a mark on a person. And it's the kind of mark that will eventually be discovered, no matter how much you try to hide it.

But walking in the way of integrity means you never have to hide. You can step freely, knowing exactly where you are headed. You can see who is walking with you—who is there for you in case you need help. You can plan for any obstacles, because they can be easily seen from a long way off. And you don't have to worry about getting lost—the straight path stretches out in front of you, leading you directly to your goal.

Walking in integrity allows you to be confident in every step you take. And knowing that, you can even run.

Day 174

SHEEP-SEEKER

For thus saith the Lord GOD; Behold, I, even I, will
both search my sheep, and seek them out. As a shepherd
seeketh out his flock in the day that he is among his
sheep that are scattered; so will I seek out my sheep,
and will deliver them out of all places where they
have been scattered in the cloudy and dark day.
 EZEKIEL 34:11–12 KJV

The Lord spoke through Ezekiel about His love for people. He shared about how God pursues them, seeks them out. Even today, God still seeks out His beloved children.

In this moment, reflect on God's love. Recall when you began a relationship with Him. Meditate on some of today's readings to remind you of God's grace and mercy upon you. For example, Proverbs 21:2–3 (NIV) says: "A person may think their own ways are right, but the LORD weighs the heart. To do what is right and just is more acceptable to the LORD than sacrifice."

God isn't looking for more sacrifice—He already took care of that on the cross. God isn't looking for you to save yourself, or put yourself in right standing with Him—He also took care of that on the cross. God just wants you, imperfections and all, to trust Him. Enter His sheep-seeker arms and rest.

Day 175

WAIT FOR GOD

I waited patiently for the LORD; he turned to me and heard my cry. He lifted me out of the slimy pit, out of the mud and mire; he set my feet on a rock and gave me a firm place to stand. He put a new song in my mouth, a hymn of praise to our God. Many will see and fear the LORD and put their trust in him.
PSALM 40:1–3 NIV

No one likes to wait. It's why many of us would rather eat substandard food from a drive-through than experience the joy of a home-cooked meal. But many blessings can only be obtained through patience and a lot of waiting.

Just look at the blessings David received because he waited. First, God heard him. Then, God lifted him out of the pit. Next, He set David on a rock and gave him a firm place to stand. Finally, God put a song of praise in David's heart.

Most of God's blessings are not of the fast-food variety. Have patience, and wait for God. You'll be glad you did.

EXPECT TROUBLE

*These things I have spoken unto you, that in me ye might
have peace. In the world ye shall have tribulation:
but be of good cheer; I have overcome the world.*

JOHN 16:33 KJV

Why do bad things happen to good people? It is an age-old question. Sometimes we expect God to surround us with an invisible shield that keeps us from all harm and disease, all hurt and disappointment. As nice as this might sound, it is simply not how life works. Christians are not exempt from trials.

In the Gospel of John, we read that Christ told His followers to *expect* trouble in this world. The good news is that we do not have to face it alone. When trials come, remember that Jesus has overcome this world. Through Him, we too are overcomers. Draw upon the promise that through Christ you can do all things. The children's song says it this way: "Jesus loves me, this I know, for the Bible tells me so. Little ones to Him belong. They are weak, but He is strong."

Expect trouble, but refuse to let it defeat you. Trials strengthen our faith and our character. No one gets excited about a trial, yet we can be assured that God is still in control even when trouble comes our way.

OVERWHELMED IS UNDERPRAYED

*Try your best to live quietly, to mind your own business,
and to work hard, just as we taught you to do. Then
you will be respected by people who are not followers of
the Lord, and you won't have to depend on anyone.*

1 THESSALONIANS 4:11–12 CEV

"Live quietly, mind your own business, work hard, serve on the PTA, chair some committees, sign the kids up for soccer, join an aerobics class. . ." Oops! Is that what it says, or did we add something to the recommendations in the Bible?

None of these things are bad or wrong. However, moving through life as a tornado, leaving destruction in your wake, affects the lives of those around you. To be an effective witness for Christ, you must be in control of your affairs. To be able to attest to the comfort and peace that Jesus provides, you cannot be frantic and out of control.

If your mantra is "I'm overwhelmed," followed by a familiar litany of tasks, duties, and deadlines, perhaps you have not fully sought the will of God regarding your schedule and commitments. His desire is not to overwhelm you. He recommends that you do your very best to lead a quiet, simple life while you work hard at the things you need to do. Find peace as you release yourself from self-imposed requirements and surrender to God's will.

A PRAYER FOR YOU

*"I am praying not only for these disciples but also for all
who will ever believe in me through their message. I pray
that they will all be one, just as you and I are one. . . . I
have given them the glory you gave me, so they may be
one as we are one. I am in them and you are in me."*

JOHN 17:20–23 NLT

Imagine this: Thousands of years ago, while He was in human
form on earth, Jesus, the Son of God, prayed a prayer for *you*. He
prayed that you and other believers would be one, just as He and
Father God are one. And He didn't stop there! He who was the
manifestation of God on earth, He who displayed every nuance
of God's character, revealed all this to His followers—so that they
could believe and reflect God's character themselves by walking
as Jesus walked!

Make this awareness part of your daily walk. Know that Jesus
has prayed for, is praying for, and will continue to pray for you.
Know that He has been to you an example, and will help you reflect
the character of Father God. And trust that you, His believing
daughter, will never be parted from either Father or Son.

Day 177

GOD'S LOVE IS BIGGER
THAN CIRCUMSTANCES

Who shall separate us from the love of Christ? Shall
trouble or hardship or persecution or famine or nakedness
or danger or sword? As it is written: "For your sake
we face death all day long; we are considered as sheep
to be slaughtered." No, in all these things we are more
than conquerors through him who loved us. For I am
convinced that neither death nor life, neither angels
nor demons, neither the present nor the future, nor
any powers, neither height nor depth, nor anything
else in all creation, will be able to separate us from
the love of God that is in Christ Jesus our Lord.

ROMANS 8:35–39 NIV

If these things cannot separate us from God's love, then they aren't an indication of the absence of God's love either. But have you noticed that we still doubt God's love based on what happens in our lives? If we get what we want, we believe God has accepted us and loves us. If we do not receive what we long for, we believe He has abandoned or rejected us.

What desperate tragedies of the heart befall us when we measure God's love by our circumstances! We pierce ourselves through when we believe that God only receives and loves us when life goes our way. We must remember that this world is not heaven; the final story will be told later. Until then, life sometimes is hard. But nothing can separate us from Christ's love. *Nothing*.

COMFORTED BY GOD

*Shout for joy, you heavens; rejoice, you earth; burst
into song, you mountains! For the LORD comforts his
people and will have compassion on his afflicted ones.*
ISAIAH 49:13 NIV

Comfort feels wonderful in a time of distress. It's like a warm blanket wrapped around a cold and lonely feeling. How do you comfort yourself? Perhaps you take a walk, bake a cake, or clean your house. Yet those things may fall short of your goal. Not to worry. For God is the best at helping you feel better. Second Corinthians 1:3 (NIV) calls Him the "God of all comfort."

David, the psalmist, considered God his shepherd, writing, "Your rod and your staff, they comfort me" (Psalm 23:4 NIV). David, once a shepherd himself, used his rod to count his sheep, his staff to guide them. He knew those tools brought his sheep *comfort*, a word which means to strengthen—as the *fort* in comfort implies.

And God doesn't just provide comfort. He is also the God of compassion, the Good Shepherd who never leaves one little lost lamb out in the cold night. In fact, He keeps a list of our tears (Psalm 56:8).

God's comfort for and compassion on the afflicted are a reason for praise. Today, join all of creation in the song of joy!

A DAY OF REST

Six days thou shalt do thy work, and on the
seventh day thou shalt rest: that thine ox and
thine ass may rest, and the son of thy handmaid,
and the stranger, may be refreshed.

EXODUS 23:12 KJV

If there is one scriptural principle that women routinely abandon, it is that of the Sabbath. Because Christ has become our rest and because we now worship on the Lord's Day, we often disregard the idea of a Sabbath rest.

Rest was at the heart of the Sabbath. One day out of seven, God's people were not to work or to make others work, so they could all be refreshed.

God Himself started the work-rest pattern before the earth was a week old. God didn't rest because He was tired; He rested because His work of creation was finished.

But a woman's work is never done! How can she rest?

It's not easy. There are always more things that can be done. But most of those things can wait a day while you recharge.

God's design for the week gives rest to the weary. Let's not neglect His provision.

Day 202

TOTAL COMFORT

"For the Lamb at the center of the throne will be their shepherd; 'he will lead them to springs of living water. And God will wipe away every tear from their eyes.'"
REVELATION 7:17 NIV

The book of Revelation contains a lot of imagery, and the precise meaning of what John saw is debated by many. However, what is *not* debatable are the words of today's verse.

Jesus, the Lamb of God, is at the center of His heavenly throne. He is the shepherd of the survivors of the end days, the ones God deemed worthy. And as their shepherd, Jesus will lead believers to the springs of living water. And God will wipe away their tears and quell their fears.

Are you craving for Jesus to quench your thirst? If so, remember Jesus' words, "Whoever believes in me, as Scripture has said, rivers of living water will flow from within them" (John 7:38 NIV). And allow the Lord your shepherd to make you lie down in green meadows and to lead you beside the quiet waters (Psalm 23:1–2). Visualize the abundant water, flowing and calm, and the fact that God will truly wipe every tear from your eyes, bringing you the peace and comfort you're longing for.

DIVINE TIMING

*Wait for the LORD; be strong and
take heart and wait for the LORD.*
PSALM 27:14 NIV

Our society has become more and more high-speed. We want instant everything—from food to news to cars to technology. We are taught life is short, time is money, and if people slow us down or cause us to lose our focus, well, maybe they should just get out of our way!

Amid the world's fast pace though, sometimes the Lord asks us to wait. And our spirits cry out, "No, not that word—*wait*—anything but that." And yet, sometimes God desires that we should wait on Him. Not because the Almighty is fickle or enjoys watching us squirm in frustration but because God is the One who made time. He is the creator and master of all of eternity. Only He knows the exact time when something should happen so that it can truly work for our good.

Take a moment to look back on your life at all the times God came to your rescue, gifted you with amazing blessings, and was your comfort and strength. What loveliness there is in the divine timing of God!

JESUS STANDS NEAR

The following night the Lord stood near Paul and said, "Take courage! As you have testified about me in Jerusalem, so you must also testify in Rome."

ACTS 23:11 NIV

Paul had been beaten, arrested, and put in chains. Some people had been ready to kill him. He had earlier escaped with his life only due to his Roman citizenship. And now he was already on the chopping block again! What would he do?

This is when the Lord stood near him, telling him to be brave and to share his testimony again. Did you catch that? *The Lord stood near him.* What strength is the believer's when he or she has Jesus literally standing near!

Christ stands with you every single day of your life. Listen. Do you hear Him now? He whispers words of affirmation, which He spoke over your ancestors, words He will speak to your descendants. Be still now. Hear Him:

"You are Mine. You are a beloved sheep of My pasture, and I am your Good Shepherd. Be bold in My name, for I have declared you more than a conqueror. I've breathed new life into you. You are cherished. Be strong and courageous because I go with you into battle. I'll help you share your story. Your testimony will draw others to My side so that I may stand near to them as well!"

REFINED AS SILVER

For You, O God, have tested us;
You have refined us as silver is refined.
PSALM 66:10 NKJV

There's no way for precious metals to be refined without going into the fire. A lovely wedding band starts as an ugly lump of ore. It's placed into a fiery furnace, where the precious is separated from the nonprecious. Only the good remains while the bad is sloughed off.

The same is true in our lives. When we go through the fire (difficult or painful seasons), we undergo a holy refining. We become who we were meant to be. The good is separated from the not-so-good. When we are purified, we become stronger. Brighter. Purer. We will stand the test of time. No longer a lump of ore, we are bright and shining witnesses of God's transforming power.

The refining process is never easy. No one wants to go through fiery trials. But, oh, to shine like silver! To know that the work God is doing in us will last for all eternity. It makes the hard times worthwhile when we realize the Lord's purification process can be trusted.

Day 206

FENCES

*"If you keep My commandments, you will abide
in My love, just as I have kept My Father's
commandments and abide in His love."*

JOHN 15:10 NKJV

People who own horses know how necessary fences are. Inside the pasture, the horses are protected from things that can harm them: wet, boggy ground can cause horses to founder, and certain plants can be poisonous to them. Inside the pasture, they can be fed properly, groomed, and exercised. The fence does not exist to keep the horse from being free; the fence exists so the horse and its owner can enjoy their relationship, and the horse can live to its fullest potential. Most dangers for the horse are outside the fence.

God's commandments are much like the pasture fence. Sin is on the other side. His laws exist to keep us in fellowship with Him and to keep us out of things that are harmful to us that can lead to bondage. We abide in the loving presence of our heavenly Father by staying within the boundaries He has set up for our own good. He has promised to care for us and to do the things needful for us. His love for us is unconditional, even when we jump the fence into sin. But by staying inside the boundaries, we enjoy intimacy with Him.

Day 207

GOD'S OPEN-ARM POLICY

*So he got up and came to his [own] father. But while
he was still a long way off, his father saw him and
was moved with pity and tenderness [for him]; and he
ran and embraced him and kissed him [fervently].*

LUKE 15:20 AMPC

In our eagerness to pave our own way, to start our life, and to find
our own purpose and direction, we may, at times, find ourselves
heading in the wrong direction or making bad choices, choices that
God wouldn't make for us. That's what happened to a rich man's
youngest boy in Jesus' parable of the prodigal son.

Son number two asked his dad for his inheritance early. With
riches in hand, the son went off and had a great time. Until the
money ran out. While feeding hogs for a farmer so he could eat,
the young man, who "could not satisfy his hunger" (Luke 15:16
AMPC), went back to his father, thinking he'd fare better working
for him.

While the son rehearsed the speech he'd give to his dad, his
dad saw him. Moved with compassion, the father ran to his son,
kissed him, and celebrated his return.

When you make a mistake, God does the same for you. It's
His open-arm policy.

AVAILABLE 24/7

I call on you, my God, for you will answer me;
turn your ear to me and hear my prayer.
PSALM 17:6 NIV

"No one is available to take your call at this time, so leave a message and we will return your call—or not—if we feel like it. . .and only between the hours of 4:00 and 4:30 p.m. Thank you for calling. Have a super day!"

We've all felt the frustration of that black hole called voice mail. It is rare to reach a real, honest-to-goodness, breathing human being the first time we dial a telephone number.

Fortunately, our God is always available. He can be reached at any hour of the day or night and every day of the year—including weekends and holidays! When we pray, we don't have to worry about disconnections, hang-ups, or poor reception. We will never be put on hold or our prayers diverted to another department. The Bible assures us that God is eager to hear our petitions and that he welcomes our prayers of thanksgiving.

The psalmist David wrote of God's response to those who put their trust in Him: "He will call upon me, and I will answer him" (Psalm 91:15 NIV). David had great confidence that God would hear his prayers. And we can too!

WHERE IS YOUR TREASURE?

"But store up for yourselves treasures in heaven,
where neither moth nor rust destroys, and where
thieves do not break in or steal; for where your
treasure is, there your heart will be also."
MATTHEW 6:20–21 NASB

Treasure maps show up regularly in children's stories and pirate movies. What is so intriguing about a treasure map? It leads to treasure! People have gone to great lengths in search of treasure, sometimes only to find in the end that the map was a hoax and no treasure existed.

Imagine a treasure map drawn of your life, with all its twists and turns. Where do you spend your time? How do you use your talents? Would the map lead to heaven, or is your treasure in earthly things?

Each day consists of twenty-four hours, regardless of how we use them. We make choices about the priorities in our lives. The world sends messages about how we should spend our time; however, if we listen to the still, small voice of God, we will learn how to "store up treasures in heaven."

Nurturing relationships and sharing Christ with others, as well as reading God's Word and getting to know Him through prayer, are examples of storing up treasures in heaven. Using our gifts for His glory is also important. The dividends of such investments are priceless.

GRASSHOPPERS AND GIANTS

*"We saw the Nephilim there (the descendants of Anak
come from the Nephilim). We seemed like grasshoppers
in our own eyes, and we looked the same to them."*
NUMBERS 13:33 NIV

Moses sent spies to explore the land of Canaan. Returning, the men said, "We went into the land to which you sent us, and it does flow with milk and honey! . . . But the people who live there are powerful, and the cities are fortified and very large" (Numbers 13:27–28 NIV).

Compared to Canaan's current inhabitants—especially the Anakims, who were known for their tall and robust stature—the Israelites were grasshoppers. And that shook their faith to its core. But amid the clamor Caleb silenced the crowd, saying, "We should go up and take possession of the land, for we can certainly do it" (verse 30 NIV). And Joshua agreed.

The ten spies believed only in what they saw, while Joshua and Caleb believed God. They dared to oppose the majority with a firm commitment to God and an unwavering confidence in God's promises to them.

Are your trials and problems too overwhelming to face? Like the ten spies, do you feel as if there is no way to conquer them? Stand on God's Word, and He will bring you to the promised land. In the process, your faith will transform you from a grasshopper into a spiritual giant!

Day 211

NO MORE TEARS

> *" 'He will wipe every tear from their eyes. There will
> be no more death' or mourning or crying or pain,
> for the old order of things has passed away."*
> REVELATION 21:4 NIV

Everyone experiences periods of sadness. Sometimes tears flow at the loss of a loved one, and the pain seems overwhelming. Yet death comes to us all, and we're powerless to stop it. Then there are the days when, for no apparent rhyme or reason, sadness just creeps in. Yet there is hope. And it's given to a believer by the God who loves her. He promises each of His daughters a world with no more tears.

In Revelation 21:4, God guarantees there will be no more sadness, mourning, pain, or death. You will no longer be separated from your loved ones. Worry and anguish will be things of the past. It will literally be a new world, a time of peace and joy!

If you are struggling with sadness, if your face is stained with tears, do not lose hope. Your current situation is temporary, and your God promises brighter days will come. The old order of things will pass away to be replaced with the blissful happiness found in dwelling in and with God.

Day 212

WHO GOD HEARS

The LORD is far from the wicked, but he
hears the prayers of the righteous.
PROVERBS 15:29 NLT

One of the countless, wonderful things about God is that He's a gentleman. As powerful as He is, He rarely pushes in where He's not wanted, except in cases where justice demands it.

God remains far from the wicked, for the wicked push Him away. They don't want Him around. They make choices against the Almighty and disregard His ways. Then, when they land themselves in trouble with no way out, help is nowhere to be found. They choose to exclude the one who could help them. In the end, they have no one.

But when the righteous call His name, He hears. Though none of us is righteous on our own, we can claim righteousness through Jesus Christ. He alone is righteous, and He covers us like a cloak. When we call on God, He sees the righteousness that covers us through Christ and recognizes us as His children. He leans over and listens carefully to our words, because we belong to Him. He loves us.

Next time it seems like God isn't listening, perhaps we should examine our hearts. Have we pushed God away? Have we accepted the price His Son, Jesus Christ, paid on our behalf? If not, we can't claim righteousness. If we have, we can trust that He's never far away. He hears us.

Day 213

UNCHANGEABLE

*LORD, hear my prayer! Listen to my plea! Don't
turn away from me in my time of distress. Bend
down to listen, and answer me quickly when I call
to you. . . . [The LORD] will listen to the prayers
of the destitute. He will not reject their pleas. . . .
You are always the same; you will live forever.*
PSALM 102:1–2, 17, 27 NLT

The world changes so quickly around us—places, faces, technology, relationships, mores, values, wars, boundaries, battles, surrenders, earthquakes, hurricanes, fires, and famine. . . .We can barely keep pace. Somedays we find ourselves breathless, not knowing what's sure and certain. We find ourselves feeling untethered, doubting the permanence of the very ground beneath our feet.

Yet we're believers in a God who never changes. He's always ready to help, teach, correct, and save. He's the one place we know we can go when we have problems and pleas. He's the one person who'll never turn from us when we're in distress.

Pray. And know that when you do, God will bend His ear. Know that He'll find coherence in your babbling. Know that He'll never reject you—but protect you.

In this world of constant change, remember that you're enveloped by the permanence of your rock and refuge, standing on Him and trusting in Him alone.

Day 214

BREAD IN THE WILDERNESS

*"I will rain down bread from heaven for you. The people
are to go out each day and gather enough for that day."*
EXODUS 16:4 NIV

Our faith is a living, breathing organism that needs to be fed every day. Christ, His Word, and His presence, are our daily manna. He has been rained down upon us, given to us by God. All we have to do is take Him into our lives, gathering a day's portion every day.

Jesus Himself knows that we need a daily portion of Him to renew ourselves. When He faced the hungry crowds in the wilderness, He showed His concern for their welfare. In Matthew 15:32 (NKJV), Jesus says, "I have compassion on the multitude, because they have now continued with Me three days and have nothing to eat. And I do not want to send them away hungry, lest they faint on the way."

Christ is so gracious to us. He gives us "each day our daily bread," nourishment that shields us against our mood swings, unrelenting problems, and the influence of unbelievers surrounding us. This miraculous, daily intake of Christ keeps us from fainting along the way!

God has provided you with the manna you need to feed your faith. Don't go away hungry. Take your daily portion each morning, just what you need, to live the victorious life.

Day 215

HOPE

"I will come to you and fulfill my good promise. . . .
For I know the plans I have for you," declares the
LORD. . ."plans to give you hope and a future."
JEREMIAH 29:10–11 NIV

Hope is beautiful. At times you see it, shining and bright, dancing ahead of you, making your steps lighter and forming a smile on your lips. These are the times when a new home, tiny new baby, or a new job fill you with expectation.

Other times, although hope may not seem apparent, it is still present. This is when you may be chilled deeply by grief, having lost a relationship, parent, or long-held dream. This is when the warmth of hope, like a well-worn quilt made by loving hands, God's hands, can be pulled around your shoulders, and you can rest under its comforting weight, snuggling up to the knowledge that one day you will again "see the goodness of the LORD in the land of the living" (Psalm 27:13 NIV).

God declares hope over, around, and through you. He has prepared a future for you and has plans for your well-being. A powerful as well as personal being, God doesn't give you someone else's future. He has made one just for you. Allow your heart to hope in Him and whatever future He has planned.

Day 216

IN HIS ARMS

I will both lay me down in peace, and sleep:
for thou, LORD, only makest me dwell in safety.
PSALM 4:8 KJV

Sally read until her eyes could no longer stay open. She closed her book, shut off the light, and let her head sink into the comfort of her pillow.

As her eyes closed, Sally's mind began to roam free. *Will seven hours be enough sleep tonight? Lord, can You make sure I'm up by six tomorrow morning? I didn't get nearly enough done today. . . . I wonder if my car will pass inspection next month. I can't afford a new one. What if it doesn't pass? Maybe I could borrow some money. . . .*

Sally shook her head, frustrated at the turn of her thoughts, the worries that crept in, fueling insecurities and fears. *This will not do!*

She rose up and turned her light back on. Reaching for her Bible, Sally opened up to a favorite verse—Psalm 4:8: "Lay me down in peace, and sleep. . .makest me dwell in safety." The words turned over and over in her mind. She smiled, closed her Bible, and turned off the light. Letting God's Word saturate her mind, Sally fell asleep, cradled in His arms.

Don't let the thoughts of days past and future keep you from catching those forty winks. Fall asleep in God's Word, rest easy, and rise refreshed.

GOD IN THE DRIVER'S SEAT

*I will instruct thee and teach thee in the way which
thou shalt go: I will guide thee with mine eye.*
PSALM 32:8 KJV

Hannah came to a fork in the road. She had to make some life-changing decisions. The hardest part was that the decisions she made would significantly affect the lives of her loved ones. What was she to do?

God tells us that whenever we have a decision to make, He will instruct and teach us. He will not let us flounder, but as we seek His face, He will provide direction, understanding, wisdom, and insight. He will teach us the way—the road, the path, or journey we need to take that is in our best interest.

We can clearly comprehend the way we should walk because God is guiding, with His eye upon us. He is omniscient, which means He knows all things. He knows our past, our present, and our future. He sees and understands what we are not able to comprehend in our finite beings. What a blessing that an all-knowing Lord will guide us!

Day 218

BEAUTIFUL CHANGES

*If you love learning, you love the discipline that goes
with it—how shortsighted to refuse correction!*
PROVERBS 12:1 MSG

Although the old and familiar are comforting, being willing to allow change within is important. For God, the only one who never changes, would like to transform you from the inside out as you move through life. This will happen, sometimes slowly, sometimes quickly, but always in a way that moves you from glory to glory.

Change occurs in you as you spend time with God, learning about Him from His Word. His truths go into the dark places of your heart and let in light. As you understand how completely you are loved and accepted, you will find the courage to let go of the ideal, of perfection. You will let go of fear and worry as you grow to trust God more and more. You will become satisfied, even overjoyed, with what God says about you, and stop seeking approval from others. Yes, woman, change can be beautiful.

When you believe deeply that God will never, ever abandon or reject you, you can let go of old habits and thought patterns that have kept you frozen in place. As you begin loving, learning, and thriving on correction, you will be find more and more pleasure in your inner beauty.

ROCK-SOLID SAVIOR

*Because of the Truth which lives and stays on in our
hearts and will be with us forever: Grace (spiritual
blessing), mercy, and [soul] peace will be with us, from
God the Father and from Jesus Christ (the Messiah),
the Father's Son, in all sincerity (truth) and love.*

2 JOHN 2–3 AMPC

How many times have you reached rock bottom only to find Jesus right there, the rock at the bottom? Throughout scripture Jesus is referred to as "the rock of your salvation." His truth is what lives in your heart and provides freedom to live your life with an eternal perspective.

Your relationship with Jesus is the only thing that really offers you safety and stability while you navigate the violent maelstroms life often brings. When you can't depend on others, and maybe don't even trust yourself, you have a trustworthy, rock-solid Savior. Forever He's the one you can always depend on. He faithfully points you in the way you should go. When life spins out of control, He stops the merry-go-round, and with His truth, helps you to focus.

Are you experiencing challenges that make you feel unstable right now? Ask Jesus to bring balance and stability today.

UNBROKEN PROMISES

*. . .in hope of eternal life which God, who
cannot lie, promised before time began.*
TITUS 1:2 NKJV

The walkway of our lives is littered with broken promises—
both those we've made and those that have been made to us. Each
time the commitment was given with wonderful intentions of
carrying through, but something happened to make it impossible
for the vow to be completed.

When we are the one who breaks the promise, guilt becomes
our companion. Knowing we've hurt others is painful. We often
vow to ourselves never to make another pledge, yet even that oath
isn't kept. The results of other people's broken promises to us are
usually disappointment and hurt. Perhaps we didn't get the raise
we counted on or an old friend backed out of a get-together. We
feel that the other person lied to us or that we weren't worthy of
his or her commitment.

God always keeps His word. The Bible is filled with the
promises of God—vows to us that we can trust will be completed.
God never lies. Lying is not in Him. He sees us as worthy of His
commitment.

The promise of eternal life—given even before time began—
is one of God's most wonderful gifts. No matter how disappointed we are with ourselves or with others, we only have to look
at the pledge God has made to be filled with a heart of praise
and gladness.

MISUNDERSTOOD?

*[Martha] said to Him, "Yes, Lord, I believe that You are
the Christ, the Son of God, who is to come into the world."*
JOHN 11:27 NKJV

When we think of Martha, we remember Jesus telling her to pay
more attention to spiritually important things than to her prepa-
rations for guests. Or perhaps we remember that she questioned
Jesus about why He didn't arrive in time to save her brother's life.
Based on these events, most people probably remember Martha
as something of a spiritual failure.

But do we remember that even before Jesus' death, this woman
understood just who Jesus was? Many religious leaders of her
day hadn't a clue—or they only began to understand after the
Resurrection.

Martha wasn't as spiritually unsophisticated as we often
consider her. Like Martha, we may be misunderstood—people
might assume that because we're single we can't be in charge of
the nursery, or because we're married, our husbands should be
considered first for any important position in the congregation.
Or maybe because we've made one mistake, people have locked
us into a certain low level of spiritual maturity.

Sometimes people's perceptions of us are inaccurate, and that
can hurt. But that shouldn't stop us in our tracks. Jesus knows
both our failures and successes. By His standards, Martha was
never a failure—and neither are we.

JUST REACH OUT!

"For I am the LORD your God, who takes hold of your
right hand and says to you, Do not fear; I will help you."
ISAIAH 41:13 NIV

Fear not! Do not be afraid! I am with you!

Hundreds of Bible verses address our emotions of fear, anxiety, and worry. Fear never discriminates and has held many of us captive since the beginning of time. Perhaps that's why in verse after verse, God continually reassures us of His presence and offers us peace, as He did for countless others.

God gave Moses and Jeremiah the right words (Exodus 4:12; Jeremiah 1:9), David the strength (1 Samuel 30:6), Solomon the wisdom (1 Kings 3:12), and Mary the courage (Luke 1:30) to rise above fear. But, when we're clutched by fear, how do we follow their lead, to trust God and rise above it?

Look at Isaiah 41:13. God is so tender here. He holds our hand and says four precious words; "I will help you." It's a direct invitation to hold on to God's hand. Just reach out!

Look to Jesus

*For unto us a child is born, unto us a son is given:
and the government shall be upon his shoulder: and his
name shall be called Wonderful, Counsellor, The mighty
God, The everlasting Father, The Prince of Peace.*

Isaiah 9:6 kjv

Troubled times lay ahead. An Assyrian invasion and a Babylonian captivity would leave gloom in their wake. But Isaiah also prophesied dawn on the horizon: "That time of darkness and despair will not go on forever. . . . There will be a time in the future when Galilee of the Gentiles. . .will be filled with glory. The people who walk in darkness will see a great light" (Isaiah 9:1–2 NLT). What was that light? A child would be born, bringing with Him the brightest ray of hope ever! God's people could look beyond the hardship to the coming Messiah.

These days, we might fear that troubled times lie ahead. Our world is aching, and there's already abundant gloom. But Isaiah's words promise dawn on the horizon. The Messiah is coming back! He's coming back to put things right for good and for certain: "His government and its peace will never end. He will rule with fairness and justice. . .for all eternity. The passionate commitment of the LORD of Heaven's Armies will make this happen!" (Isaiah 9:7 NLT). Look beyond any hardship to the returning King.

DRINK OF HIS GLORY

*I saw the Lord sitting on a throne, high and lifted up,
and the train of His robe filled the temple. Above it stood
seraphim; each one had six wings: with two he covered
his face, with two he covered his feet, and with two he
flew. And one cried to another and said: "Holy, holy, holy
is the LORD of hosts; the whole earth is full of His glory!"*

ISAIAH 6:1–3 NKJV

The earth truly is full of God's glory. In the busyness of life, so
filled with distractions, it's easy to miss the wonder and majesty
of His glory. Yet each new day, God takes the time to paint the
sunrise and fill the evening sky with a light show.

Consider the works of His hands—the beauty and variety of
flowers growing wildly, the powerful crashes of the ocean's waves,
the majestic heights of a mountain range.

He wants you to step outside of the everyday chaos that tries
to hem you in to experience His presence and His glory. He speaks
to you in the little and big things found in His creation. Your
heavenly Father pours out His artistic beauty simply for your joy
and pleasure.

Day 225

OPEN WIDE

You called in distress and I delivered you. . . .
O Israel, if you would listen to Me! . . . I am the
Lord your God, Who brought you up out of the land
of Egypt. Open your mouth wide and I will fill it.
PSALM 81:7–8, 10 AMPC

God is longing for His people to trust in Him. Over and over again, He's rescued the Israelites from peril. And over and over again, they turn away after His deliverance. Thus, He laments, "If only they would listen to Me!"

God can do anything, rescue us from any situation. He'll walk with us through our wilderness. He'll carry us like a mother does a nursing child. Like a hen, He'll cover us with His feathers until we're able to go on again. And most fantastic of all, if we open ourselves all the way up to Him, He'll overflow us, so boundless are His blessings.

All it takes on your part is belief, listening to Jesus, your "Bread of Life" (John 6:35 AMPC) and living water (John 4:10, 14), trusting in Him above all else, and relying on Him more than your family, other people, society, institutions, or yourself—your abilities, knowledge, intuition, gut-feeling, intelligence, money, whatever.

Jesus is all you need for true fulfillment. Just listen. And get ready to receive.

Day 226

RELAX

*"You will not have to fight this battle. Take
up your positions; stand firm and see the
deliverance the Lord will give you."*
2 Chronicles 20:17 niv

Why do we always feel we need to fight our own battles?

Oh, God wants us to use common sense and stand up for others and ourselves when it's appropriate. But sometimes, it's best not to defend ourselves at all. Sometimes, when we know we've done no wrong, when we know we stand innocent before God in whatever situation we find ourselves, it's good just to remain still and calm and let God be our defender.

Truly, the more we defend ourselves, the guiltier we sound sometimes. But when we can stand before God with clean hands and a pure heart, God will deliver us. Oh, it may not be in the way we want. It may not happen as quickly as we'd like. But when we decide to stand firm, to continue living godly lives, to continue seeking His approval in our words, thoughts, and actions, we can trust Him.

Let's remember today to rest in His goodness, despite the battles that rage around us. We don't have to live our lives fighting. We can relax. Our Father is the judge, and He will deliver us.

Day 227

GOD SEES YOU

She answered GOD by name, praying to the
God who spoke to her, "You're the God who sees
me! Yes! He saw me; and then I saw him!"
GENESIS 16:13 MSG

As women, we have an innate need to be seen. There's a deep desire inside where we want others to know us—to know those things that help us and hurt us. Even more, we want others to *want* to know! It's about being pursued and appreciated. It's about being worth the time and effort of others. It's about being important enough for someone to want to learn about us—learn what matters most to our heart.

While you may crave that from those around you, it's important to remember that God already knows you better than you know yourself. He's your creator, and He has firsthand knowledge of what makes you tick. He understands what delights your heart and has knowledge of what hurts it. God knows everything there is to know about you.

That means you are fully known and fully seen right now. Your heart's desire for that kind of intimacy has been met. And even more, your heavenly Father is crazy about you.

The next time you feel unloved or unwanted, remember that God sees you and loves you willingly and completely.

GOD'S PROMISES

"God is not human, that he should lie, not a human being, that he should change his mind. Does he speak and then not act? Does he promise and not fulfill?"
NUMBERS 23:19 NIV

Our opinions of God are often shaped by our experiences with people. When we've been hurt, we see God as hurtful. When people lie to us, we subconsciously think of God as a liar. After all, if humans are created in His image, it only stands to reason that God would be like the people in our lives. Right?

Well, no. Yes, we were created in God's image. But we humans are a fallen, broken race. We're sinful. God is without sin.

Humans lie. God doesn't.

Humans go back on their word. God doesn't.

Humans can be mean and hurtful. God is love, and He only acts in love.

God promised good things to those who love Him, those who live and act according to His will. That doesn't mean others won't hurt us or that we won't experience the effects of living in a sin-infested world. But where there's pain, we have a healer. Where there's brokenness, we have a comforter. And where we feel alone, we know we have a friend.

And one day we'll experience the perfect fulfillment of all His promises without the burdens of this world to weigh us down.

Now that's something to look forward to.

Day 221

KNOWN AND LOVED

"I am the good shepherd; I know my sheep and my sheep know me—just as the Father knows me and I know the Father—and I lay down my life for the sheep."
JOHN 10:14–15 NIV

Do you fear being known and rejected? Do you feel that if someone truly knew you they couldn't possibly love you? In these verses, Christ asserts that He knows you. He doesn't just know you as a casual acquaintance or even an intimate friend. His knowledge runs deeper than that. He knows you in the same way that He knows the Father.

In the Trinity, Jesus and the Father are one. So He is saying that He knows you in the same way that He knows Himself. There could not be a deeper or more intimate knowledge. He knows all the things that you hide from everyone else—He knows the temptations, the frustrations, the lost hopes, the rejections, the insecurities, and the deep desires that you may hardly acknowledge to yourself.

Even though Christ knows the darkest and most secret parts of you, He still loves you. He doesn't love you because He can gain something from it. He doesn't love you on a surface, nonchalant level. He *laid down His life* for you. There is no greater love. He knows you better than anyone else does, and yet He loves you with a deeper, purer love than anyone else can give you. You are deeply known and deeply loved.

BOARD GOD'S BOAT

*Then, because so many people were coming and
going that they did not even have a chance
to eat, he said to them, "Come with me by
yourselves to a quiet place and get some rest."*
MARK 6:31 NIV

Are you "missing the boat" to a quieter place of rest with God? You
mean to slow down, but your church, work, and family responsibilities pile higher than a stack of recyclables. Just when you think a
free moment is yours, the phone rings, a needy friend stops by, or
your child announces she needs you to bake cookies for tomorrow's
school fund-raiser.

The apostles ministered tirelessly—so much so, they had little
time to eat. As they gathered around Jesus to report their activities, the Lord noticed that they had neglected to take time for
themselves. Sensitive to their needs, the Savior instructed them
to retreat by boat with Him to a solitary place of rest where He
was able to minister to them.

Often we allow the hectic pace of daily life to drain us physically and spiritually, and in the process, we deny ourselves time
alone to pray and read God's Word. Meanwhile, God patiently
waits. So perhaps it's time to board God's boat to a quieter place.
Don't jump ship!

HE CARRIES US

*In his love and mercy he redeemed them. He lifted
them up and carried them through all the years.*
ISAIAH 63:9 NLT

Are you feeling broken today? Depressed? Defeated? Run to God,
not away from Him.

When we suffer, He cries. Isaiah 63:9 (NLT) says, "In all their
suffering he also suffered, and he personally rescued them. In his
love and mercy he redeemed them. He lifted them up and carried
them through all the years."

He will carry us—no matter what pain we have to endure. No
matter what happens to us. God sent Jesus to be our redeemer.
He knew the world would hate, malign, and kill Jesus. Yet He
allowed His very flesh to writhe in agony on the cross—so that
we could also become His sons and daughters. He loved me, and
you, that much.

One day, we will be with Him. "Beloved," He will say, "no
more tears. No more pain." He will lift us up and hold us in His
mighty arms, and then He will show us His kingdom, and we will,
finally, be whole.

Be Glad

The Lord has done it this very day;
let us rejoice today and be glad.
Psalm 118:24 niv

The feeling of gladness often carries with it a sense of relief and gratitude. A student may be glad to find out she passed the driving test. A husband and wife may be glad to hear the news that they are pregnant (or not!). An employee is glad to receive a raise.

This psalmist was very glad. He had been surrounded by his enemies. He had been pushed back and was about to fall down and be conquered, but the Lord helped him. God came to the rescue, and instead of dying that day, the writer had lived. He says, "The Lord is my strength and my defense; he has become my salvation. Shouts of joy and victory resound" (Psalm 118:14–15 niv).

What has God done for you already this day? Open your eyes and see the works He has performed. Maybe He kept you safe on your commute to work. Maybe He sent rain to water dry fields. Maybe He cleared the clouds and gave you a bit of sunshine to start your morning. God shows His love and care for you every day all day long in both big and small ways. Don't forget to look around and see what God is doing for you and for others today. Then rejoice and be glad!

THE WINNING TEAM

If God is for us, who can be against us?
ROMANS 8:31 NIV

We always *know* God is for us, but it doesn't always *feel* that way. Even though we know the end of the story, even though we know we are on the winning team, sometimes it feels like we're losing battle after battle.

It can feel like cancer is winning. Or the chemo or radiation that goes along with cancer feels like it's whipping us. Sometimes our relationships are difficult, and we feel like we're on the losing team.

We can make sure God really is on our team, in the little battles, when we conduct ourselves in a way that honors Him. If we've been in the wrong, we can't claim that God is on our side in that battle. But when we love God with all our hearts, when we serve Him and serve others, when we keep our promises and make the people around us feel loved and valued and cherished, we can know God is pleased. We can know that He will stand behind us, defend us, and support us.

And ultimately, no matter how many battles we may feel like we're losing, if we stand with God, we will stand victorious. The other team may score a few points here and there. But when we're on God's team, we know we're the winners.

PRAISE AND THANKSGIVING

*Enter his gates with thanksgiving and his courts
with praise; give thanks to him and praise his name.*
PSALM 100:4 NIV

In Old Testament times, people went to the temple to meet with God. God's presence resided there just once a year after the sacrifice had been made on the Day of Atonement, but people came many times a year for festivals and to offer sacrifices for sin. The gates were the entrance to the temple grounds, and through the gates were the courts. They were the outside area where the people gathered. Part of this area was dedicated to altars for sacrifices.

Now that God lives within us through His Holy Spirit, we don't have to go to the temple or church to find Him. He is always with us. How, then, should this verse impact our relationship with God now? When we go to Him in prayer, let's consider starting with thanksgiving and moving into praise. Thanksgiving is thanking God for what He has done for us and how He has provided for us. Praise is identifying and acknowledging the characteristics of God, such as His creating, healing, righteousness, mercy, and love.

We are commanded to give thanks and praise God's name. As we do so, our worries, fears, confessions, and requests fall into their proper place.

No Worries

*"So don't worry about tomorrow, for tomorrow will bring
its own worries. Today's trouble is enough for today."*
MATTHEW 6:34 NLT

It has been said that today is the tomorrow you worried about yesterday. Isn't it true? How many of the things you worry about actually happen?

Worry is a thief. It robs us of the joy of the moment and plants us firmly in the future, where we have absolutely no control. Instead of focusing on the problems that this day brings, we propel ourselves into an unknown tomorrow. In living this way, we miss out on all the little moments that make life precious.

The antidote to worry is to focus on today—this hour, this moment in time. What is happening now? Experience it with all five of your senses. Allow the wonder of today to touch your heart and settle it down. Sure, there is trouble today, and there are problems to solve, but Jesus is right here with us. We have the gift of the Holy Spirit who can counsel and comfort us and help us get through any and every situation. There is nothing you can't face with Jesus by your side. When you focus on what He can do instead of what you can't do, you will experience a deep and abiding peace that comes only from Him.

Day 236

STRENGTH IN THE LORD

The LORD is my light and my salvation—
whom shall I fear? The LORD is the stronghold
of my life—of whom shall I be afraid?
PSALM 27:1 NIV

Even when it seems that everything is piling up around you, Christ is there for you. Take heart! He is your stronghold, a very present help right in the midst of your trial. Regardless of what comes against you in this life, you have the Lord on your side. He is your light in the darkness and your salvation from eternal separation from God. You have nothing to fear.

At times, this world can be a tough, unfair, lonely place. Since the fall of man in the garden, things have not been as God originally intended. The Bible assures us that we will face trials in this life, but it also exclaims that we are more than conquerors through Christ who is in us! When you find yourself up against a tribulation that seems insurmountable, *look up.* Christ is there. He goes before you, stands with you, and is backing you up in your time of need. You may lose everyone and everything else in this life, but nothing has the power to separate you from the love of Christ. Nothing.

Day 231

BEAUTY AND BRAINS

This man's name was Nabal, and his wife,
Abigail, was a sensible and beautiful woman.
1 SAMUEL 25:3 NLT

Abigail is the only woman in the Bible whose brains are mentioned before her beauty. And how well she used them! She stood before a furious king and his army, calming him with just her words. She returned home at the end of the day but wisely chose just the right time to tell her quarrelsome husband the news. Her wisdom and grace made her so memorable that when her husband died, David sent for her and made her his bride.

With the stressful and fast-paced lives we live today, we can easily believe that women in the Bible have little to teach us. After all, they lived thousands of years ago, without the headaches of today's world. Yet our concerns are not that different. We still worry about our families, seek to act responsibly in God's eyes, and strive to do our work with diligence.

And the wisdom to handle those concerns still comes from the same source: God. Just as He granted Abigail the wisdom to soothe a king, the Lord will grant us the wisdom and intelligence to handle whatever today's world throws at us.

All we have to do is ask.

Day 238

CRY OUT TO GOD

GOD, you're my last chance of the day.
I spend the night on my knees before you.
PSALM 88:1 MSG

The psalmist was in misery and cried out to God. He felt as though he were near death. Ever been there?

In one form or another, every woman experiences extreme despair in her life. It may be due to the loss of a loved one. You may find yourself abandoned by a family member, dealing with a chronic illness, or desperate over a prodigal child who makes one bad choice after another.

Whatever the cause of your heartache, if you have not yet been in the depths of despair, at some point in your life you will be. Human existence brings with it times that are simply unbearable on your own.

During such times, you must rely on God. You may not feel Him or sense His presence, but His Word declares that He will never leave you nor forsake you.

Talk to God first thing in the morning and just before your head hits the pillow at night. He is your refuge and your strong tower in times of trouble. A brighter day will come. Joy comes in the morning. Hold on tight to God. Find strength in knowing you are never, ever alone.

ANSWER ME!

*Answer me when I call to you, my righteous
God. Give me relief from my distress; have
mercy on me and hear my prayer.*
PSALM 4:1 NIV

Have you ever felt like God wasn't listening? We've all felt that from time to time. David felt it when he slept in a cold, hard cave night after night, while being pursued by Saul's men. He felt it when his son Absalom turned against him. Time and again in his life, David felt abandoned by God. And yet David was called a man after God's own heart.

No matter our maturity level, there will be times when we feel abandoned by God. There will be times when our faith wavers and our fortitude wanes. That's okay. It's normal.

But David didn't give up. He kept crying out to God, kept falling to his knees in worship, kept storming God's presence with his pleas.

David knew God wouldn't hide His face for long, for he knew what we might sometimes forget: God is love. He loves us without condition and without limit. And He is never far from those He loves.

No matter how distant God may seem, we need to keep talking to Him. Keep praying. Keep pouring out our hearts. We can know, as David knew, that God will answer in His time.

Day 240

LIVING WATER

The woman said to him, "Sir, give me this water so that I won't get thirsty and have to keep coming here to draw water."

JOHN 4:15 NIV

The Samaritan woman who came to draw water from Jacob's well didn't know she would meet Someone who would change her life drastically. Her life had been filled with relationships that didn't work. She may have felt worthless and used. That day may have started out like every other day in her life, but when she approached the well, Jesus was waiting. He asked her for a drink. When she questioned His reason, He in turn offered her water—living water. If she drank of it, she would never thirst again. She was all for never having to come to the well again to draw water, not realizing Jesus was offering her spiritual life, not a physical refreshment. As they talked, she found living water that gave her a new lease on life.

Some days life can seem like one endless task after another; it exhibits a sameness that makes us weary. We thirst for something better, or maybe just different. Maybe it's time for a trip to the well. As we come to Christ in prayer, seeking a much-needed drink, we will find Him waiting at the well, offering the same living water to each of us that He offered to the Samaritan woman. Are there any among us who don't need times of spiritual refreshing in our lives? Grab a bucket and go to the well. Jesus is waiting.

A Sure Foundation

Therefore, this is what the Sovereign LORD says: "Look!
I am placing a foundation stone in Jerusalem, a firm
and tested stone. It is a precious cornerstone that is safe
to build on. Whoever believes need never be shaken."
ISAIAH 28:16 NLT

When a foundation stone is selected for a building, the largest and best is chosen. It must be straight and solid, able to hold all the weight that will be placed on it. The "foundation stone" that God is referring to in the verse above is Jesus Christ. Jesus is the "precious cornerstone" and He alone is safe to build your life on.

You can trust Jesus to be your home base, the starting point of all your hopes, an unfailing infrastructure. He meets your needs when others fail you. He holds you close when you're afraid. He heals your wounds. He successfully plans your future. He brings peace to chaos.

No matter how tumultuous your circumstances, the promise is that you will not be shaken. What threatens to throw you off balance today? What potential calamity is stealing your confidence? Jesus is bigger than any problem you face. Put your trust in Him alone.

INTIMACY

*Aware of this, Jesus said to them, "Why are you
bothering this woman? She has done a beautiful
thing to me. . . . When she poured this perfume on
my body, she did it to prepare me for burial."*
MATTHEW 26:10, 12 NIV

The woman who anointed Jesus understood who He was and
what was about to happen. Even the men who walked daily with
Jesus didn't get it. To her, no gift was too lavish. No words were
adequate to express her gratitude for what He was about to relinquish—His life!

The beauty of it all? He knew her very soul! He knew her heart
longed to give more. He knew her message, beyond any words,
was a pale reflection of her gratitude. He knew her soul so wholly,
so intimately, so deeply. What a connectedness they shared. That
is why He said, "What she has done will always be remembered."

This intimate loving Lord is the same Lord today. He hasn't
changed. He knows the depths of our hearts. He knows what we
try to express but fall short. He sees our intentions. Take comfort
in His level of understanding and in the intimate relationship
He wants with us. Its depth is beyond any friendship, parental
devotion, or even earthly marital union. It is a spiritual melding
of souls. An amazing truth of a perfect, loving Bridegroom becoming one with His bride by laying down His life for her.

Day 243

A STANDING INVITATION

*The LORD said to Moses, "Come up to me on the
mountain and stay here, and I will give you the
tablets of stone with the law and commandments
I have written for their instruction."*
EXODUS 24:12 NIV

God wants to spend time with you. Just like a human parent yearns
to have a connection with her own child, the Lord craves a relationship with you. You may feel rejection here on earth from friends
and family, but you will never experience that from your heavenly
Daddy. People may make you feel unwanted, but God never will.
And although you may have experienced abandonment, times
when no one would stand with you, God will never forsake you.

God's invitation is a standing one. Whether it be one o'clock
in the afternoon or one o'clock in the wee hours of the morning,
God is available. No matter how many times you've shared your
thoughts and feelings with Him before, He'll listen again for
He welcomes you into His presence whenever you want and
wherever you are.

What keeps you from reaching out to God? Is it a busy sched-
ule? Do you feel like an annoyance? Is it pride? Do you think
He has bigger fish to fry? Well, friend, just like He did for
Moses, God is inviting you to come and spend time with Him.
Why not right now?

Day 244

BREATH OF LIFE

He heals the brokenhearted and binds up their
wounds [curing their pains and their sorrows].
PSALM 147:3 AMPC

As a result of sin, every person on the earth is born into a fallen world. The sinful condition brings hurt and heartache to all men—those who serve the Lord and those who don't. The good news is, as a child of God, you have a hope and eternal future in Christ. Jesus said, "I have told you all this so that you may have peace in me. Here on earth you will have many trials and sorrows. But take heart, because I have overcome the world" (John 16:33 NLT).

When your life brings disappointment, hurt, and pain that are almost unbearable, remember that you serve the one who heals hearts. He knows you best and loves you most. When the wind is knocked out of you and you feel like there is no oxygen left in the room, let God provide you with the air you need to breathe. Breathe out a prayer to Him and breathe in His peace and comfort today.

Day 245

NEVER ALONE

God has said, "Never will I leave you;
never will I forsake you."
HEBREWS 13:5 NIV

Life is full of disappointments, broken promises, failed relationships, and loneliness. It may seem like you are the only person you can really trust. But the Lord will never desert you or forsake you. He promises to be with you through this life and the next. When all else feels hopeless, know that He remains steadfast.

For those who have trusted people in the past but have been let down, this may be a hard concept to accept. But this is no idle promise based on the feeling of a moment. When Christ hung on the cross, He was forsaken by God. The sin that was laid on Him was so horrific and abhorrent that the Father, who was one with Jesus, could not look at Him. In the most heart-wrenching act of history, the holy Father turned His face away from His once blameless Son. Because Christ was willing to be forsaken and utterly alone, you never will be. God won't ever have to turn away from you—you now bear the pure innocence of Christ. Christ took your sins upon Himself so you would never have to experience what it's like to be completely alone and forsaken by God.

WHAT IS A TRUE FRIEND?

There are "friends" who destroy each other,
but a real friend sticks closer than a brother.
PROVERBS 18:24 NLT

In today's world we use the term *friend* loosely. Unable to describe a hypothetical, indefinable somebody, we often say, "I have a friend who. . ." The person usually is a distant acquaintance, but because we are unable to determine what to call them, we clump them into the multifaceted category of "friend."

An ancient proverb, however, captures the essence and beauty of true friendship. It says, "Ah, the beauty of being at peace with another, neither having to weigh thoughts or measure words, but spilling time out just as they are, chaff and grain together, certain that a faithful hand will keep what is worth keeping and with a breath of kindness, blow the rest away."

Friends find the good in us and dismiss the rest. We can be ourselves in their presence and not worry about misunderstandings or saying the wrong thing.

Jesus is that kind of friend. He sticks close by us at our most undesirable, least lovable moments. We can tell Him anything and He understands. In fact, He knows everything about us and loves us anyway. Like a true friend, Jesus enhances our good qualities and, with a breath of kindness, blows the rest away.

GPS

Whether you turn to the right or to the
left, your ears will hear a voice behind you,
saying, "This is the way; walk in it."
ISAIAH 30:21 NIV

Many times in life we find ourselves at a crossroads, faced with a pivotal choice about the direction of the future. Israel was at such a juncture, challenged by the prophet Isaiah to return to a lifestyle that embraced their compassionate and gracious God. Rejection of the challenge would result in desolation; repentance would bring the blessings of a restored relationship.

Monumental decisions are not unique to people of faith, but Isaiah's verse offers encouragement and hope to those who call upon the name of the Lord while making crucial choices. This verse speaks directly to the GPS (God Positioning System) eternally available to each of us. This GPS brings the voice of God directly into our lives.

When we walk with God and use His navigational system, we can rest assured that His map for our lives is trustworthy. He will never lead us down dead-end roads, or route us onto nonexistent streets. Instead, He promises to hear us when we cry for help (Isaiah 30:19). And from that request, He gives direction that is unequaled by any earthly system.

INSTANTANEOUS ANSWERS

*"As soon as you began to pray, a word went out, which
I have come to tell you, for you are highly esteemed."*
DANIEL 9:23 NIV

Daniel was an upright Jewish man, carried off into captivity as the Babylonians conquered Jerusalem. Enrolled in King Nebuchadnezzar's indoctrination program, Daniel spent three years learning the culture of Babylon before becoming one of the king's most trusted advisors. Living in exile for most of his life, Daniel nevertheless remained faithful to God, and his heart broke for the cumulative sins of the people of Israel.

In the middle of pouring out his heart to God one day, Daniel's prayer is interrupted by the appearance of the angel Gabriel. Bringing insight and understanding (Daniel 9:22), Gabriel's message contains the interesting concept that in the instant that Daniel began to pray, the answer was already on its way.

Before Daniel got past his salutation, God knew Daniel's heart and had already set in motion the response to Daniel's unfinished prayer.

As He did for Daniel, God knows our needs even before we give voice to them in prayer. We can rest in the knowledge that even before the words leave our lips, God has already heard them, and He has already answered them.

In Anxiety, God Comforts

In the multitude of my anxieties within me,
Your comforts delight my soul.
Psalm 94:19 nkjv

Do you worry when evil people seem to prosper and when life gets in your way? You are not alone.

We don't know for sure who wrote Psalm 94, but we can be certain that the psalmist was annoyed and anxious when he wrote it. He cries out to God, asking Him to "render punishment to the proud" (verse 2 nkjv). Then, he goes on with a list of accusations about the evil ones. The psalmist's anxiety builds until finally, in verses 8–11, he warns his enemies to shape up and start following God. Verse 19 is the turning point—the place in the psalm where the writer is at a loss for words. Completely and utterly exasperated, he turns from his rant and starts praising God. "In the multitude of my anxieties within me," he says, "Your comforts delight my soul" (nkjv).

"In the multitude of my anxieties within me." Does that phrase describe you? When anxiety overwhelms us, we find relief in the words of Psalm 94:19. When we turn our anxious thoughts over to God, He brings contentment to our souls.

YOU NEVER WALK ALONE

"But the Advocate, the Holy Spirit, whom the Father
will send in my name, will teach you all things and
will remind you of everything I have said to you."
JOHN 14:26 NIV

Jesus' earthly missionary journey was about to end and—in this passage—the master prepared His disciples for His departure.

The disciples were confused and frightened, so Jesus comforted them with words of assurance, comfort, and hope: "Do not let your hearts be troubled and do not be afraid" (John 14:27 NIV).

At first, Jesus' followers thought they would be left alone. But Jesus assured them He would send the Father's ambassador to teach, direct, guide, and remind them of every word He had told them.

Jesus called the Holy Spirit "the Advocate," a translation of the Greek word *parakletos*: "one called alongside to help." It can also indicate strengthener, comforter, helper, adviser, counselor, intercessor, ally, and friend.

The Holy Spirit walks with us to help, instruct, comfort, and accomplish God's work on earth. Through His presence inside us, we know the Father. In our deepest time of need, He is there. He comforts and reveals to us the truth of God's Word.

Jesus is always with us because His Spirit lives in our hearts. No Christian ever walks alone!

WHEN YOU FEEL REJECTED

*But he replied, "I must preach the Good
News of the Kingdom of God in other towns,
too, because that is why I was sent."*

LUKE 4:43 NLT

Jesus was rejected when preaching in His boyhood hometown of Nazareth. Yet that didn't stop Him from continuing to cast out demons and heal people in other towns. Jesus was committed to "preach the Good News of the Kingdom of God" for He knew that's why God had sent Him.

Yet in Nazareth, Jesus' hometown, the people were furious at the words He said, so they mobbed Him and tried to force Him to the edge of the hill on which the town was built, intending to push Him off the cliff! Thankfully, Jesus was able to pass through the crowd and went on His way.

You too have been called by God to do some amazing things for the faith. Sometimes you might receive great opposition. But keep stepping out in faith. Don't give up. Remember you were called for a divine purpose, which is to live for Christ. More specifically, God has given you a ministry to focus on. When the pressure is on and it feels like no one is supporting you, remember *God* loves and supports you!

Day 252

YOU ARE GOD'S SPECIAL POSSESSION

"For the people of Israel belong to the LORD;
Jacob is his special possession. He found them in
a desert land, in an empty, howling wasteland.
He surrounded them and watched over them; he
guarded them as he would guard his own eyes."
DEUTERONOMY 32:9–10 NLT

Imagine a family heirloom—a crystal bowl that's been handed down for multiple generations. It's priceless to you. You keep it in a special place on display for all to see. When people stop by, you point it out and tell the story behind it. If you lost this special treasure, you would be devastated. If broken, you would never forgive yourself.

The Israelites were priceless to God, and so are you. He took great care, moving them from place to place. Just as you wrapped that fragile crystal bowl, He took the time to make special provision for His people. As we learn in today's verses, God surrounded His children and watched over them. He guarded them at every turn—think of their crossing the Red Sea, fleeing from the Egyptians, and so on.

God cares just as much about you and is watching over you even now. How priceless you are to your heavenly Father!

SECOND CHANCES

*"But if wicked people turn away from all their sins
and begin to obey my decrees and do what is just
and right, they will surely live and not die. All
their past sins will be forgotten, and they will live
because of the righteous things they have done."*
 EZEKIEL 18:21–22 NLT

God has always been in the business of giving second chances,
from Old Testament times until now. He has requirements for
good living, of course, but for those who choose Him over their
mistakes of yesterday, all sins (and that truly means *all* sins) will
be forgotten.

In Psalm 103:12, we learn that God casts our sin as far as
the east is from the west. That's a great distance. Picture your
mistakes and misdeeds flying all the way from Texas to China,
from India to Chile! He wants us to have that visual so that we
won't be held back by our past. It's so far behind us that we can't
even see it anymore.

Have you turned away from the things that are separating you
from God? If not, this is the perfect day to do so. Turn. . .and live!

UNFAILING LOVE

"But then I will win her back once again. I will lead
her into the desert and speak tenderly to her there. I
will return her vineyards to her and transform the
Valley of Trouble into a gateway of hope. She will give
herself to me there, as she did long ago when she was
young, when I freed her from her captivity in Egypt."

HOSEA 2:14–15 NLT

Oh, how God loves Israel! He has chased her, caught her, lost
her, chased her again. Over and over He's proven His love to her.

That same love that propelled God to chase after His beloved
Israel also propels Him to chase after you. No matter how far you
wander, no matter how stubborn you get, He won't give up on
you. You're His daughter, His beloved. He adores you, even on
the days when you're grumpy, bloated, and just want to pull the
covers over your head.

Isn't the image of God speaking tenderly to you, the one He
loves, so precious? He's not standing next to you, berating you or
beating you over the head for your mistakes. Quite the opposite,
in fact! His words are laced with love. And because you know
you're loved, it's so easy to slip your hand into His for a "happily
ever after."

Day 255

EVERLASTING PEACE

*Peace I leave with you; My [own] peace I now give
and bequeath to you. Not as the world gives do I give
to you. Do not let your hearts be troubled, neither let
them be afraid. [Stop allowing yourselves to be agitated
and disturbed; and do not permit yourselves to be
fearful and intimidated and cowardly and unsettled.]*
JOHN 14:27 AMPC

Do you want to be free of worry and fear? Want to live a life filled with peace and calm? Jesus holds the answer!

Yes, Jesus has left His peace with you. And this peace, *His* peace, is not the kind of peace the world holds. His is a supernatural peace. And it is found in the presence and strength of God and His Word. *But,* you may be asking, *How can this be? How can I access this amazing and unsurpassed peace Jesus talks about?* By calling on the Comforter, aka the "Counselor, Helper, Intercessor, Advocate, Strengthener, Standby" (John 14:26 AMPC). You know, the Holy Spirit, the one God sent down in Jesus' name to teach you and remind you of things Jesus has already told you in His Word (John 14:26).

Today, stop allowing yourself to be frightened and freaked out. Instead, seek God's presence and receive His peace.

GOD WILL FIGHT FOR YOU

When all our enemies heard about this, all the
surrounding nations were afraid and lost their
self-confidence, because they realized that this
work had been done with the help of our God.
NEHEMIAH 6:16 NIV

The Israelites faced much opposition when rebuilding the wall of Jerusalem—insults, threats, weariness, and hardships. But they knew that their God would fight for them. And He was indeed faithful.

We may not be building a city wall, but we will face any number of hardships in our lives. Perhaps a wayward teenaged daughter will come home pregnant. Or you will face the sudden disloyalty within a lifelong friendship. Maybe you will suffer the bullying of a boss or the tremendous challenges and disappointments in a career you thought was tailormade by God. Perhaps the painful issues will be health or marriage related, or you may have bouts of poverty or depression or experience ridicule because of your faith in Christ. Life can be brutal at times, but God *will* fight for us, for you.

Stay close to God and ask Him to come alongside you. The Lord is willing and waiting, and He is full of love and mercy.

Day 251

ROCK OF REFUGE

*But the LORD is my fortress; my God is the
mighty rock where I hide. God will turn
the sins of evil people back on them.*
PSALM 94:22–23 NLT

A lot has changed since the psalms were written. But while modern society is different from the ancient world, much remains the same. Reading through the psalms, we see that the people of biblical times were no strangers to just how wicked humankind could be. Evil people were doing evil things way back then too, and God's people called out to Him to make things right.

Yet even before God righted the wrongs, His people observed how He was still active in positive ways in their individual lives: "Joyful are those you discipline, LORD, those you teach with your instructions. You give them relief from troubled times until a pit is dug to capture the wicked" (Psalm 94:12–13 NLT). And again, "Unless the LORD had helped me, I would soon have settled in the silence of the grave. I cried out, 'I am slipping!' but your unfailing love, O LORD, supported me. When doubts filled my mind, your comfort gave me renewed hope and cheer" (verses 17–19 NLT).

God *always* brings His goodness into the bad. Until that day when He abolishes all evil, we can look to Him, our fortress and rock of refuge.

TRUE BEAUTY

Your beauty should not come from outward adornment,
such as elaborate hairstyles and the wearing of gold
jewelry or fine clothes. Rather, it should be that of
your inner self, the unfading beauty of a gentle and
quiet spirit, which is of great worth in God's sight.
1 PETER 3:3–4 NIV

Chances are you are inundated by ads for beauty enhancement products and services. Expensive makeup items, hair products, diet aids, clothing, the list goes on and on. The message you get is that beauty is something you can purchase. Yet these material things only enhance your outward appearance. Although they may make you more attractive to yourself or others, Peter reminds you that true beauty cannot be bought but comes from within.

What God values more than anything is your inner self because *that* person is your true being. And having a quiet and gentle spirit is what pleases your Lord.

In Proverbs 31, you can read the description of a woman of noble character. Take particular note of verse 30 (NIV), which says, "Charm is deceptive, and beauty is fleeting; but a woman who fears the LORD is to be praised." Today and every day, remember that outward beauty is indeed fleeting. But inward beauty never fades, never develops wrinkles, never declines in health. This kind of beauty is readily available to all of us.

Day 251

OUR STRONG ARM

*But LORD, be merciful to us, for we have
waited for you. Be our strong arm each day
and our salvation in times of trouble.*

ISAIAH 33:2 NLT

At times we may feel weak and discouraged. We don't even have the energy to lift our heads up and take on the next challenge. But God can turn us around. When we go to Him, when we seek His face, when we put all our cares on His shoulders, He comes to our rescue.

God not only willingly takes our burdens away but also becomes our arm of strength. Through Him, we find more than enough energy to change the next diaper, tackle another project at work, seek a new path for our lives, deal with our teens and aging parents, cope with an illness, and find a way through a difficult relationship.

Only God can turn our challenges into opportunities for Him to show His power. Just be patient. Wait on Him. And He will do more than see you through.

STARTING OVER

Then Peter came to Jesus and asked, "Lord, how many times shall I forgive my brother or sister who sins against me? Up to seven times?" Jesus answered, "I tell you, not seven times, but seventy-seven times."
MATTHEW 18:21–22 NIV

Picture this: You're in the middle of a heated conversation with a friend. The two of you are at odds. You say something. She says something back. You respond, determined to make your point. She does the same, her jaw clenched. Things escalate, and before long you spout something mean-spirited and completely out of character for you. *Ugh.*

There's no taking that back, is there? Words stick. At times like this, you really wish you could have a do-over. If only you could hit the REWIND button! The good news is, you can.

With God's help, you can have countless do-overs. Sure, there will still be a mess to clean up, but He's pretty good at that part too! Why else do you think He told Peter there would be so many opportunities to forgive?

FREE THROUGH CHRIST

*Stand fast therefore in the liberty wherewith
Christ hath made us free, and be not entangled
again with the yoke of bondage.*
GALATIANS 5:1 KJV

At seventeen, Teresa ran away from home and became a topless dancer. Eventually, alcohol, drugs, and prostitution became the norm. She made lots of money, but she wasn't happy.

Teresa consumed alcohol and drugs to face the life she had chosen for herself. One day she overdosed and landed in the hospital. Afterward, she visited a church one night and there gave her heart to Christ. He set her free from the bondage of drugs and prostitution. Today, Teresa is a tireless witness for Christ. In her book, *Sold to the Highest Bidder*, she boldly shares her testimony of how Christ has set her free. She stands on God's Word and in the liberty Christ gave her. She works to help others find the same freedom she has found.

No matter what our past or present, Christ can set us free. There is no bondage that He cannot break, no power that can defeat Him. We become new creations in Christ when we surrender our lives to Him.

When we allow Jesus complete control of our lives, we can stand fast in the liberty through which He has set us free. And there is no better freedom than that.

FRIENDS WITH JESUS

"You are my friends when you do the things I command you. I'm no longer calling you servants because servants don't understand what their master is thinking and planning. No, I've named you friends because I've let you in on everything I've heard from the Father."
JOHN 15:11–15 MSG

Imagine what it must have been like to be among Jesus' friends while He lived on earth. Wouldn't you have loved to go wherever He went, to hear Him speak, and to see the miracles? The Gospels give us a glimpse of some of His companions, who were ordinary people like us. They weren't perfect. The twelve disciples squabbled among themselves sometimes. Mary and Martha too. And yet Jesus counted those select few among His closest friends. They understood more than anyone what Jesus thought and planned.

The Bible never gives the impression that people have to be super-spiritual to be Jesus' followers. Look at Peter, the disciple many of us can identify with because he seemed to speak before he thought. It was important to include some of Peter's failures in scripture, and he wasn't alone. When we read about the disappointing acts of Jesus' friends, we don't have to despair when our own lives don't measure up.

Yes, they failed sometimes—but they repented and never gave up. Because they kept trying, Jesus called them friends. He is the same now as He was then, so we can be assured we are His friends too.

Day 263

TAKE THE IF OUT OF THE EQUATION

Lord, I believe! [Constantly] help my weakness of faith!
MARK 9:24 AMPC

A man's young son had issues. He would go into convulsions, foam at the mouth, grind his teeth, and then fall into a stupor. The danger was that the boy would be thrown into fire and water. The loving yet desperate father said to Jesus, "If You can do anything, do have pity on us and help us" (Mark 9:22 AMPC).

Jesus replied, "[You say to Me], If You can do anything? [Why,] all things can be (are possible) to him who believes!" (Mark 9:23 AMPC). That's when the father asked Jesus to constantly help him with his weakness of faith. Moments later, Jesus healed the boy of his affliction.

Jesus has one request when you ask for help with your own issues: Take the *if* out of the equation when it comes to believing in His power. Have faith that *He can do* anything in your life, that for Him *nothing is impossible*.

But when you do fall short in faith, know that the Lord will constantly help you, pouring on you more than a sufficient amount of grace, enabling Him to work even through your weakness.

No matter what your level of faith, constantly call on Jesus. He will come, grip your hand, and lift you up into a life of seemingly impossible miracles.

BATTLE PLANS

"See, I have delivered Jericho into your hands."
JOSHUA 6:2 NIV

It would be interesting to test out God's battle strategy on some military commanders today: "Want to take over that city full of hostile terrorists? Just march around it once a day for six days. Then on the seventh day, march around the city seven times and blow your trumpets. What? You don't have trumpets? Well, go get some!"

It's safe to say that plan wouldn't go over so well. But you know it did, in fact, work very well for Joshua and the Israelites. They followed God's instructions and took the whole city of Jericho without really any kind of serious opposition.

But isn't that the way with God's plans? They never look like the ones you'd come up with—not in a million years. Love your enemies. Give more than what's required. Sell all you have. Turn the other cheek. Give up your life to gain the world. Follow the star to a see the poor baby who will be the king of creation. Watch an innocent man suffering and dying to save the world.

No, His plans don't look like yours. Isn't that a very good thing?

His Eye Is on the Sparrow

*I am like a pelican of the wilderness; I am
like an owl of the desert. I lie awake, and am
like a sparrow alone on the housetop.*
Psalm 102:6–7 nkjv

The circumstances of the psalmist's prayer could have been anything—chronic pain, an enemy's affliction—but the psalmist lays it all out before the Lord, describing how his "bones burn like glowing embers" and he is "reduced to skin and bones" (Psalm 102:3, 5 niv). In his suffering, he felt alone, like a solitary bird on the roof.

Though the psalmist felt alone—as maybe you sometimes do—it doesn't mean he was overlooked. For God sees every sparrow, and His children are worth much more than the birds of the air (Matthew 10:29–31). You are seen; your pain does not go unnoticed.

As tempting as it is to put on a brave front and swallow your pain, don't withhold your lament from the Lord. Lamenting is different from complaining—it's not blaming God but crying out for His mercy. Follow the psalmists' example: There are more psalms of lament than any other type. Lamenting is part of abiding—for it is waiting patiently through your tears, waiting in expectant hope for the help of the one who hears, the one who will answer.

OUT OF NOWHERE

He opened the rock, and water gushed out;
it flowed like a river in the desert.
PSALM 105:41 NIV

Has a blessing ever appeared in your life that seemingly came out of nowhere?

The Israelites experienced this phenomenon time and time again as God led them out of Egypt. He opened the Red Sea, and they walked right through it on dry ground. He fed them bread from heaven called manna. He even opened a rock, and water gushed forth to sustain them.

You may be walking through a desert right now in your own life. Perhaps the job that seemed so secure is suddenly gone. Or a relationship has crumbled around you. Or a loved one has passed away. Regardless of the barren land in which you find yourself, know God hasn't forgotten you.

Abide in Christ. Read His Word. Stand on His promises. He has called you more than a conqueror (Romans 8:37), has promised you hope and a future (Jeremiah 29:11), and will never leave nor forsake you (Hebrews 13:5).

You may never see water flood out of a rock, but get ready. There are blessings ahead of you that will seem to come out of nowhere! God has a bright future in store for you and is able to do above and beyond what you can imagine in your wildest dreams.

Day 261

YOU ARE LOVED

*For great is your love, higher than the heavens;
your faithfulness reaches to the skies.*
PSALM 108:4 NIV

God's love for you is higher than the heavens. His faithfulness reaches to the skies—and beyond. Rest in that love today.

Regardless of where "love" has led you in the past, you can trust God. He will never withdraw His love from you—no matter what. Perhaps a man pledged his love to you at an altar and you believed in him, later to be left with a big, expensive photo album full of memories—no husband in sight. Perhaps earthly parents let you down in some way. Siblings turned their backs on you. Friends who pledged their love and loyalty forever have dropped out of sight.

Let those hurts and memories go. And know this: God loves you. He is your true husband, father, brother, and friend. He has your name written on the palms of His hands (Isaiah 49:16). And He will love you from here to eternity. For "He is good; his love endures forever" (2 Chronicles 5:13 NIV).

With God, there is no time or space. He is not limited by feelings or circumstances. He has no earthly constraints. He promises in His Word that He will never leave you. Bank on it. Today, start living like a daughter of the King. Hold your head high. You are dearly and infinitely loved.

Day 268

FIGHTING FOR US

"With him is only the arm of flesh, but with us is the
Lord our God to help us and to fight our battles."
2 CHRONICLES 32:8 NIV

Hezekiah had been working hard for God, undertaking the service of God's temple. But after all this hard work, King Sennacherib of Assyria came to make war against Jerusalem.

Hezekiah gathered his people and made plans. He delivered a rousing speech that could have come straight out of a Hollywood movie—telling his people not to be afraid of the king of Assyria, "for there is a greater power with us than with him" (2 Chronicles 32:7 NIV). And it worked! The people "gained confidence" (verse 8 NIV) and stood up to the Assyrian army.

Then Hezekiah and Isaiah prayed and the Lord sent an angel "who annihilated all the fighting men" of Assyria (2 Chronicles 32:21 NIV). So the Lord saved Hezekiah and Jerusalem, just as He had saved His people before, and just as He would do again and again.

This same God is continuing to fight for you today—answering your prayers and giving you confidence to do battle against any kind of power that seeks to control your heart. You can count on your Lord to give you strength to defend your peace.

Day 261

MADE NEW

Therefore if any person is [ingrafted] in Christ (the Messiah) he is a new creation (a new creature altogether); the old [previous moral and spiritual condition] has passed away. Behold, the fresh and new has come!

2 CORINTHIANS 5:17 AMPC

The day had started with a shining sun, but suddenly you find yourself caught in a heavy downpour of rain. Short on time and patience, you tighten your grip on your bags of just-bought groceries and walk briskly to your car. Once behind the wheel, you realize you are completely soaked, but you don't even care.

Some days everything seems to go wrong and you just want to sit down and cry. Maybe you need a good cry. Just don't forget to follow it up with prayer. Let God know you need more of Him. That your focus has been elsewhere. You have let too many things get in the way. Ask Him to wash away the old and tired, and bring back the new—the dedication and love you experienced when you first came to know Him.

Then take a deep breath. Feel His embrace. He will help you make a clean start.

ISOLATED BUT NOT ALONE

*"Can a mother forget the baby at her breast and
have no compassion on the child she has borne?
Though she may forget, I will not forget you! See, I
have engraved you on the palms of my hands."*
ISAIAH 49:15–16 NIV

Jesus prayed in the garden of Gethsemane. He knew He stood
on the brink of the biggest battle of His earthly life. He craved
companionship—support from His friends. He asked His disciples,
those closest to Him, to pray, but He discovered them sleeping
instead. Then in the night, Judas gave Him away with a kiss. His
disciples abandoned Him, friends forgot Him, and Peter, the one
who promised to have His back, denied even knowing Him.

As Jesus' captors dragged Him away, He saw no supportive,
familiar faces in the crowd. Isolated, He held tight to God. Even
when the Father turned away, Jesus called to Him for assurance.
Jesus gave up His life and died, fully committed to the Father's
plan. He faced death, burial, and resurrection—isolated but not
alone. His faith remained unshaken because He knew God would
never abandon Him.

No matter what circumstances you are facing today, God has
not forgotten you. When you feel isolated, remember that you
are never alone.

CAST IT ON GOD

Humble yourselves, therefore, under God's mighty hand, that he may lift you up in due time. Cast all your anxiety on him because he cares for you.
1 PETER 5:6–7 NIV

Can you even fathom it? The almighty God of the universe cares about the ins and outs of your daily life. He is not an indifferent, uninvolved God, leaving you to fend for yourself. He is personal and present, desiring that you should cast your anxieties on Him. This truth should be soothing to your soul. It's a salve that you can apply whenever you are afraid or troubled.

The problem is that casting your burdens on the Lord is often easier said than done. You might be born with a tendency to cling stubbornly to your problems, believing you alone are capable of ironing out the wrinkles and restoring control. You may think having a white-knuckled grip on your worries will somehow solve them. But in reality, only God is in control. In the stormy seas of life, He is the only thing that remains steadfast and unshakable. Unless you are holding on to Him, you will be tossed unceasingly on the waves.

So how do you let go? You can begin by humbling yourself before God, acknowledging His might and ability to care for you. You can bask in the incredible knowledge that He eagerly desires to relieve you of your burdens.

TRIALS AND WISDOM

*Consider it pure joy, my brothers and sisters, whenever
you face trials of many kinds, because you know that
the testing of your faith produces perseverance. Let
perseverance finish its work so that you may be mature
and complete, not lacking anything. If any of you lacks
wisdom, you should ask God, who gives generously to
all without finding fault, and it will be given to you.*

JAMES 1:2–5 NIV

Trials and troubles are an everyday part of living here in a fallen
world. Pastor and author Max Lucado says, "Lower your expectations of earth. This isn't heaven, so don't expect it to be."

Things won't be easy and simple until we get to heaven. So
how can we lift our chins and head into tomorrow without suc-
cumbing to discouragement? We remember that God is good.
We trust His faithfulness. We ask for His presence and peace during each moment. We pray for wisdom and believe that the God
who holds the universe in His hands is working every single trial
and triumph together for our good and for His glory.

This passage in James tells us that when we lack wisdom we
should simply ask God for it. We don't have to face our problems
alone. We don't have to worry that God will hold our past mistakes
against us. Be encouraged that the Lord will give you wisdom
generously without finding fault!

THE LORD IS CLOSE

*Everything the LORD does is right. He is loyal to
all he has made. The LORD is close to everyone who
prays to him, to all who truly pray to him.*

PSALM 145:17–18 NCV

Do you ever feel like you go to God in prayer with the same things
over and over again? Is your prayer life in need of a little lift? The
psalms are full of prayers and truth. To find a road map for prayers
and promises, look to the psalms.

The authors of the psalms knew the truth of this scripture—that
the Lord is close to those who pray to Him. They expressed their
honest emotions to God—their joy, their fears, their praise. They
understood that God loved them and wanted to have a personal
relationship with them—just like He does with us.

If you're struggling with how to pray to God or what to pray
about, use the psalms as your guide. Pray through a psalm every
day. Add your own personal thoughts and feelings as you pray.
Pretty soon, you'll realize that you have begun a personal friendship with the creator of the universe.

Day 274

GOD ALLOWS REDOS

"I, even I, am he who blots out your transgressions,
for my own sake, and remembers your sins no more."
ISAIAH 43:25 NIV

How many of us have hung our heads low, knowing we really messed up? Wishing we could redo that homework assignment, take back the unkind words that leaped from our mouths without thinking, or even pull back that email message right after we clicked SEND. We've all done something we wished we could undo. Often, we think we have failed not only ourselves but also God.

In fact, the Bible is full of people that God used despite their errors. Moses had an anger problem. David was lustful. Jacob was deceptive. The wonderful thing about our faith is that we serve a God of second chances. Not only is He willing, but He also wants us to confess our sins so He can forgive us. Sing praises for the wonderful blessing of starting over!

BE HAPPY DESPITE IT ALL

*A twinkle in the eye means joy in the heart,
and good news makes you feel fit as a fiddle.*
PROVERBS 15:30 MSG

The apostle Paul had much he could've grumbled about. He was beaten, jailed, shipwrecked, and nearly drowned; yet through it all, he discovered God was the source of his contentment. Paul understood God was in control of his life, even when he was in those overwhelming, tragic situations. Remember his songs of praise from the jail cell (Acts 16)?

Sometimes we find ourselves in hard places, and life isn't going the way we planned. This is the time we have to look for the positive. We have to make the choice to "bloom where we're planted," and God will meet us there. In our songs of praise amid the difficulties, God will come. The Holy Spirit, the Comforter, will minister to our needs. The Lord has promised to never leave or forsake us, so if He is present, we should have no fear or worry. Without fear or worry, we can learn to be content. No fretting, no regretting, just trusting the Word is truth.

When we place our hope in Christ and He's our guide, He will give us the ability to walk satisfied, no matter our circumstances. He is our all in all.

O THE DEEP, DEEP LOVE OF JESUS

*I pray that out of his glorious riches he may strengthen
you with power through his Spirit in your inner
being, so that Christ may dwell in your hearts
through faith. And I pray that you, being rooted
and established in love, may have power, together
with all the Lord's holy people, to grasp how wide
and long and high and deep is the love of Christ.*

EPHESIANS 3:16–18 NIV

The apostle Paul encouraged the people in Ephesus with his words
in an effort to explain how far-reaching God's love was.

In the late 1800s, the lyricist Samuel Trevor Francis enter-
tained the idea of ending his own life. In the midst of despair, he
felt God reach out to him, and he wrote a stirring hymn echoing
Paul's words:

O the deep, deep love of Jesus,
vast, unmeasured, boundless, free!
Rolling as a mighty ocean
in its fullness over me!

What an amazing picture. That He should care for us in such
a way is almost incomprehensible. Despite our shortcomings,
our sin, He loves us. It takes a measure of faith to believe in His
love. When we feel a nagging thought of unworthiness, of being
unlovable, trust in the Word and sing a new song. For His love
is deep and wide.

Day 277

OPEN THE BOOK

*For everything that was written in the past was
written to teach us, so that through the endurance
taught in the Scriptures and the encouragement
they provide we might have hope.*
ROMANS 15:4 NIV

"Out with the old and in with the new!" is unfortunately some
Christians' philosophy about the Bible. Yet the Old Testament
scriptures are vital to every believer. We cannot understand the
power of the New Testament until we embrace the teachings,
wisdom, and moral laws of God revealed in the Old Testament.
After all, the Old Testament points directly to the coming of the
Messiah, Jesus, and our salvation.

The apostle Paul reminds us that everything in the Bible was
written with purpose—to teach us that through our trials and the
encouragement of God's Word we might have hope.

Life is tough, after all. We get discouraged and, at times, disheartened to the point of such despair it's hard to recover. Yet the
Word of God ignites the power of a positive, godly fire within.

Reading *all* of God's Word is paramount. It is the source
of hope, peace, encouragement, salvation, and so much more.
It moves people to take action while diminishing depression
and discouragement. As the writer of Hebrews put it, "For the
word of God is alive and active. Sharper than any double-edged
sword. . ." (Hebrews 4:12 NIV).

Need some encouragement? Open the Book.

Day 278

WONDERFUL YOU

*For you created my inmost being; you knit me
together in my mother's womb. I praise you because
I am fearfully and wonderfully made; your
works are wonderful, I know that full well.*

PSALM 139:13–14 NIV

Many of us look at ourselves and find something we want to change:

"I wish I had Julie's figure. I hate my hips."

"I love Marcia's curly hair. Mine is so straight and hard to manage."

"Maybe I will color my hair auburn. Brown looks mousy."

And yet, many of the very things we may not like are what make us unique. The psalmist says that we are fearfully and wonderfully made. That means that we are made in such a way to produce reverence and inspire awe. Our bodies are complicated and wondrous in the way they work and heal.

By looking at ourselves the way God looks at us, we can see that our differences are reason to praise Him and acknowledge that it is right to honor, love, and be grateful for all of His creation—including ourselves. Though we may not understand why He gave us the physical attributes that He did, we can praise Him, knowing He took great love and pleasure in creating us.

GOD IS UNSTOPPABLE

And Jonathan said to his young armor-bearer,
Come, and let us go over to the garrison of these
uncircumcised; it may be that the Lord will
work for us. For there is nothing to prevent
the Lord from saving by many or by few.

1 SAMUEL 14:6 AMPC

We serve a mighty God who always wins. He has been, He is, and He will always be victorious because He is above all. God's plans are perfect, and His will is wonderful. There is nothing to prevent the Lord from doing what He sees fit to do.

Nothing.

Please let that truth comfort you. The Word clearly states over and over again that God is for you, that He loves you, and that His plans for you are good! That means that if you take a wrong turn in life or have a bad season of sinning, God's plans still win. If it's His will, *it will happen.*

Talk about taking away the pressure to perform or be perfect! Friend, your job is to keep taking the next right step, developing a relationship with Him, confessing and repenting your struggles, and trusting God's power over your circumstances. He's inviting you to live in a place of rest in Him.

Let God do the heavy lifting. Activate your faith in His abilities, because, unlike you, He is unstoppable.

Day 280

WE WON'T BE SHAKEN

*I know the LORD is always with me. I will
not be shaken, for he is right beside me.*
PSALM 16:8 NLT

When crisis strikes, people often drift away from the Lord. As each day passes, another part of them either dies or regains life. Though they may believe nothing ever could have prepared them for such pain, the everyday choices they've made throughout life determine what they will be like on the other side.

Every day we have a choice to trust God and the opportunity to put things in His hands and look eagerly for the way He will work them out. Every day we are developing a relationship with Him. We are choosing whether we will invest or neglect. Build up or break down. Draw closer or walk farther. It is how we handle ourselves in our daily lives that determines the amount of faith we'll have when a crisis comes.

Maybe our hearts will still break, but we will know who to turn to. We will trust and believe when everything is dark, because we have walked many roads with Him. We know His character. We know He is good. We know that though we don't understand, *He does*. And because He does, we can rest in His love. We don't need to know the reason, only that He is with us.

BANK ON HIS GENEROSITY

*"You may ask, 'What will we eat in the seventh
year if we do not plant or harvest our crops?' I
will send you such a blessing in the sixth year that
the land will yield enough for three years."*

LEVITICUS 25:20–21 NIV

Can you imagine regularly taking a year off work and having no worries whatsoever? Today's scripture gives a fascinating look at God's generosity and provision: Every seventh year, the Israelites were to leave the land fallow, a sabbath to the Lord (Leviticus 25:4). If the Israelites were obedient in this, God promised to provide extra for their needs, far beyond the bare minimum, so they and the land could rest that year.

God's abundance is also seen in Mark, as Jesus feeds the multitude (five thousand men, besides women and children) who had followed Him into the countryside to hear Him preach. There were twelve baskets of leftover food after the people "ate and were satisfied" (6:42 NIV).

Jehovah Jireh, our provider, is delighted to care for His people. What have you been waiting for God to provide? All throughout His Word is evidence of His generosity and compassion. He will provide for your needs for today and for tomorrow—you can bank on it.

AWESTRUCK WITH WONDER

*The whole earth is filled with awe at your
wonders; where morning dawns, where
evening fades, you call forth songs of joy.*
PSALM 65:8 NIV

We serve a remarkable God! His mighty hand is at work in creation around us. With the tip of a finger, He draws canyons out of rock. With just a breath, He moves ocean waves to and from the shore. With just a word, He bids the sun and moon to light our path.

The evidence of God's trustfulness is evident if we're paying attention. The tide continues to roll in, day after day. The sun continues to rise, morning after morning. Dew covers the earth in a cool, damp blanket, causing things to grow. Trees shoot up in magnificent splendor, shedding their leaves in autumn and springing back to life after snowy winter frosts melt away.

All of nature, from the tiniest caterpillar to majestic mountain peaks, stands as a testimony to the fact that God is trustworthy. If He can take care of even the smallest creature, if He can remind the moon to cast its glow, surely He can care for you, even when you walk through dark valleys.

PROMISES FULFILLED

*Not one of all the LORD's good promises
to Israel failed; every one was fulfilled.*
JOSHUA 21:45 NIV

Have you ever been lied to? Ever been on the end of a broken promise? There's nothing worse than waiting for someone to carry through. . .only to find they never planned to. The disappointment is like a knife to the heart, especially coming from one you trusted.

Perhaps you've been on the opposite end of the story. Maybe you made promises to someone—a child, a spouse, a friend—and then went back on your word. Now you're regretting the pain you caused and you're wondering how to make things right again.

Thank goodness, God isn't like us. He doesn't make promises and then break them. If He said it, He will carry through. You won't have to wonder if He will make good on His promises to you. He is who He says He is and He'll do what He says He'll do.

Today, look at several of the promises in God's Word. Put your name in each sentence, personalizing each promise. Then claim each promise as your own and watch in wonder as God brings every one of them to pass in your life.

A Simple Thing

*"Thus says the LORD: 'Make this valley full of ditches
. . . . You shall not see wind, nor shall you see rain; yet
that valley shall be filled with water, so that you. . .may
drink.' And this is a simple matter in the sight of the
LORD; He will also deliver the Moabites into your hand."*
2 KINGS 3:16–18 NKJV

Some days you may have no idea how to "fix" a situation. And
so with your shoulders drooped, you come before the Lord. He
tells you the impossible will happen in a way you never imagined.
You'll be well-provided for. You're going to be victorious against
whatever's coming at you. Not only that, but all these things are
simple for the Lord! But you have to trust God will do as He says:
you have to dig ditches to ready the dry earth to receive the water,
full of faith that a miracle is imminent.

Jesus' apostles' readying work was to trust God and expect the
miraculous. That's how it came to be that "at night an angel of the
Lord opened the prison doors and brought them out" (Acts 5:19
NKJV). Their part was to then go and preach in the temple, bringing
more believers into the fold.

Trust God. Expect Him to work. Know that for God, providing
the miraculous is a simple thing.

Day 285

FROM GLOOM TO BLOOM

Let all that I am praise the LORD; may I never forget
the good things he does for me. . . . He fills my life with
good things. My youth is renewed like the eagle's!
PSALM 103:2, 5 NLT

Some days it's easy to feel we are sinking beneath the waves of bad news flowing out to us. To have the negativity of the world become like seaweed wrapped around our minds. But God would have us look not to our circumstances but to Him. To trust not in events but in His power. To focus not on our afflictions but our blessings. For when we change our perspective from one of "me" to "He," everything looks better and brighter.

What if you looked at the things that happen as neither good nor bad? What if you constantly remembered God is in your corner, on your side (Psalm 118:6)? What if you understood and kept in mind the idea that God has everything rigged in your favor?

To be sure, there are times when you need to grieve the loss of someone or something. Times when you need to regroup and take stock of what's happening. But the majority of the time, looking at things as being rigged by God in your favor may just change your life from gloom to bloom!

PEACE

For God is not a God of disorder but of peace.
1 CORINTHIANS 14:33 NIV

Orderliness in life brings peace, whereas disorderliness leads to confusion and chaos. This is a simple truth from God. Like warm, clean, colorful laundry tossed together, the moments and activities of our day need sorting into harmony. Balance rest with work, reflection with business, and togetherness with solitude. Determine ways to let your day and week reflect the orderliness of God.

Because you are made in God's image, you have a great capacity to bring tranquility from disorder in your home. Does your home feel tranquil? If not, consider giving away extra items.

Along with not being a God of disorder, God is also not a God of confusion. So take time to consider your emotions and thoughts. Sort through them and ask the Holy Spirit to guide you into peace. Your inner world of thoughts and feelings thrive when you slow down for reflection. Is there something that needs to be said? Is there a trouble that needs to be given to God in prayer? You can be certain Jesus, your Prince of Peace, will lead you from confusion to calm if you will only ask Him.

WORKING FOR PEACE
WHEREVER YOU ARE

*"Work for the peace and prosperity of the city
where I sent you into exile. Pray to the LORD for
it, for its welfare will determine your welfare."*
JEREMIAH 29:7 NLT

You've moved somewhere you never wanted to go. You're stuck in a job you never wanted to do. You're trapped in a class you don't want to take. You find yourself in a crowd where you don't feel welcome.

There are many times in our lives when we feel like strangers in strange lands. The Israelites who were exiled to Babylon certainly felt this way. But God gave them interesting advice. Instead of telling them to keep to their own kind, He told them to go out and build new lives there. He told them literally to put roots down, to have children and grandchildren. He told them to work hard and make sure this land—this land of their enemies—prospered.

Next time you find yourself feeling stuck someplace you don't want to be, don't get caught up in planning your exit. Instead, think about how you can make the best of the situation. Ask God to help you to reach out to strangers. Think about ways you can help those around you succeed—no matter who they are or how welcome (or not) they've made you feel. Dig in. Participate. Join the team. Make solid connections. And trust that God will bless your efforts.

Day 288

HOPE IS YOURS

*For thus says the LORD to the
house of Israel: "Seek Me and live."*
AMOS 5:4 NKJV

Through prophets, God in His mercy frequently warned His chosen ones, long before they reaped the negative consequences for their sin. In Amos 4:6–6:14, we learn Israel had not returned to God. In a time of peace and prosperity, this selfish and materialist society had become indifferent toward Him. Yet Amos stood courageously for God in front of a people who didn't want to hear the truth God had instructed him to boldly declare.

In Amos 5, the people who gathered to hear the prophet's message believed everything was going well. They were shocked and perplexed as Amos began a song of grief, crying out as if the people of Israel had already been destroyed. (You might liken it to going to church in your Sunday best only to discover the minister preaching your funeral—and the funeral for most of your fellow citizens!) But God's message of death continued with a promise from Him: "If you seek Me, you can live."

As you read the book of Amos, you'll very easily see similarities between the Israelites' culture and the one you live in today. From the beginning of time until the end, sin seeks to destroy. . .but hope is yours when you seek God.

Day 287

FILLED WITH JOY

*But let all who take refuge in you rejoice; let them sing
joyful praises forever. Spread your protection over them,
that all who love your name may be filled with joy.*

PSALM 5:11 NLT

Joy is often confused with happiness. While joy may be similar
to happiness, the two concepts have entirely different sources.
Happiness is based on what's happening right now. Joy is based
on an assured, victorious future.

When we're in trouble, we can take refuge in God, and we
can rejoice! We can—and will—sing His praises forever. All who
love God, all who are called His children will be filled with joy!

The reason for that joy is that we know, despite our present
trouble, we have hope. We have the promise of a good future filled
with love and peace, and absent from suffering and trials of every
kind. Though we may not feel happy about our current circum-
stance, we can rejoice, because we know how our story will end.

Day 210

JOY IS JESUS

Though you have not seen him [Jesus], you love him; and even though you do not see him now, you believe in him and are filled with an inexpressible and glorious joy, for you are receiving the end result of your faith, the salvation of your souls.
1 PETER 1:8–9 NIV

As children we find joy in the smallest things: a rose in bloom, a ladybug at rest, the circles a pebble makes when dropped in water. Then somewhere between pigtails and pantyhose, our joy wanes and eventually evaporates in the desert of difficulties.

But when we find Jesus, "all things become new" as the Bible promises, and once again, we view the world through a child's eyes. Excitedly, we experience the "inexpressible and glorious joy" that salvation brings.

We learn that God's joy isn't based on our circumstances; rather, its roots begin with the seed of God's Word planted in our hearts. Suddenly, our hearts spill over with joy, knowing that God loves and forgives us and that He is in complete control of our lives. We have joy because we know this world is not our permanent home and a mansion awaits us in glory.

Joy comes as a result of whom we trust, not in what we have. Joy is Jesus.

A MATTER OF PRIORITIES

*To everything there is a season, a time
for every purpose under heaven.*
ECCLESIASTES 3:1 NKJV

Change is a regular part of modern life, as routine as an afternoon thunderstorm—and often just as messy. Jobs shift or disappear. Friends move. Babies are born, and children graduate and marry. On top of lives already crammed to the brim with responsibilities and stress, change comes to all of us.

Only one thing in our lives never changes: God. When our world swirls and threatens to shift out of control, we can know that God is never surprised, never caught off guard by anything that happens. Just as He guided David through dark nights and Joseph through his time in prison, God can show us a secure way through any difficulty. He can turn the roughest times to good.

Just as He supported His servants in times past, He will always be with us, watching and loving.

EYE CARE

For thus says the LORD of hosts. . ."he who
touches you touches the apple of His eye."
ZECHARIAH 2:8 NKJV

The apple of the eye refers to the pupil—the very center, or heart, of the eye. Consider the lengths we go to in order to protect our eyes. We wear protective glasses in some workplaces. We close our eyes or squint in windstorms or bright light. When dust blows, we turn our heads or put up our hands to keep the dirt from ending up in our eyes.

When we do get something in an eye, the ache and discomfort are instant. Tears form, and we seek to get the particle out as quickly as possible to stop the pain. If we are unable to remove the offending bit, we often become unable to do anything but focus on the discomfort.

To think that we are the apple of God's eye is incredible. Consider the care He must take for us. He will go to great lengths to protect us from harm. When something or someone does attack us, God feels our pain. He is instantly aware of our discomfort, for it is His own. When the storms of life come, we must remember how God feels each twinge of suffering. Despite the adversity, we can praise God for He is sheltering us.

Day 213

DON'T BE ANXIOUS?

*Do not be anxious about anything, but in
every situation, by prayer and petition, with
thanksgiving, present your requests to God.*
PHILIPPIANS 4:6 NIV

Today's world does not make worry-free living easy. With all of
our commitments and responsibilities, stress tends to overwhelm
us. Instead of putting things into perspective, we let our anxieties
spiral out of control. Often we rely on our own means to solve
problems, accomplish interminable to-do lists, and balance overfull
lives. When we trust in ourselves to deal with life's pressures, we
become bogged down, weary, and disheartened.

In this verse, Paul urges his readers not to be anxious about
anything. Instead, he writes that we should present all of our
requests—with expressions of gratitude—to God. We find these
words extremely challenging to integrate into our daily lives. *Don't
be anxious? Be thankful instead?*

Paul was certainly familiar with trials. His words to the Philippians are actually written from jail. Undoubtedly, he could
have succumbed to anxiety and worry. Yet he writes to the Philippians with thanksgiving and joy. Paul knows that we will
experience hardship and adversity. However, he has experienced
the solace that comes from trusting God with every aspect of
life. While this way of life is admittedly a challenge, Paul assures
us that relying on God for all of our concerns—and giving
thanks all the while—is both comforting and rewarding.

Day 214

FINDING BALANCE

Hope deferred makes the heart sick,
but when the desire comes, it is a tree of life.
PROVERBS 13:12 NKJV

Our minds are full of the things we are trying to fix in our lives—
strained relationships, financial worries, stress, health concerns.

Too much too fast is overwhelming. Looking for balance can
leave us lost, not knowing which way to turn. The best way to gain
balance is to stop moving and regain focus.

Jesus is your hope! He stands a short distance away bidding
you to take a walk on water—a step of faith toward Him. Dis-
regarding the distractions can be hard, but the rough waters can
become silent as you turn your eyes, your thoughts, and your
emotions to Him.

You can tackle the tough things as you maintain your focus.
Let Him direct you over the rough waters of life, overcoming
each obstacle one opportunity at a time. Don't look at the big
picture in the midst of the storm, but focus on the one thing
you can do at the moment to help your immediate situation—
one step at a time.

The Promise of Joy

Weeping may endure for a night,
but joy cometh in the morning.
Psalm 30:5 kjv

Have you experienced suffering? Perhaps you are hurting even now. Tough times are a reality for all of us.

The psalmist David was well acquainted with hardship. He used phrases such as "the depths," "the pit," and even "the grave" to describe them. Although he was known as a man after God's own heart, at times David was pursued by his enemies and forced to run for his life. He also lived with the consequences of committing murder and adultery, even long after receiving God's forgiveness.

God is faithful, and suffering is temporary. This is a promise we can claim, as David did, when facing difficulty or depression. David experienced God's faithfulness throughout the ups and downs of his life.

King Solomon, one of the wisest men who ever lived, concludes in the third chapter of Ecclesiastes that there is a time for everything, including "a time to weep and a time to laugh" (verse 4 niv).

Some trials are short-lived. Others are more complex. As believers, we can find joy in the Lord even as certain trials remain a backdrop in our lives. All suffering will end one day when we meet Jesus. The Bible assures us that in heaven there will be no tears.

TO BE OR TO DO?

They did not conquer the land with their swords; it was not their own strong arm that gave them victory. It was your right hand and strong arm and the blinding light from your face that helped them, for you loved them.

PSALM 44:3 NLT

She stared out the window, misty-eyed. *What's wrong with me?* she wondered. *I should do more for the Lord, but I'm so tired.* Unfounded guilt weighed upon her spirit. The young woman seldom felt that she did enough, though she gave of her time and talents regularly.

Still immersed in thought, she sensed the gentle nudge of the Holy Spirit. *"I don't want you to do, as much as I want you to be."*

Women are conditioned to "do it all." And most of the time, we do. But our personal expectations are unreasonable and self-defeating if we think we must accomplish all tasks by our own strength and skills.

As Christian women, we must remember the basic precepts of our walk with God. Namely, Jesus saved us because He loves us. God cares more about who we are and what characteristics we develop through the work of the Holy Spirit than what we do in the work of ministry.

God requires us to *be*. To be faithful to Him through Bible study and prayer. To be obedient. And to be ourselves. That makes God smile.

SMELLING THE ROSES

I know that nothing is better for them than to rejoice, and to do good in their lives, and also that every man should eat and drink and enjoy the good of all his labor—it is the gift of God.
ECCLESIASTES 3:12–13 NKJV

Women today work hard—sometimes the labor seems endless. We care for our homes, families, employers, and churches. We cook, sort, haul, clean, and nurture, and that's before we even leave for our jobs outside the home. We run errands at lunch and often eat more meals behind the steering wheel than at the dinner table. Our days start early and end late, and we head for our beds as if sleep were a luxury instead of a necessity.

Yet constant work is not what God intended for our lives. We should work hard, yes, but not to the exclusion of rest and times of renewal for our minds and souls. As the author of Ecclesiastes points out, our work and the results of it—our food, homes, and friendships—are gifts that God meant for us to enjoy and appreciate.

Finding time isn't always easy, but the rewards of a calmer mind and a grateful heart will be well worth the effort.

THE REWARDS OF SACRIFICE

*And the young men that were spies went in,
and brought out Rahab, and her father, and her
mother, and her brethren, and all that she had.*

JOSHUA 6:23 KJV

Rahab, one of the most dynamic women in the Bible, took risks that would make most of us today shudder. She believed in the majesty and truth of the God of the Israelites when everyone around her worshipped pagan idols. Every citizen of Jericho knew the power the Lord held, yet they chose to rely on the safety of the city's infamous walls. Rahab saw that God not only destroyed His enemies but safeguarded those who followed Him.

Because of her beliefs, Rahab opened her home to the two spies, an act that easily could have gotten her and her entire family executed. She risked everything to protect the spies from the king, asking in exchange that the Israelites spare her family in the destruction to come (Joshua 2:12–13). They did, and the ultimate reward for her faithfulness was a place in the lineage of Christ.

We may not be called to take the chances Rahab did. Yet, as mothers, sisters, and daughters, we are called upon every day to stand up for our beliefs. Rahab is a reminder that God does, indeed, provide for those who love and believe in Him.

GOD KNOWS YOUR NAME

*But now, this is what the LORD says—he who
created you, Jacob, he who formed you, Israel:
"Do not fear, for I have redeemed you; I have
summoned you by name; you are mine."*

ISAIAH 43:1 NIV

Do you remember your first day of school? The teacher called the roll, and you waited for your name to be announced. When it was, you knew that you were a part of that class—you belonged there.

We wait for our names to be called a lot in life: when captains pick teams, while sitting in a doctor's waiting room, or to be called in for a job interview. There is comfort in hearing our own names, in being recognized.

God knows your name. He created you and redeemed you from sin through His Son, Jesus, if you have accepted Him as your personal Savior. He knows you. He put together your personality and topped off His masterpiece by giving you all sorts of likes and dislikes, dreams and desires, passions and preferences. You are His unique design, His daughter, His beloved one.

No matter if you feel you don't belong, *you belong to God*. He takes great joy in you. You are His treasure. He sent Jesus to die on the cross to give you an abundant life. He wants to spend eternity with you! He calls you by name, and your name is music to your Father's ears.

Day 300

GOOD FOR THE SOUL

*When I kept silent about my sin, my body
wasted away through my groaning all day long.*
PSALM 32:3 NASB

The shame was too great to bear. Tina could hardly lift her head, let alone face her family. For weeks she was miserable—couldn't eat, couldn't sleep—the burden weighed more heavily on her every day. Finally, she gathered the courage to talk with her mother.

Tina was shocked when her mother received her with open arms. She felt as if a weight had been lifted from her shoulders. She was forgiven, released from the pain of the past.

Shame is a powerful silencer. When we feel guilty and ashamed about our actions, the last thing we want to do is speak of them. However, Psalm 32:3 reminds us of the pain silence can cause. Keeping silent about our sin can literally make us feel as if we were dying.

God does not want His children to live in silent shame. Saying what we've done wrong out loud is the first step to healing. Confession is merely agreeing with God about our actions. While other people may not always forgive us, God promises that if we confess our sins He will forgive us and cleanse us from our unrighteousness.

Grace. A clean slate. It's ours for the asking.

Day 301

WHEN TROUBLE COMES. . .

*When you pass through the waters, I will be with you;
and when you pass through the rivers, they will not
sweep over you. When you walk through the fire, you
will not be burned; the flames will not set you ablaze.*

ISAIAH 43:2 NIV

This is one of the most comforting verses in the Bible. It is God's promise that when we face trials in our lives, He will not abandon us.

The Bible offers literal examples of this. When Moses and the Israelites approached the Red Sea, with the Egyptian army in hot pursuit, God literally parted the water and allowed the Israelites to escape from their enemies (Exodus 14:10–31). When Shadrach, Meshach, and Abednego were cast into a fiery furnace for refusing to bow down to a golden idol, God brought them out of the fire unscathed. He was literally there in the fire with the three young men, seen as a fourth person (Daniel 3).

Isaiah 43:2 doesn't say "*If* you pass through the waters." It says *when*. When we face trouble in our lives, God is with us. Jesus repeats this promise in John 16:33 (NIV), "In this world you will have trouble. But take heart! I have overcome the world."

MORE THAN WE CAN IMAGINE

Now unto him that is able to do exceeding
abundantly above all that we ask or think,
according to the power that worketh in us. . .
EPHESIANS 3:20 KJV

This scripture concludes Paul's prayer for the Ephesian church for spiritual growth, inner strength, and knowledge of God's love (verses 14–19). The passage is a doxology giving praise to God and assurance to every believer of the omnipotence of our loving Lord.

The apostle declares that God is able to do "exceeding abundantly." The Greek word *huperekperissou* is a rare double compound meaning that God is not only able to accomplish all things, but does so "superabundantly above the greatest abundance"—or "beyond measure."

"Above all that we ask or think" is just that. Imagine every good thing that God has promised in His Word—or things you've only dreamed about. Think of wonderful things that exceed the limits of human comprehension or description, then imagine that God is able and *willing* to do even more!

The last part of this verse indicates that the Holy Spirit works within the Christian's life to accomplish the seemingly impossible. Our highest aspirations are within God's power—but like Paul, we must pray. When we do, God does far more for us than we could ever guess.

Day 303

STRENGTH THAT DOES NOT FAIL

*But [Joseph's] bow remained strong and steady
and rested in the Strength that does not fail him,
for the arms of his hands were made strong and
active by the hands of the Mighty God of Jacob, by
the name of the Shepherd, the Rock of Israel.*

GENESIS 49:24 AMPC

It's easy to try to fight the battle on your own or attempt to fix things yourself, failing to remember that God stands ready to supply you with His strength. Whether the fight you face is physical or spiritual in nature, your rescue depends on your willingness to invite God to step in.

Joseph endured great adversity, starting with his older brothers selling him into slavery as a young boy. Each battle Joseph faced required courage and faith in God to rescue him and provide him with strength. Joseph's bow remained strong because he relied on God's strength. God's hands supported Joseph as he used his weapon against his enemies.

As you endure difficulties, burdens, and persecution, remember that you don't have to fight alone. God is with you and has provided you with the strength that does not fail.

LOVE GOD? THINGS WILL WORK OUT

*And we know that all things work together
for good to them that love God, to them who
are the called according to his purpose.*

ROMANS 8:28 KJV

"God won't give me more than I can handle." You hear this phrase a lot. Is it true? Does the Bible say this?

The origin of this phrase is 1 Corinthians 10:13, which is actually dealing with the idea of temptation and says that God "will not allow you to be tempted beyond what you are able, but with the temptation will also make the way of escape, that you may be able to bear it" (NKJV).

Sadly, this verse is used by many who do not know Christ but who find some measure of mental comfort in the idea that, no matter what they are experiencing, even if it is the consequences of sinful choices, God is not allowing them to bear too much. This just isn't so. Proverbs 13:15 (KJV) declares that "the way of transgressors is hard." The crushing consequences of sin will break you and cast you aside.

Only the ones who are following Christ can lay claim to the promise that God will work all things together for good. Those who trust and obey can rest in the assurance that everything (the good and the bad) fits together in the pattern He has laid out for them.

KEEP ASKING

You shall have charge over my house, and all my
people shall be governed according to your word
[with reverence, submission, and obedience]. Only in
matters of the throne will I be greater than you are.

GENESIS 41:40 AMPC

And just like that, Joseph went from a prisoner to second in command in Egypt. Talk about an immediate promotion! One minute he was in jail for a crime he didn't commit, and the next Joseph is interpreting a dream for the king and is elevated to Pharaoh's number two. For years Joseph had been praying and hoping for his situation to change, and when God's plan called for a move . . .a move happened.

Let this encourage you! Sometimes it's hard to continue praying for God's intervention over and over and over again. Our perseverance peters out. We worry He may grow tired of our request, or we give up altogether because we think His answer is a firm *no*. But the truth is that it's not yet time for the next right step.

It's hard to understand God's timing, so we have to choose to trust it because God is God and we are not. Yet we need not grow weary of asking, for we won't wear God out. And we'll have peace if we live our lives knowing that when it *is* the right time, God's answers *will* come.

Day 306

STEADFAST LOVE

*Give thanks to the LORD, for he is
good; his love endures forever.*
PSALM 107:1 NIV

When the sea of life batters us, it's easy to forget the Lord's goodness. Caught up in our own storms, tunnel vision afflicts us as we view the troubles before us. We may even doubt the Lord whom we serve. Though we might not consciously separate ourselves from Him, deep inside we fear He won't act to save us—or that He won't act in time.

That's a good time to stop and give thanks to God, who never stops being good or ends His love for us. Our situations change, our love fails, but God never varies. He entirely controls all creation, and His character never changes. The darkest circumstances we face will not last eternally. Life moves on and alters. But God never deserts us.

Even when our troubles seem to be in control, they aren't. God has not changed, and our doubts cannot make alteration in Him. If we allow faith to take control, we will realize that and turn again to Him.

Facing troubles? Give thanks to the Lord. He is good. He hasn't deserted you, no matter what you face, and His goodness will never end. He won't fail us.

Rod and Staff

*Even though I walk through the darkest valley,
I will fear no evil, for you are with me; your
rod and your staff, they comfort me.*
Psalm 23:4 niv

Do a rod and a staff sound comforting to you? These well-known Bible verses bring hope to many people, yet little is mentioned about the shepherd's tools—the rod and staff.

Sheep traveled into valleys for food and water, but the valleys also contained danger. The high ridges created perfect places for lions and coyotes to wait to snatch an innocent lamb.

Anticipating new grass, sheep often wandered away where they slipped into swamps or fell down steep cliffs. Tiny flies bit their ears.

But the shepherd was prepared. He constantly watched over his flock for any signs of danger. With his tall staff with crooked end, he could snare a sheep from a swamp or guide him in fast-moving waters.

His rod, a short stick with leather strips on the end, kept the flies and mosquitoes away—and could be used in cleaning and grooming.

As stubborn, somewhat dumb creatures, we (like sheep) get into dangerous situations in the valleys of life. But the Lord stays with us, protecting us from the nuisances, cleaning us of our sins, and redeeming us when we fall.

GROWTH IS GOD'S SPECIALTY

"Though it is the smallest of all seeds, yet when it grows,
it is the largest of garden plants and becomes a tree,
so that the birds come and perch in its branches."
MATTHEW 13:32 NIV

Insignificant beginnings can lead to magnificent finishes. Jesus picked up the tiniest of all seeds—a mustard seed—to show the disciples. This seed is about the size of the point of a sharpened pencil tip.

Once planted, the seed grows slowly in a gradual process. The seedling takes days or even weeks before it gives any sign of breaking through the ground. Why does growth drag on slowly?

The mustard seed requires deep roots. The plant grows its roots three times faster than the stalk in order to be well grounded. Mustard trees grow up to twenty-one feet tall with the roots reaching down to sixty-three feet in the ground.

God planted mustard-seed-sized faith within each of us. Our faith may seem inadequate and so small we no longer think it exists. But often during these times we are not aware of the deep transformation occurring within our souls.

God is pushing our roots deeper. We can help nourish this growth through prayer and studying His Word.

Miraculous growth from a very small seed is only possible through the work of the Master Gardener.

KEY TO HAPPINESS

He will be the sure foundation for your times,
a rich store of salvation and wisdom and knowledge;
the fear of the LORD is the key to this treasure.
ISAIAH 33:6 NIV

During the days of Isaiah, things were downright scary in Jerusalem. The Assyrian army was ravaging everything in sight, threatening Jerusalem's very existence. But Isaiah was the voice of calm, revealing God's words to His people, assuring them that God would save them.

The words of Isaiah resonated with the people then as they do now. The key, as Isaiah tells us, is to fear the Lord. In this case, the word *fear* does not mean to be afraid but rather to have respect and reverence. This is the same way we "fear" our parents or those in authority.

What is "this treasure" of which Isaiah speaks? Unlike a chest overflowing with gold and jewels, Isaiah refers to a treasure far more valuable. This treasure offers safety, peace of mind, knowledge, and wisdom. As Proverbs 8:11 (NIV) tells us, "Wisdom is more precious than rubies, and nothing you desire can compare with her."

Remember to let God be your foundation, and you will certainly reap the bounty of His treasure.

KNOWING GOD

*Jesus shouted to the crowds, "If you trust me, you
are trusting not only me, but also God who sent
me. For when you see me, you are seeing the one
who sent me. I have come as a light to shine in
this dark world, so that all who put their trust
in me will no longer remain in the dark."*

JOHN 12:44–46 NLT

Not sure what God is all about? Uncertain as to His true character? You need not look any further than Jesus Christ. When you know Him, you'll know God. When you trust Him, you're trusting God. For Jesus was God in the flesh.

Study His compassion for the mourning, the lame, the weak, the blind, the leper, the sinner. Read of His attitude toward the political and religious leaders of His day. Walk with His disciples as they follow Him, forever trying to understand and often falling a little bit short. Allow Him to open up your eyes to what He reveals in the scriptures. Make a list of all the statements He begins with the words, *I am.* And then find proof of His identity in the Word and in your own life.

Trust in Jesus. Love, worship, and believe in Him—and you'll find yourself living in His light, understanding God, and finding a peace beyond compare.

Day 311

GOD'S WILL AND WAY

He walked away, about a stone's throw, and knelt down and prayed, "Father, if you are willing, please take this cup of suffering away from me. Yet I want your will to be done, not mine." Then an angel from heaven appeared and strengthened him.

LUKE 22:41–43 NLT

There may be times of hardship in our lives. Times when things don't go the way we think they should. But when we desire God's will above our own, we can trust Him to help us—no matter what. And when we do, we know He'll strengthen us by supernatural means.

Throughout His story, God has strengthened and directed those who are following His will. Regarding the Exodus, the psalmist wrote, "Your road led through the sea, your pathway through the mighty waters—a pathway no one knew was there! You led your people along that road like a flock of sheep, with Moses and Aaron as their shepherds" (Psalm 77:19–20 NLT).

Trust the will of your Good Shepherd, the one who knows best. Not only will He send you supernatural aid, He'll reveal a pathway no one knew existed!

Day 312

OUTSIDE OF TIME

*"Only I can tell you the future before it
even happens. Everything I plan will come
to pass, for I do whatever I wish."*
ISAIAH 46:10 NLT

Time ticks away, fleeting past as we go about our busy day. How often have you wished time would stop—stand still for moments, hours, or even days? It's normal to want to capture the good times in our lives and hold them tightly.

As an eternal being, God stands outside of time. He *was, is,* and always *will be.* We live in the moment—the sliver of time we call today, and that is where our focus often stays. But what if we looked at our lives from God's perspective? He created us to live for all eternity with Him. He didn't intend for us to live our lives here on earth, die, and then begin eternity with Him.

Eternity is now! It starts with the realization that your salvation has granted you a never-ending story—a life without end. Sure, you'll leave this earth at some point, but you'll carry on as a child of God with Him forever and ever. You can live outside of time knowing there is really no end to your time with Him.

HOLD ON!

Let us not become weary in doing good, for at the proper time we will reap a harvest if we do not give up.
GALATIANS 6:9 NIV

Have you ever felt that God abandoned you? Have the difficulties in your life pressed you to physical and mental exhaustion? Do you feel your labor is in vain and no one appreciates the sacrifices you have made?

When Elijah fled for his life in fear of Jezebel's wrath, depression and discouragement tormented him. Exhausted, he prayed for God to take his life, and then he fell asleep. When he awoke, God sent an angel with provisions to strengthen his weakened body. Only then was he able to hear God's revelation that provided the direction and assistance he needed.

God hears our pleas even when He seems silent. The problem is that we cannot hear Him because of physical and mental exhaustion. Rest is key to our restoration.

Just when the prophet thought he could go on no longer, God provided the strength, peace, and encouragement to continue. He does the same for us today. When we come to the end of our rope, God ties a knot. And like Elijah, God will do great things in and through us, if we will just hold on.

THE GREAT GIFT GIVER

*Every good and perfect gift is from above, coming
down from the Father of the heavenly lights,
who does not change like shifting shadows.*

JAMES 1:17 NIV

Do you know a true gift giver? We all give gifts on birthdays and at Christmas, when we receive wedding invitations, and when a baby is born. But do you know someone with a real knack for gift giving? She finds all sorts of excuses for giving gifts. She delights in it. A true gift giver has an ability to locate that "something special." When shopping for a gift, she examines many items before making her selection. She knows the interests and preferences, the tastes and favorites of her friends and family members. She chooses gifts they will like—gifts that suit them well.

God is a gift giver. He is, in fact, the creator of all good gifts. He finds great joy in blessing you. The God who made you certainly knows you by name. He knows your tastes and preferences. He even knows your favorites and your dreams. Most important, God knows your needs.

So in seasons of waiting in your life, rest assured that gifts chosen and presented to you by the hand of God will be worth the wait.

Day 315

FIRSTFRUITS

Honor the LORD from your wealth, and from the first of all your produce; then your barns will be filled with plenty, and your vats will overflow with new wine.

PROVERBS 3:9–10 NASB

Perhaps you think this verse doesn't apply to you because you don't consider yourself wealthy. The only "produce" you have comes from the grocery store. Barns and vats of wine may not be your top priority.

But this verse still applies. Read these words: *"Honor the LORD . . .from the first of all."* Our God is not a God of leftovers. He wants us to put Him first.

One way to honor God is to give Him our "firstfruits," the best we have to offer. The truth is that everything we have comes from God. The Bible calls us to cheerfully give back to the Lord one-tenth of all we earn.

Giving to God has great reward. You may not have barns you need God to fill, but you will reap the benefit in other ways. When believers honor God by giving to Him, we can trust that He will provide for our needs. In Malachi 3:10, we are challenged to test God in our tithing.

Start with your next paycheck. Make the check that you dedicate to God's kingdom work the first one you write. See if God is faithful to provide for you throughout the month.

Day 316

COUNT ON HOLY STRENGTH

Then Asa cried out to the LORD his God, "O LORD, no one but you can help the powerless against the mighty! Help us, O LORD our God, for we trust in you alone. It is in your name that we have come against this vast horde. O LORD, you are our God; do not let mere men prevail against you!"

2 CHRONICLES 14:11 NLT

When you have strengths, abilities, and resources within yourself, it's easy to look to yourself to solve problems and make things happen. But God created you so that He could do life *with* you all the time, not just when you need His help. When you include God in your daily ups and down, that fellowship allows Him to fill you with His power.

Complete dependence on God doesn't mean you're weak, passive, or unproductive. It means you're allowing His power to make you more effective for Him, enabling you to do so much more, often with eternal value.

If you're facing battles you feel you can't possibly win, don't give up. Study Asa who, when standing against immense throngs of enemy soldiers, realized how incapable he was without God's holy power. When He prayed for God's intervention, God came through, supernaturally and stupendously. In all things, trust in God alone.

A Cornerstone

*As the Scriptures say, "I am placing a cornerstone in
Jerusalem, chosen for great honor, and anyone who
trusts in him will never be disgraced." Yes, you who
trust him recognize the honor God has given him.
But for those who reject him, "The stone that the
builders rejected has now become the cornerstone."*

1 Peter 2:6–7 NLT

Today's scripture, written by the apostle Peter, incorporates Old
Testament words found in Isaiah 28:16 and Psalm 118:22. Peter
was saying that although Jesus, the cornerstone, was rejected by
people, He was chosen by God for great honor.

Although Peter, whose name means "rock," denied knowing
Jesus before He was crucified, God still forgave him. In fact, God
used Peter, who had once stumbled over the cornerstone, to help
spread the Gospel and encourage other believers.

Like Peter who fell short, stumbled, and showed his imperfections, you too may need a fresh start. Know that with Jesus as
the cornerstone in your life, even when you trip up, you'll meet
up with God's grace and mercy. So thank Him, praise Him, and
trust Him to catch you when you fall. Know you can stand tall on
the cornerstone in your life and that, when you trust in Him, you
will "never be disgraced."

BELOVED SHEEP

"I myself will gather the remnant of my flock out of all the countries where I have driven them and will bring them back to their pasture, where they will be fruitful and increase in number. I will place shepherds over them who will tend them, and they will no longer be afraid or terrified, nor will any be missing."

JEREMIAH 23:3–4 NIV

If you ever have an identity crisis, here is a beautiful reality to fall back on. You are God's beloved sheep. This truth is enough to outshine everything the world tells you that you are not. You can be confident that God has set you securely in His fold. He has elaborate plans to care for you, make you successful, and eradicate your fear and dismay.

Because your trustworthy shepherd loves each member of His flock, you can trust Him to care for those you love as well as yourself.

Being God's sheep means that you (or *ewe*) can reside in a peaceful pasture, green with peace and gladness at any time or place. When you feel a little beat up by life outside the pasture, you can remember that your Good Shepherd understands. He promises not to lose even one of His fold. He keeps a careful headcount and goes in search of those who wander off.

Day 317

When You Can't Pray

*And the Holy Spirit helps us in our weakness. For
example, we don't know what God wants us to pray for.
But the Holy Spirit prays for us with groanings that
cannot be expressed in words. And the Father who knows
all hearts knows what the Spirit is saying, for the Spirit
pleads for us believers in harmony with God's own will.*

Romans 8:26–27 nlt

Sometimes we literally cannot pray. The Holy Spirit takes over on such occasions. Go before God; enter into His presence in a quiet spot where there will not be interruptions. And just be still before the Lord.

When your heart is broken, the Holy Spirit will intercede for you. When you have lost someone or something precious, the Holy Spirit will go before the Father on your behalf. When you are weak, the Comforter will ask the Father to strengthen you. When you are confused and anxious about a decision that looms before you, the Counselor will seek God's best for you. You are not alone.

You are a precious daughter of the Living God. And when Christ ascended back into heaven, He did not leave you on this earth to forge through the wilderness on your own. He sent a Comforter, a Counselor, the Holy Ghost, the Spirit of Truth. When you don't know what to pray, the Bible promises that the Spirit has you covered.

Day 320

TRUE LOVE

*Love is patient, love is kind. It does not envy, it does
not boast, it is not proud. It does not dishonor others,
it is not self-seeking, it is not easily angered, it keeps
no record of wrongs. Love does not delight in evil but
rejoices with the truth. It always protects, always trusts,
always hopes, always perseveres. Love never fails.*

1 CORINTHIANS 13:4–8 NIV

Imagine the daunting task of accurately defining *love*. Most dictionaries rely on synonymous phrases: Love is "a strong affection," "a warm attachment," "a benevolent concern for others." Dictionaries define love through the language of emotion.

The apostle Paul understood that love is more than a feeling. When he sat down to write his famous description of love in 1 Corinthians 13:4–8, instead of defining the word *love*, he explained what love is—love is the demonstration of selfless acts toward others.

Paul explained that true love is displayed through the unselfish behaviors of patience, kindness, humility, forgiveness, protection, trust, hopefulness, and perseverance. This is the kind of love that Jesus showed toward others and that God shows toward us every day. God's kind of love never fails.

The words "I love you" slip easily from the lips and drift away. The passionate feeling of love sometimes grows cold. But God's love doesn't change. It is always pure, unconditional, and forever.

FINDING JOY

*And now, dear brothers and sisters, one final thing.
Fix your thoughts on what is true, and honorable,
and right, and pure, and lovely, and admirable. Think
about things that are excellent and worthy of praise.
Keep putting into practice all you learned and received
from me—everything you heard from me and saw
me doing. Then the God of peace will be with you.*
PHILIPPIANS 4:8–9 NLT

Your mind is powerful. The thoughts you choose to dwell on have the power to determine the outcome of your day. They can pave the way for a calm and grateful heart, or set a course for cynicism and disbelief.

There is such a benefit to fixing your thoughts on things that are good, pleasing, and perfect. God was not being legalistic when he said to think on these things. He was giving us sound advice. He was showing us the path to peace. What makes your heart beat a little faster? What brings joy to your heart and a smile to your lips? What makes your eyes crinkle with laughter and your feet step a little lighter? Think about these things.

Life is meant to be enjoyed. Relish the simple things! God made the playful puppies, galloping horses, and singing birds. He enjoys them, and He invites you to enjoy them too.

A Piece of Work

*For we are God's masterpiece. He has created
us anew in Christ Jesus, so we can do the
good things he planned for us long ago.*
Ephesians 2:10 nlt

The most beautiful pieces of pottery are those where you can see the work of someone's hands in the object. They are not uniform pieces—each is unique, with little differences in shape or style. Sometimes, if you look closely, you can see the line formed by the person's thumb sliding along the wet clay. Or a faint impression of a fingerprint pattern at the bottom of a mug, where the artist gave the clay one last touch.

But if you saw the work before the potter began, all you would see is a gray lump of wet clay. No form, no function, no fingerprints. Just a gray lump, waiting to be shaped.

There are days when we may resemble masses more than masterpieces. Sometimes we are stubborn and refuse to be shaped. Sometimes we are frozen in our uncertainty and cannot be moved. Sometimes we just can't even see our own beauty.

But God wants to use us. He works with us and through us and for us. We can trust His hands to make us into masterpieces, ready to do what He has planned for us long, long ago.

OUR ONE DEFENSE

*I will give thanks to the LORD because of
his righteousness; I will sing the praises of
the name of the LORD Most High.*
PSALM 7:17 NIV

Do you know the old hymn "The Solid Rock"? The songwriter is clear that our hope is built on "nothing less than Jesus' blood and righteousness." And when we stand before the throne, we are dressed in the righteousness of Christ. He is our only defense and the reason we stand before God without fault or stain.

Think about that for a moment. What images come to mind? Do you see yourself hidden in Christ before God? Do you see God looking upon you with love? Can you see that nothing we could possibly do will make God love us any more or less? Do you know for sure that you cannot earn your way to a right relationship with God?

Christ is our one defense. We stand before God without stain or blemish because of Christ. We are made perfect in God's sight because of Christ. We are wholly and dearly loved children of God—completely acceptable in His sight.

All because of Jesus.

Day 324

"I Am Your God"

Fear not [there is nothing to fear], for I am with you; do not look around you in terror and be dismayed, for I am your God. I will strengthen and harden you to difficulties, yes, I will help you; yes, I will hold you up and retain you with My [victorious] right hand of rightness and justice.

ISAIAH 41:10 AMPC

Have you ever woken up in the middle of the night and found yourself unable to get back to sleep? The previous day's conversations, events, what-ifs, and more are playing over in your mind, keeping Mr. Sandman at bay.

That's when you know the challenge is on. You get up quietly, careful not to disturb your snoring dog, cat, husband, child—whatever—and head for where you left your Bible the night before. You sit down and open God's Book to the verse above, then read Isaiah 41:13: "For I the Lord your God hold your right hand; I am the Lord, Who says to you, Fear not; I will help you!" (AMPC).

Having set a firm foundation of faith, you enter into the psalms, reading aloud King David's words of praise. As the minutes tick by, you feel God's presence. As you abide in Him, your eyes grow heavy and you find sleep in His arms.

Day 325

WHOLEHEARTEDNESS

"For I will set My eyes on them for good, and I will bring
them back to this land; I will build them and not pull
them down, and I will plant them and not pluck them
up. Then I will give them a heart to know Me, that I am
the LORD; and they shall be My people, and I will be their
God, for they shall return to Me with their whole heart."

JEREMIAH 24:6–7 NKJV

God is wholehearted. He is present in the moment. He does not love partially but completely. God loves enthusiastically with all His passion, and that is how He desires you to love Him.

Life may have left your heart bruised and broken, but God can do what no one else can. He can give you a new heart—one that comprehends His greatness.

Who else but God can rescue you from your wanderings? Who else can build you up, layer upon layer of strength and courage? Only God can plant your roots deeply in a place that becomes a lasting home.

Your heart is safe with your faithful God. It can expand and dream.

Return to Him now. Discover the freedom of hoping in a future that is good. Find your ease in loving God with your whole heart. Grasp the deep and abiding love with which He first loved you.

GOD HAS EARNED OUR CONFIDENCE

For you have been my hope, Sovereign LORD,
my confidence since my youth.
PSALM 71:5 NIV

Internal clues suggest that the psalmist wrote Psalm 71 during a troublesome time. In the midst of recounting his situation, he asserted that God had been his hope and confidence since his youth. As Paul later outlined in Romans 5, his previous experiences built that hope.

Psalm 71:5 is an example of synonymous parallelism in Hebrew poetry. The two lines express nearly the same thought, the second expanding on the idea expressed in the first.

"You have been my hope": I have a trustful expectation that You will fulfill Your promises.

"You have been my confidence": I not only expect You to fulfill Your promises, I am certain You will.

Although translations alternate between "trust" and "confidence" in this verse, either translation is appropriate. Confidence makes a slightly stronger, in-your-face statement of trust. It's like looking at today's news in tomorrow's newspaper. The game is fixed and the outcome predetermined.

Confidence in the Lord allows us to face disasters without fear (Proverbs 3:25–26); to live in peace (Isaiah 32:17); and to approach God (Ephesians 3:12).

In an unpredictable world, we serve an unchanging God who has earned our confidence.

HOW LONG HAS IT BEEN?

*Trust in him at all times, you people; pour out
your hearts to him, for God is our refuge.*
PSALM 62:8 NIV

An early twentieth-century hymn goes like this:

Go to the deeps of God's promise;
Ask freely of Him, and receive;
All good may be had for the asking,
If, seeking, you truly believe. . . .

Has it been a long time since you've completely poured out
your heart to God? Not just your everyday prayers for family and
friends, but a complete and exhaustive outpouring of your heart
to the Lord? Oftentimes we run to friends or spiritual counselors
in times of heartache and trouble, but God wants us to pour out
our hearts to Him first. He is our refuge, and we can trust Him to
heal our hearts completely.

The next time you reach for the phone to call up a friend and
share all of your feelings, stop and pray first. Share your heart with
God and gain His perspective on your troubles. The God who
created you knows you better than anyone. Let Him be your first
point of contact in any situation.

HIS MAJESTY

God's voice thunders in marvelous ways; he does
great things beyond our understanding.
JOB 37:5 NIV

God is both great and good at the same time.

As far as being great, He is *El*, which means God in full power. He is the awesome creator of everything we see. He is in control of the rain, snow, and sun. He holds the earth together with His thoughts. He is God of unlimited might.

At the same time and to the same degree, God is good. He is marvelously and unsurpassably good. There is no darkness or evil in Him. He is 100 percent kind, loving, and merciful all the time.

Together, His greatness and His goodness means that we can trust Him to work in our lives in an amazing way. We can trust that even when we struggle with hardships, He is working things out for our best. We can trust that when we experience success, it has been a good gift from His hand.

No matter what the circumstances of your life, you can lift our eyes to God whose voice thunders mightily. You can gratefully and humbly trust the way your great and good God designs your day.

Day 321

CONFIDENCE

And now, little children, abide in him; that,
when he shall appear, we may have confidence,
and not be ashamed before him at his coming.
1 JOHN 2:28 KJV

Someday each one of us will stand before our Maker. It is difficult to imagine how we will react. Will we run to Him with open arms or shrink back with embarrassment? Will we desire to sit at His feet or retreat to a far-off corner of heaven? Our reaction then will depend on our relationship with Him now.

We have the opportunity to enter into a personal relationship with our heavenly Father through Jesus Christ. The acceptance of this invitation by faith assures us of eternal life. Yet many people who profess faith in Jesus never grow in their relationship with Him. They stick their ticket to heaven in their back hip pocket, never realizing there is so much more!

Jesus came to give us eternal life in heaven as well as abundant life on earth. As we allow His Word to speak to our hearts, we grow in our relationship with Him. He becomes our friend, our confidant, our Good Shepherd. We know Him intimately. We communicate with Him constantly. We love Him deeply. Let's get to know the Lord now. Then we will anticipate our face-to-face meeting with excitement and confidence!

NEED WISDOM? JUST ASK

*"Call to me and I will answer you and tell you
great and unsearchable things you do not know."*
JEREMIAH 33:3 NIV

In this verse, God is speaking directly to the prophet Jeremiah.

For forty years, Jeremiah had been warning that Judah and Jerusalem would be destroyed for their sins. Now, his predictions were coming true: The Babylonian army was poised to attack. King Zedekiah commanded that Jeremiah be thrown into prison for speaking the words of God. While Jeremiah was there, God commanded him to pray. "Call to Me," He said, "and I will answer you" (Jeremiah 33:3 NASB).

Jeremiah 33:3 teaches that if we pray to God, He will answer us with wisdom. In the King James Version of the Bible, the word *pray* is listed more than five hundred times. God wants us to pray. When we call on Him in prayer, we know that He hears us (1 John 5:15).

Proverbs 2:6 (NASB) says, "For the LORD gives wisdom; from His mouth come knowledge and understanding." God knows us fully, and He is able to direct us in wisdom and guide us through the works of His Holy Spirit.

Just as God gave Jeremiah wisdom when he prayed, He will do the same for you if you call on Him in faith (James 1:5–6).

SUCH AS I HAVE

Then Peter said, Silver and gold have I none;
but such as I have give I thee: In the name of
Jesus Christ of Nazareth rise up and walk.
ACTS 3:6 KJV

Have you ever been asked to fill a position for which you felt unqualified? Your first thought is to say no. Surely there is someone better qualified than you for the job. Satan doesn't make your decision any easier. He whispers negative thoughts into your ears. "You can't do that; you're not good at it." "Everyone's looking at you and thinking what a bad job you're doing." "You're making a mess of this. Let someone else do it." All of his thoughts are lies of course. Maybe you aren't as experienced as the last person who had the job, but you're the one God chose. You may not have the abilities or talents of others, but you have something God can use.

When Peter and John approached the lame man at the gate of the temple, Peter didn't hesitate to tell him they didn't have any silver or gold for him. But he had something the man could use. He said, "What I do have I give you" (NKJV). God is looking for those who are willing to give what they do have. He knew before He called you what you could do, and He also has the ability to qualify you to do whatsoever He requires. Give God whatever You have and allow Him to use it.

CURE FOR DISCONTENT

...always giving thanks to God the Father for everything, in the name of our Lord Jesus Christ.
EPHESIANS 5:20 NIV

Do you struggle with being satisfied with your current situation in life? Discontent is a heart disease that manifests in comparing, coveting, and complaining. What is the cure? The habit of gratitude. Thanking God for everything—the good and the bad—means we accept it as His will, even if we don't like it.

Sometimes we receive birthday or Christmas gifts we have no desire for, but we still thank the giver. God is the good giver of every perfect gift (James 1:17). Failing to thank Him is rebellion against His wisdom and ways. If we expect Him to do things the way we want or to give us more, we forget that God owes us nothing.

When God commands thanksgiving, He is not mandating our feelings but rather our submission. However, because thankfulness changes our attitude and outlook, it does affect our feelings. Discontent and resentment cannot coexist with humble acceptance of what happens to us. Therefore, thanking God must become our lifelong habit. When we turn out the light every night, we can review our day and thank God for each event—good and bad—because He allowed it, and He is good. We can be satisfied with that.

WAKE UP IN SAFETY

I lay down and slept, yet I woke up in safety, for the
LORD was watching over me. I am not afraid of ten
thousand enemies who surround me on every side.
PSALM 3:5–6 NLT

There was a time when the average person would never have known what it was like to have thousands of enemies. To achieve those numbers, one might have to be a celebrity—perhaps a hated villain in a movie, or the quarterback who choked in the championship game, or a radio host who opened his big mouth one too many times.

But in this age of social media, one wrong post can earn you millions of followers in seconds. And those millions might not like your message. In fact, they may well hate you for it. They also might just tell you about it. A lot.

But our mighty God knows what it's like to be surrounded by enemy voices. He knows what it's like to have insults hurled at Him. He knows what it's like to have crowds shouting out His name—not in support, but in rage.

The one who faced such hatred is watching over you. He is surrounding you too—but with His love and strength. Wake up in safety and don't be afraid.

Day 334

FAITH IS THE VICTORY

For we live by faith, not by sight.
2 CORINTHIANS 5:7 NIV

When we find ourselves in the dark, our first response is to find a flashlight. We like to see where we are stepping. . .in the backyard as well as in life. We prefer knowing which direction, how fast, and how long the journey will take at every turn. We are, however, called to walk by faith, which usually means "lights out." Yet when confusion and uncertainty cause darkness, we try to regain control, a wild scramble to stop the pain of walking in the dark.

Uncertainty is uncomfortable. Yet in these situations, we are to remember that faith is the victory, not the outcome. God is responsible for the results. Our job is the faith.

Trusting that God will take care of the outcome is a muscle that gets stronger each time you practice it. Instead of worrying over the test results, the job interview, or the bill payment, tell God you trust Him to take care of you. Tell Him that over and over until both your mind and heart believe it. Know that no matter how the details play out at the end, God is most assuredly in control and working for your best.

BEAUTIFUL FOR THE KING

*Before each young woman was taken to the king's bed,
she was given the prescribed twelve months of beauty
treatments—six months with oil of myrrh, followed
by six months with special perfumes and ointments.*
ESTHER 2:12 NLT

Esther was just one of many women who had to take her turn at a full year of beauty treatments before being taken to the king. What a regimen!

Sometimes just one morning at the cosmetics counter in a department store can seem like forever, browsing through all of the choices of creams, colors, and scents. Although it's fun to peruse the products and buy some necessities—maybe even a luxury or two—it's important that we not focus more on our outward appearance than we should.

Our King does expect us to take care of our bodies. After all, He created us and wants us to maintain our optimal health. However, He doesn't expect us to be supermodels. No matter what impossible standards culture presents, we are beautiful in the eyes of the One who created the whole earth.

Aren't you thankful that the King of kings doesn't require you to endure year-long beauty treatments or be camera-ready for Him? He truly loves you just as you are—created in His image and special to Him.

NOTHING TO FEAR

Precious in the sight of the LORD
is the death of His saints.
PSALM 116:15 NKJV

Benjamin Franklin said, "Two things in life are certain, death and taxes."

We can sometimes escape paying a tax, but we cannot escape death. Every one of us will die someday.

In Psalm 116, the psalmist tells of his cries to God for mercy. He cried out to God because he was afraid. "The cords of death entangled me, the anguish of the grave came over me" (verse 3 NIV). Then he goes on to praise God for saving him. We can't know if the psalmist was literally saved from dying, or if his words were a metaphor. But we do know from reading Psalm 116 that God saves our souls from dying (verse 8).

The Twenty-Third Psalm holds the familiar words "Yea, though I walk through the valley of the shadow of death, I will fear no evil: for thou art with me" (verse 4 KJV). Through our belief in Jesus Christ, we know that we are saved; we become God's "saints."

Psalm 116:15 assures us that our transition from this world to heaven is precious in God's sight. God paid the price of our eternal life through the sacrifice of His only Son. In death, we have nothing to fear.

TOTAL KNOWLEDGE, TOTAL LOVE

Your eyes saw my unformed body. All the
days ordained for me were written in your
book before one of them came to be.

PSALM 139:16 NIV

The psalmist states it in a dozen poetic ways: God knows everything about us. He knows where we are at all times. He knows what we are going to say before we open our mouths. In fact, He knows every one of our days and has since before our conception.

The Bible talks about several people God set apart from birth: Samson, the first candidate for the "world's strongest man"; Jeremiah, prophet to the nations; John the Baptist, called to prepare the way of the Lord.

But God also knows the days of ordinary people. Job said, "a person's days are determined; you have decreed the number of his months" (Job 14:5 NIV). The same knowledge applies to our new birth. He created us anew in Christ Jesus for good works "which God prepared in advance for us to do" (Ephesians 2:10 NIV).

The God who knows everything about us still loves us. With the psalmist, let us declare, "Such knowledge is too wonderful for me, too lofty for me to attain" (139:6 NIV).

GOD IS COMMITTED TO US

*"In that day," declares the LORD, "you will call me 'my
husband'; you will no longer call me 'my master.' "*
HOSEA 2:16 NIV

This Old Testament book tells the story of the faithful and forgiving
Hosea, married to the prostitute Gomer. Hosea represents God's
deep love and commitment to His people. Gomer, in her sinful
and wandering ways, symbolizes Israel.

God based this illustration on the marriage relationship. God
is the loving husband, fully devoted to His wife, even considering
her infidelity. He never gives up and continually searches for her,
protecting her, restoring her to His side. God's forgiveness and
love redeem that relationship.

God also wants *our* hearts. He desires a relationship with us
based on love and forgiveness. He enters into a covenant with us,
like the marriage between Hosea and Gomer. God is the loving,
faithful husband, constantly pursuing us no matter what we do or
where we roam. Though it is difficult to grasp how much He loves
us, we find hope in His promise. God will keep His commitment
to us. His love song to us is forgiveness, and His wedding vow is
unconditional love.

MORE THAN SPARROWS

"You are worth more than many sparrows."
MATTHEW 10:31 NIV

Sparrows are not rare birds. The little gray, white, and black bodies can be spotted all over the world. They hang out in hedges and graze on grassland. They are about as common as field mice and rabbits.

As common as they are, God knows these creatures. He knows the seeds they like to eat and when they molt. He knows they like to bathe in the dust and congregate in talkative groups. He knows the feathers on their heads and the bird's-eye views they have seen.

God cares about sparrows. He cares about caterpillars and ants and rabbits and mice as well. If our great God cares about these little creatures that come and go and do as they please, how much more do you think He cares about you? Even when you're struggling to follow Him, and when you sing the wrong notes in all the right praise songs, and when you forget to pray, and when you forget you know Him—in all these times, the God of the sparrows and the grass in the field and the mountaintops and the nations knows you, and claims you as His child.

Never worry about what you are worth to your Father. He loves you more than the wildflowers growing in the field. He loves you more than the flutter of a million sparrows' wings. He sees you and everything you do from his God's-eye view, and He loves you still.

JESUS IS ALWAYS RIGHT ON TIME

When Mary came where Jesus was, and saw Him,
she fell down at His feet, saying to Him, "Lord, if You
had been here, my brother would not have died."

JOHN 11:32 NKJV

When Jesus arrived, Mary thought He was too late. She knew Jesus, the Son of God, could have saved her brother. But now her beloved Lazarus was dead.

Yet, the fact is that Jesus is always right on time. This is hard for us to understand because we are human. And humans operate on an earthly timetable. But Jesus, the Son of God, is beyond time and space. He can always be trusted to do what is right. He didn't "mess up" and have to fix any mistake in the story of Lazarus's death.

Lazarus had been dead four days. And yet Jesus asked that the stone blocking the entrance to the tomb be moved. An unusual request. But that's because something unusual was about to happen.

Jesus called for Lazarus to "come forth" (John 11:43 NKJV), and Lazarus did! The Savior had shown up and given life back to a dead man.

"Trust in the LORD with all your heart and lean not on your own understanding" (Proverbs 3:5 NIV). Looking for a miracle in your life? Hold on. Jesus is never late.

Day 341

GET ABOVE IT ALL

Set your minds and keep them set on what is above (the higher things), not on the things that are on the earth.
COLOSSIANS 3:2 AMPC

If you've ever taken a trip by airplane, you know with one glimpse from the window at thirty thousand feet how the world seems small. With your feet on the ground, you may feel small in a big world; and it's easy for the challenges of life and the circumstances from day to day to press in on you. But looking down from above the clouds, things can become clear as you have the opportunity to get above it all.

Sometimes the most difficult challenges you face play out in your head—where a struggle to control the outcome and work out the details of life can consume you. Once removed—far away from the details—you can see things from a higher perspective. Close your eyes and push out the thoughts that try to grab you and keep you tied to the things of the world.

Reach out to God and let your spirit soar. Give your concerns to Him and let Him work out the details. Rest in Him and He'll carry you above it all, every step of the way.

Day 342

GRACE IN THE DESERT

"They found grace out in the desert. . . . Israel, out looking for a place to rest, met God out looking for them!" GOD told them, "I've never quit loving you and never will. Expect love, love, and more love!"

JEREMIAH 31:2–3 MSG

Grace out in the desert. What a refreshing thought. Have you been in a desert place, lost, lonely, disappointed, feeling the pain of rejection? Often our immediate response is to berate ourselves, look within to see how we have been the one lacking, plummeting our self-esteem. Dejected we crawl to that desert place to lick our wounds.

Behold! God is in our desert place. He longs to fill our dry hearts with His healing love and mercy. Yet it's so hard for us—with our finite minds—to grasp that the creator of the universe cares for us and loves us with an everlasting love, no matter what.

Despite their transgressions, God told the Israelites He never quit loving them. That is true for you today. Look beyond any circumstances and you will discover God looking at you, His eyes filled with love. Scripture promises an overwhelming, unexpected river of love that will pour out when we trust the Lord our God. Rest today in His Word. Expect God's love, love, and more love to fill that empty place in your life.

Day 343

GOD GIVES HOPE

*"For I know the plans I have for you," declares
the Lord, "plans to prosper you and not to harm
you, plans to give you hope and a future."*
JEREMIAH 29:11 NIV

When God promises something, He is sure to deliver.

Due to their sin and rebellion, the Jews were held hostage by Babylon. At the end of Israel's seventy-year captivity, Jeremiah prophesied that their deliverance was near. God promised that if the people would pray and seek Him with all their heart, He would listen and be found (verses 12–14).

In Jeremiah 29:11, the prophet's reassuring words of hope must have soothed and refreshed like cool water on parched lips. The same is true today.

Sometimes hope comes in the form of a second chance, easing our sense of failure. Other times it's clothed in the words of a doctor who informs his patient that a full recovery is near. Hope thrives in the fertile soil of a heart restored by a loving gesture, a compassionate embrace, or an encouraging word. It is one of God's most precious gifts.

God *wants* to forgive our sins and lead us on the paths of righteousness—just as He did for the Israelites of old. He has great plans for us. That's His promise, and our blessed hope.

QUEEN OF THE HILL

*Though the sheep pens are sheepless and the cattle barns
empty, I'm singing joyful praise to G*OD*. I'm turning
cartwheels of joy to my Savior God. Counting on
G*OD*'s Rule to prevail, I take heart and gain strength.
I run like a deer. I feel like I'm king of the mountain!*
HABAKKUK 3:17–19 MSG

You haven't had a raise in five years. Your love life is dismal at
best. Your kids aren't living up to your expectations. Your sister is
ill. You've just totaled your brand-new car. Your mom recently
passed away. And you don't have enough money for groceries this
week. Your spirits are lower than low.

What's a woman to do?

It's simple. Change your lament of "Woe is me" to a song of
joyful praise to God. Jump up and down, start skipping as you
rejoice in your Lord. And before you know it, His strength will
begin welling up within you. He'll make your heart truly sing.
Instead of your being buried by your misfortunes, you'll be standing on top of them. Because of God and His amazing power,
you are now Queen of the Hill. Your footing is sure. You have
conquered your calamities! You are no longer a victim but a victor!

Day 345

TOUCHING JESUS

*When she had heard of Jesus, [she] came in the
press behind, and touched his garment. For she said,
If I may touch but his clothes, I shall be whole.*

MARK 5:27–28 KJV

The woman with the issue of blood suffered for twelve years, and even though she had seen several physicians and spent all her money, she wasn't any better. She must have felt she was at the end of her rope. Then she heard about Jesus.

At times, we've all reached the end of our rope. We did all we knew to do and it didn't solve a thing. But in our efforts, we missed the secret this woman discovered. She made her way to Him, in spite of the challenges, pushing through a throng of people who jostled each other in their eagerness to be near Jesus too. They may not have wanted to give way to this woman, but she pressed on—and when she reached Jesus, she touched His clothes and received healing.

The secret to solving any problem is to touch Jesus. We can't do that in the flesh today, but we can touch Him anytime through prayer and His Word. Like the woman in this story, we must press through whatever may hinder us. Don't give up! Touching Jesus is all that matters.

Day 346

NO CONDEMNATION

Who is he who condemns? It is Christ who died, and furthermore is also risen, who is even at the right hand of God, who also makes intercession for us.
ROMANS 8:34 NKJV

We know someone condemns us. Satan whispers lies continually into our minds: "You're worthless." "You've gone too far; God doesn't love you anymore." "No one could forgive someone like you." The accusations go on and on, but we don't have to believe them.

No matter what the devil says, his lies don't change God's mind, and we shouldn't pay any attention to him. The enemy is very convincing when he reminds us of our mistakes. We know he's right—we've blown it. He pollutes our minds and muddles our thoughts.

But Jesus is in heaven, at God's right hand. They are side by side, one mind, one heart. Jesus essentially says to the Father, "Satan is telling our kids lies again, making them think we won't forgive them. But all they have to do is repent, ask for forgiveness, and ignore his voice."

God the Father sees us through His Son. Jesus is eager to forgive the worst sinner. When we turn to Him, all our sins are washed away in His blood; we're spotless. And there's a glorious celebration in heaven whenever a sinner turns to Jesus.

No matter how filthy we feel, we're never more than a prayer away from being clean, as pure as if we never sinned.

Day 347

YOUR FOREVER GOD

We pondered your love-in-action, God. . .
Your name, God, evokes a train of Hallelujahs
wherever it is spoken, near and far; your arms
are heaped with goodness-in-action. . . . Our God
forever, who guides us till the end of time.
PSALM 48:9–10, 14 MSG

When spending time in God's presence, you can feel His love and light reaching out and enfolding you. In response, you cannot help but praise Him for all He has done for you, in you, with you, and by you.

It seems almost impossible to imagine that God is with you now, surrounding you with His protection and strength. That He will be with you when it's time for you to cross over to heaven, giving you all the peace and comfort you need before being with Him in an entirely new way. And that He will be with you for all eternity, when there will be no more sorrow, pain, war, or death itself.

Although this constant presence of a living Lord may seem impossible, Jesus assures you that "all things are possible with God" (Mark 10:27 AMPC). So rest easy every moment of every day, knowing you will be forever guided by the one who loves you with all of His being.

Day 348

GOD'S GRACE THROUGH THE DETOUR

*But he said to me, "My grace is sufficient for
you, for my power is made perfect in weakness."
Therefore I will boast all the more gladly about my
weaknesses, so that Christ's power may rest on me.*

2 CORINTHIANS 12:9 NIV

You may be struggling. A situation is out of your control. Someone
has made a decision that affects you—and you are not very happy
about it.

Take heart. Such things happen often throughout life. You
thought you were on a particular path, but the plans, circumstances,
or parameters changed. And right now you may feel as though
God interrupted your life. But here's the thing: God always has
permission to interrupt. And even though you may be having
a hard time understanding what it all means, rest assured that
you are just on a detour right now—and you cannot detour out of
the reach of God's grace.

So there's no need to worry—a detour always puts you right
back on the path you are supposed to be on!

Your job is just to take this time to relax and enjoy the scenery.

WORRY VS. PRAYER

*Don't worry about anything; instead, pray
about everything. Tell God what you need,
and thank him for all he has done.*
PHILIPPIANS 4:6 NLT

Do not worry. This is a tall order for women. We are worriers by nature, aren't we? We worry about our children and friends. We worry about what people think of us and what we will do if such-and-such happens. We are the queens of the what-if's! But the Bible tells us not to worry about *anything*.

In the book of Matthew, we are reminded that if God cares for the birds of the air, providing them with food as they need it, He is certain to take care of His children! But if we give up worrying, what will we do with all the time we spent being anxious? Exchange it for time in prayer.

Go before God with your concerns. Cast all your cares on Him, for He promises to care for you. Tell God what you need, and thank Him in advance for what He will do. God will always provide. He will always show up. He does not want you to worry.

MOST SATISFIED

Oh, the depth of the riches both of the wisdom and knowledge of God! How unsearchable are His judgments and His ways past finding out! "For who has known the mind of the LORD? Or who has become His counselor?" "Or who has first given to Him and it shall be repaid to him?" For of Him and through Him and to Him are all things, to whom be glory forever. Amen.

ROMANS 11:33–36 NKJV

We know that no one has lent God anything, nor has anyone given God advice. We were made in His image, but He is nothing like us and we are nothing like Him.

Everything, from the bright spring breeze to a newborn's laugh, was created by Him. God does not depend on anyone or anything. It is because He doesn't rely on anyone that He can love perfectly. How often do we seek man's acceptance over God's acceptance? How often are our motives tainted with manipulation because we want to please or be pleased?

God is impervious to manipulation; it is not in His character. He will never tweak His ways to get us to like or accept Him. His complete independency means we can trust His love. He withholds things for our good; He grants things for our good. But don't miss the pinnacle part of Paul's message, "to whom be glory forever." Everything you do as a child of God is for His glory, and everything God does is for His glory.

We are most satisfied when God is most glorified.

GOD IS FOR US

*You keep track of all my sorrows. You have collected
all my tears in your bottle. You have recorded each one
in your book. . . . This I know: God is on my side! I
praise God for what he has promised; yes, I praise the
LORD for what he has promised. I trust in God, so why
should I be afraid? What can mere mortals do to me?*

PSALM 56:8–11 NLT

When you're in the middle of a rough season, does it ever feel as
if no one else, including God, notices what you're going through?

In Psalm 56, David recounted when he was in a tough spot.
From morning till night, the Philistines lurked and threatened
and trampled him. Yes, David was greatly troubled, but he knew
one thing: God was for him. God had not overlooked what was
happening; in fact, He was keeping track of every sorrow, collecting
every tear. In his trouble, David trusted God all the more, because
only that trust—only God Himself—could rescue him from despair.
No wonder the shepherd-boy-turned-king advised, "O my people,
trust in him at all times. Pour out your heart to him, for God is
our refuge" (Psalm 62:8 NLT).

God is on your side! Turn to Him when rough times pull you
down. He'll pull you back up.

His Love Never Quits

Give thanks to GOD—he is good and his love never quits. Say, "Save us, Savior God, round us up and get us out of these godless places, so we can give thanks to your holy Name, and bask in your life of praise."

1 CHRONICLES 16:34–36 MSG

God's Word tells us in Psalm 139 that we can never escape the presence of God. He is with us always, no matter where we go or what we do. His love never quits on us. First John 4:10 (NIV) says, "This is love: not that we loved God, but that he loved us and sent his Son as an atoning sacrifice for our sins." God doesn't love us because we did a lot of good things for Him. He doesn't love us because of our last names or because of the jobs we do. He can't love us any more or any less than He already does. He loves us simply because He is our Father and our creator. In fact, He gave up His very life to show you how much.

You may have had a parent, friend, or spouse abandon you at some point in your life. God won't do that. You may feel alone and fearful. God won't leave you. You may feel sad and crushed. God says He is close to the brokenhearted and saves those who are crushed in Spirit (Psalm 34:18).

Day 353

NO FEAR

*Surely the righteous will never be shaken; they will
be remembered forever. They will have no fear of
bad news; their hearts are steadfast, trusting in the
LORD. Their hearts are secure, they will have no fear;
in the end they will look in triumph on their foes.*
PSALM 112:6–8 NIV

We dread the phone call. We wait anxiously for the test results.
We have nightmares about the stories we see on the internet. We
fret over what tomorrow will bring, because there never seems to
be a shortage of bad news, right? But here's the good news! The
Bible says that the righteous—people who revere God and want
to obey Him (Psalm 112:1)—can be fearless in the face of bad
news. Their hearts stay steadfast and secure by trusting in God,
who watches over them and is sovereign over all. God is so very
great that our biggest fears vanish in His shadow.

Each time you feel your heart tugged toward fear, tug it back
toward God with these words: "The LORD is high above all nations,
and his glory above the heavens! Who is like the LORD our God,
who is seated on high, who looks far down on the heavens and the
earth? He raises the poor from the dust and lifts the needy from
the ash heap, to make them sit with princes" (Psalm 113:4–8 ESV).

FATHER TO THE FATHERLESS

Father to the fatherless, defender of widows—
this is God, whose dwelling is holy.
PSALM 68:5 NLT

Doesn't your heart ache for the fatherless children in this world? Many of these little ones weep for the daddy they never had. Others have gone without for so long that they don't know any other way of life. They don't even know how to mourn for what they've never had.

As members of Christ's body, we've an obligation to care for those in need and fill in the gap when parents are missing. But we also have an obligation to share the good news that God is the best Daddy of all. Our Abba Father sweeps in like a knight on a white steed, ready to show His sons and daughters that He'll care for them, no matter what they're going through. He's a fierce protector, one who cares greatly about those who've been overlooked or abused.

Perhaps you're in need of a reminder that God is *your* Daddy. Lift your hands toward heaven and let Him sweep you up into His arms. Even now, He's dancing and singing over you, longing to fill the voids in your heart.

Day 355

His Healing Abundance

"Behold, I will bring it health and healing;
I will heal them and reveal to them the
abundance of peace and truth."
Jeremiah 33:6 nkjv

Our health—physical, mental, emotional, and spiritual—is important to God. He longs to see us whole in every area of our lives. As believers in His grace and goodness, we ought to be diligent about seeking health so that we can be good stewards of His gifts.

If we confess our sins to God, He will bring relief to our souls. When we're distressed, we have Jesus, the Prince of Peace, to give us peace. When our emotions threaten to overwhelm us, we can implore Jehovah Rapha—the God who heals—to calm our anxious hearts. When we're physically sick, we can cry out to Jesus, our great physician. While He may not always heal us in the ways we might like, He will always give us strength, courage, and peace.

So whether our problems affect us physically, spiritually, mentally, or emotionally, we can trust that God will come to us and bring us healing. And beyond our temporal lives, we can look forward with hope to our heavenly lives. There we will be healthy, whole, and alive—forever.

Day 356

ACCESS TO GOD'S POWER

*Jesus was baptized. As he was praying, the sky opened up
and the Holy Spirit, like a dove descending, came down
on him. And along with the Spirit, a voice: "You are my
Son, chosen and marked by my love, pride of my life."*
LUKE 3:21–22 MSG

Jesus' baptism. What a wondrous example of the power of prayer—
and of the Three-in-One God in action.

Jesus, the one who opens doors that no one can shut, is an
amazingly powerful prayer, for, as He's praying, the sky actually
opens up! Then the Holy Spirit, like a dove alighting from the
heavens, descends on Him. At the same time, God's voice booms
out, "You are My Son, My Beloved! In You I am well pleased and
find delight!" (Luke 3:22 AMPC).

What a great example of the power you have access to in your
life! Just as Jesus' prayers could open up the sky, your prayers can
move mountains. You also have a three-man team on your side.
Like Jesus, you have a Father God who loved you—before you ever
loved Him (Romans 5:8). Because of this great love, this Father
God sent His Son not only to seek you—but to save you (Luke
19:10). And then He left behind the Spirit to draw you to Him
(John 16:13–14).

What more could a woman want—or need?

THE PEACE OF CHRIST

*Let the peace of Christ rule in your hearts,
since as members of one body you were
called to peace. And be thankful.*
COLOSSIANS 3:15 NIV

How do we let the peace of Christ rule in our hearts? One way is to take every thought captive and make it obedient to Christ (2 Corinthians 10:5). That means when an unkind or impure thought comes into our minds, we take it straight to the cross of Christ.

Instead of obsessing over conversations and what other people might be thinking of you, you focus on Jesus. Sometimes just saying the name of Jesus out loud when you have a negative thought can stop the thought in its tracks and refocus your mind.

After allowing Jesus into your thought process, thank God for your blessings. Thank Him for His great love for you and others. Ask Him to give you something else to think about instead of going back to that original thought.

If you're having a convicting thought, take that to God as well. Ask Him to reveal what is true and right and what your response should be.

Surrendering our thoughts to Christ naturally leads to surrendering our actions to Him too. When our hearts and minds are surrendered to Christ, the peace of Christ is free to rule in our lives.

Day 358

YOU ARE IN GOD'S MIND

*I know and am acquainted with all the birds of
the mountains, and the wild animals of the field
are Mine and are with Me, in My mind.*
PSALM 50:11 AMPC

So many things that may be out of your reach are at God's command. Look at birds. They are not only in His sight and in His company—they are in His mind. He has knowledge of their position, their power, their prowess, their prey. He knows every feather and feature of every fowl.

And He is more than acquainted with all the wild animals in the field. They too reside in His mind and are at His command. He knows their movement, color, conquest, and conflict.

In the same way that God knows His birds and animals, He knows you. He sees your struggles, has memorized your features, and knows the number of hairs on your head.

No matter where you go or what you do, you are with Him. You are in God's mind. There is nothing you can hide from your Master, your Creator.

Allow His Word, His voice, to speak to you. Meld your mind with His. Seek the wisdom He is bursting to share. Know Him as He knows you. Love Him as He loves you.

For when you become one with the great I AM, nothing He has will ever be out of your reach.

Day 351

MY CHILD

After this manner therefore pray ye:
Our Father which art in heaven. . .
MATTHEW 6:9 KJV

The famous theologian Charles Spurgeon said the Lord's Prayer "begins where all true prayer must commence, with the spirit of adoption, 'Our Father.' There is no acceptable prayer until we can say, 'I will arise, and go unto my Father.'"

What a beautiful word picture this paints: a child in supplication before his heavenly Father. Not a stranger before an unknown god but a child of the King. Yet it takes faith to receive and believe that picture. Our lives on this earth burden us with negative thought patterns, ripping us from the arms of Jesus into self-condemnation and guilt. To absolve ourselves from this recurring problem seems impossible. "No one else has—" We can fill in the blank with feelings of unworthiness and doubt.

Know this: The enemy loves to divide and destroy by isolating us and making us feel rejected. What a liar he is. We are loved with a great love by the creator and must allow that thought to permeate our souls. God loves us so much He sent His Son to teach a pattern of prayer. And that pattern begins with the words that give us heart-knowledge: We are His children.

Day 360

REDEMPTION IS NEAR

"When these things begin to take place, stand up and lift up your heads, because your redemption is drawing near."
LUKE 21:28 NIV

Take one look at the world news, and there is no doubt. The events Jesus speaks of in Luke 21 are certainly happening. Nations are at war. Kingdoms are shattered. Every day the news tells us of earthquakes, plagues, famine, and terrors so great we can hardly speak of them. As if this isn't enough, throughout the world, followers of Christ are being persecuted. It's easy to be discouraged. Who wouldn't be? Even if you knew your favorite team was ultimately going to win the game, it would be difficult to see them take such a beating.

But Jesus exhorts us to take a posture of victory—backs straight, heads held high. His promise is clear and rings through the centuries since He first spoke these words. Redemption is near! The battle is fierce, but the war is already won. Soon, all the pain and sorrow will be a distant memory. In the light of Jesus' face, the pain will dim as we rise victorious to reign with Him forever.

Stand tall. Hold tight to the promise. Jesus is near.

Day 361

STAND FIRM!

"But the one who stands firm to the end will be saved."
MATTHEW 24:13 NIV

In Matthew 24, Jesus describes signs of the end-times. His comments come just after His triumphal entry into Jerusalem and His condemnation of the scribes and Pharisees.

While the disciples admire Jerusalem's temple and the fine things inside, Jesus is unimpressed. When He tells them that the temple will be completely destroyed, the disciples are shocked. The temple is the center of their universe—its destruction equals the end of the world.

Later, on the Mount of Olives, the disciples ask Jesus when the temple will be destroyed, and what signs will indicate the end of the age. Jesus warns them of deceit and wars, famine and earthquakes. Then He says, "You will be handed over to be persecuted and put to death, and you will be hated by all nations because of me" (Matthew 24:9 NIV). Imagine how the disciples felt about that—but in Matthew 24:13, Jesus gave them hope, saying, "But the one who stands firm to the end will be saved."

During troubled times, we too can find hope in Matthew 24:13. When we stand firm in Christ, we will certainly receive His promise of eternal life.

Day 362

MY STRENGTH

I love you, LORD, my strength.
PSALM 18:1 NIV

Ever feel like you want to crawl into a hole and pull the earth in around you? Most of us have felt that way at some point. Sometimes life overwhelms us, and we feel like we will drown at any moment.

At times like that, we often don't have the strength to even pray. We don't know what to say to God, and we don't have the energy to form the correct words or thoughts. That's when we need to keep it simple. "I love You, Lord," is all we need to say.

When we utter those three little words to God, we bend His ear to us. We bend His heart to us. When we whisper our love for Him, though we don't have strength to say another word, He shows up and becomes our strength. He wraps His mighty arms around us, pulls us into His lap of love and comfort, and pours His life and love into our spirits.

Truly, it is in those moments of weakness, when we have nothing else to offer God, that He is made strong in us. He longs for our love above all else. When we give it, as weak as we may feel, He becomes strength for us.

ABSOLUTELY NOTHING

*For I am convinced that neither death nor life, neither
angels nor demons, neither the present nor the future,
nor any powers, neither height nor depth, nor anything
else in all creation, will be able to separate us from
the love of God that is in Christ Jesus our Lord.*
ROMANS 8:38–39 NIV

Sometimes, when our circumstances spiral downward and we feel like we're living a nightmare, we wonder where God went. His love, which is supposed to be never-ending, seems out of reach. We pray, but our words seem to bounce off the ceiling and fall flat on the floor.

But it doesn't matter how we feel. God promised that nothing can separate us from His overwhelming, magnificent, powerful love. And though our circumstances may numb our sensors, making it seem like His love is absent, we can fall back on faith in God's promises. His love is there, enveloping us, whether we feel it or not. Nothing in this world can keep His love from us. Absolutely nothing.

Cancer may destroy our flesh, but it won't destroy God's love. Bills may deplete our finances, but they can't deplete His love. Relationships may break our hearts, but they will never break His love. We don't have to face any of life's difficulties alone, for our Creator loves us. He will hold our hands through it all. And when we are too weak to face another day, His love will carry us.

THE BLESSING OF PEACE

Therefore, since we have been justified through faith, we have peace with God through our Lord Jesus Christ.
ROMANS 5:1 NIV

The type of peace this verse is talking about isn't a feeling. It's the kind of peace that's like a treaty. When we ask Jesus to be Lord of our lives, our status and relationship with God change. We go from being His enemies to being His friends. Additionally, we have a sense of relief that His wrath and the punishment for our sins are no longer hanging over our heads.

We also can celebrate that peace with God is not just a one-time event. Rather, it is an ongoing source of blessing. Peace *with* God leads to peace *from* God. This peace is not just the absence of turmoil and trouble, but a real sense that God is in control. It's a small representation of heaven here on earth. His peace brings the confidence that He is working things out in our lives, even if we can't understand it all.

Satan would love to steal our peace. He can't change our relationship with God, but we can give Satan a foothold when we worry and ruminate and fuss over our circumstances instead of turning them over to God. Give your troubles to God and rest in His peace.

Day 365

GOD IS GOOD

*"Will you discredit my justice and condemn me
just to prove you are right? Are you as strong as
God? Can you thunder with a voice like his?"*
JOB 40:8–9 NLT

While God loves us unconditionally and wants to bless and love us, we must remember that He is first and foremost the one and only God. He is the last word—the final judge. Have you spent time reading through the Old Testament? There we see God display His power. We see Him destroy entire people groups. We see Him do some scary stuff that is hard to accept.

Seeing this side of God can strike fear in us—and it should. We should learn to fear God, because as the scripture says, His ways are higher than our ways, His thoughts higher than our thoughts. He will do things we don't understand.

But while He is huge and terrifying and sometimes confusing, we know we can trust Him. As you continue to read through the Bible, you'll also see that He protects, provides for, and unconditionally loves the people who trust Him. Not the people who are perfect, *the people who trust Him.*

CONTRIBUTORS

Terry Allburger, Emily Biggers, Joanna Bloss, Renae Brumbaugh, Dana Christensen, Karin Dahl Silver, Dena Dyer, Tina Elacqua, Nancy Farrier, Jean Fischer, Carol Lynn Fitzpatrick, Darlene Franklin, Anna Gindlesperger, Shanna Gregor, Linda Hang, June Hetzel, Anita Higman, Marcia Hornok, Austine Keller, Eileen Key, Ardythe Kolb, Tina Krause, Kristen Larson, P. J. Lehman, Marian Leslie, Donna Maltese, Emily Marsh, Sabrina McDonald, Pamela McQuade, Helen Middlebrooke, Lydia Mindling, Mandy Nydegger, Nicole O'Dell, Betty Ost-Everley, MariLee Parrish, Vickie Phelps, Rachael Phillips, Valorie Quesenberry, Julie Rayburn, Ramona Richards, Kate Schmelzer, Shana Schutte, Carey Scott, Leah Slawson, Janice Thompson, Stacey Thureen, Lisa Toner, Amy Trent, Jennifer Vander Klipp, Jean Wise

Scripture permissions

Scripture Index

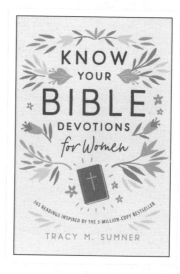